BBC
RADIO **2**

SOUNDS OF THE SIXTIES

THE ULTIMATE SIXTIES MUSIC COMPANION

by Phil Swern

First published November 2016
by Red Planet Publishing Ltd

Text © Phil Swern 2016
This work © Red Planet Publishing Ltd

Paperback ISBN: 978 1 9059 59 78 5

Printed in the UK by CPI Group

For more information about our music books visit:
www.musicbookclub.co.uk

BBC Radio 2 logo used by permission

Red Planet is an imprint of Red Planet Publishing Ltd

Foreword

Sounds Of The Sixties was first broadcast on BBC Radio 2 on 12 February, 1983, when it was introduced by Keith Fordyce. It was decided in the Eighties to give it to a different presenter every week – with many famous names being involved including Alvin Stardust, Tom Jones, Duane Eddy, Donovan, Neil Sedaka, Frankie Valli and many, many more. In 1988, then-producer Stuart Hobday persuaded Simon Dee to present the show but after six months, it was decided that his contract would not be renewed.

At this point I was invited to take over the slot as regular presenter. I was more than happy to do so and made my first appearance on 31 March, 1990. Apart from a few weeks off here and there to sort out health issues, I have been turning up every week for 26 years to introduce an endless stream of Sixties music.

In March, 2015 I was asked to introduce an edition to celebrate my 25th Anniversary on the show and I selected 10 of my all-time favourite Sixties records; I was honoured to broadcast recorded tributes from Ray Davies, Petula Clark, Helen Shapiro, Paul Jones and Marty Wilde. I am delighted that a *Sounds Of The Sixties* book has finally been published with so many amazing stories about such a large variety of tracks and so many different genres of Sixties music.

I hope you enjoy the read and that you'll continue to listen to the show every Saturday morning on BBC Radio 2.

Brian Matthew

About Brian

Brian Matthew started broadcasting in 1948 in Germany, and trained as an actor at RADA before joining the BBC in 1954. His great love of the theatre allowed him to perform in many well-known venues and he even has his own 50-seat theatre in his home in Kent.

For many years he hosted two of the top pop shows on the BBC's Light Programme – *Saturday Club* and *Easy Beat* – and the long-running TV pop show, *Thank Your Lucky Stars*. Brian was one of the first DJs on Radio 2, and hosted *Late Night Extra*, as well as the hugely successful *Round Midnight*, which won the 1987 Pulitzer Publishing Award.

Brian has presented *Sounds of the Sixties* (winner of a Gold Sony Radio Award in 1996) since 1990, the same year he received a Broadcasting Press Guild Award for Outstanding Contribution to Radio.

Contents

SOUNDS OF THE SIXTIES

The Hits

The first section of the Sounds Of The Sixties book will deal with 100 hit singles, all with a story to tell...

1. DAYS The Kinks (1968) *UK No 12*

At the end of June 1968, The Kinks released the single 'Days', which reached number 12 in the United Kingdom. It was a top-20 hit in several other countries in the summer of that year but despite their popularity in America, it failed to chart there. It is also notable as the last recording made by the original line-up of the group; in fact, Ray Davies claimed the song was composed in part as an emotional farewell to the original members.

2. RUDI'S IN LOVE The Locomotive (1968) *UK No 25*

The Birmingham-based band were first called The Kansas City Seven, a name that was later considered too jazzy for an act who were including lots of blues and soul numbers into their show. The band gained recognition for their energetic live performances and soon had bookings in London, where they played many times. 1966 saw various personnel changes and by the end of the year, only trumpeter Jim Simpson remained of the original line-up.

In 1967, keyboard player Norman Haines became part of the new line-up and his songwriting talent played a major part in their future. Their first single, 'Broken Heart', failed to chart but the follow-up, 'Rudi's In Love', released in October of 1968, and also composed by Norman Haines, proved very popular on the dance floor and reached number 25 during its eight-week stay in the charts, giving them their only hit single.

3. I FEEL LOVE COMIN' ON Felice Taylor (1967) *UK No 11*

'I Feel Love Comin' On' was a one-hit wonder for the Californian-born Diana Ross-sound-alike Felice Taylor, who began singing with her sisters Darlene and Norma. Together, they formed girl group The Sweets who recorded one single in 1965, 'The Richest Girl'. Felice then recorded one single, 'Think About Me' under the name of Florian Taylor before signing to Bob Keane's Mustang label. There, she worked with Barry White who wrote and produced 'It May Be Winter Outside (But In My Heart It's Spring)' and 'I'm Under The Influence Of Love'. It was

Felice's third single, 'I Feel Love Comin' On' (also written and produced by White) that was to become a UK hit for her.

4. ANYTHING GOES Harpers Bizarre (1967) *US No 43/UK No 33*

Harpers Bizarre were formed out of a band from California called The Tikis, who got hold of the Paul Simon song 'The 59th Street Bridge Song (Feelin' Groovy)' and were determined to release their version of it. After acquiring a deal with Warner Brothers, the band changed their name to Harpers Bizarre – after the famous magazine. Their release of 'The 59th Street Bridge Song' reached the American top 20, prompting the label to call for an album, which they duly produced and creatively titled *Feelin' Groovy*. 'Anything Goes', a cover of the Cole Porter song, was the title track from their second album release. Group member Ted Templeman, who began as the drummer but later moved to guitar and vocals, went on to become a successful record producer for such artists as The Doobie Brothers, Van Morrison, Carly Simon and Eric Clapton.

5. MOTHER-IN-LAW Ernie K Doe (1961) *US No 1/UK No 29*

Ernie was born Ernest Kador Jnr in New Orleans and was the ninth of 11 children. His father was a Baptist minister and young Ernest began singing in his church choir. When he signed his first record deal it was decided that Kador was too difficult to pronounce so he became Ernie K Doe. The song 'Mother-In Law' had been discarded by Toussaint (who wrote and produced it) as he thought it worthless; but Ernie, who was having marital problems and put part of the blame on his in-laws, found the song and decided to record it. The deep bass voice belongs to Benny Spellman, and Ernie returned the favour the following year by singing backing vocals on his single 'Lipstick Traces'.

6. ALL ALONG THE WATCHTOWER The Jimi Hendrix Experience (1968) *US No 20/UK No 5*

This track, written by Bob Dylan for his album *John Wesley Harding*, was a song that Dylan had performed more often in concerts than any other of his compositions. Hendrix began work on his version in January 1968, with Dave Mason on guitar. Halfway through the session, bass player Noel Redding got fed up with the arguments amongst the other musicians, so he packed up and left. Mason then took over the bass part that eventually was played by Hendrix himself. Hendrix was still dissatisfied with the final result and continued to make changes to the track, overdubbing guitar parts for months to come. Becoming increasingly unhappy with the results, he continued to make changes until finally the finished version was released on his album *Electric Ladyland* in September 1968.

7. LET'S GO TO SAN FRANCISCO The Flowerpot Men (1967)
UK No 4

The group came about as a result of a single written and recorded by ex-Ivy League members John Carter and Ken Lewis. They licensed the track to Decca's Deram label where it became an instant hit; but the company found themselves with a big chart record and no one to promote it as neither John nor Ken had the appetite for touring or appearing on television again. The decision was taken to put together a group from some of the top session musicians and singers, which included vocalist Tony Burrows.

8. DEAD END STREET The Kinks (1966) *UK No 5*

'Dead End Street' is Dave Davies' (fellow band member and brother of Kinks' frontman/composer) favourite Kinks' singles. Many years after it was used as the setting for the single's promotional film, back in the Sixties, Dave helped campaigners in their plight to save a 300-year old street in Kentish Town. In the promo film, Dave, dressed as a Victorian undertaker, is taken by surprise as a corpse leaps out of a coffin and chases police down the street. The local council had planned to turn Little Green Street, the oldest road in Kentish Town, into a through-road for heavy-duty vehicles.

9. NEW YORK MINING DISASTER 1941 The Bee Gees (1967)
US No 14/UK No 12

This was the first major hit for The Bee Gees. The first part of the song was written when the group had arrived in the UK from Australia and were living in a rented house in Hendon. They went to their record company offices to play them some of their demos when there was a power cut. They sat on the stairs waiting for power to be restored and imagined what it must have been like to be trapped down the mines, and that inspired them to create the song sitting on the record company's stairwell.

Stevie Wonder in 1968, aged 18, around the time of 'For Once in My Life', his biggest UK yet back then

10. FOR ONCE IN MY LIFE Stevie Wonder (1968)
US No 2/UK No 3

This became Stevie's biggest UK hit to date. It was written by Ron Miller and Orlando Murden and was originally recorded by Jean DuShon as a demo for the writers. They were so impressed with her performance, they convinced Chess Records to release it as a single on their Cadet label in early 1966. As Miller was a staff writer for Motown's publishing company, label boss Berry Gordy was furious that he'd given the song away to an outside artist and insisted he made it available to his own signing, Barbara McNair, who then included it on her album *Here I Am*. In 1967, Stevie decided to record his own version but Gordy hated his treatment and vetoed it being released. Finally, in October 1968, he was convinced by the head of the label's quality control to allow it to be issued as a single. Many other artists have covered the song including Tony Bennett, Frank Sinatra, Ella Fitzgerald and The Temptations.

11. I GET AROUND The Beach Boys (1964) *US No 1/UK No 7*

Written by Brian Wilson and his cousin, Mike Love, it became their first single in the UK to break through the top 20 barrier and also their first to top the American charts. In November 1969, Brian Wilson's father sold many of the group's copyrights to an American music publisher for an undisclosed amount of money. More than 23 years later, Brian successfully claimed back many of the titles – at which point, Mike

Love filed a lawsuit against Brian, claiming he hadn't been given credit on many of the songs and therefore had received no royalties. One of the songs was 'I Get Around', originally credited to only Wilson, but Love insisted that he had come up with the 'round, round, I get around' hook. Now the credits have been amended and both writers are receiving their royalties.

12. SEA OF HEARTBREAK Don Gibson (1961) *US No 21/UK No 14*

This was Gibson's only UK hit as a performer, although he wrote several hits for other artists including 'I Can't Stop Loving You' for Ray Charles (which has subsequently been recorded by over 700 other artists) and 'Too Soon To Know' for Roy Orbison. Gibson was born in Shelby, North Carolina, into a poor working-class family and formed his first band, Sons Of The Soil, in 1948. In 1958 he went to Nashville to record his own versions of 'I Can't Stop Loving You' and 'Oh Lonesome Me', giving him a double A-sided hit. His nickname was 'The Sad Poet' because he constantly wrote songs about loneliness and lost love.

13. SOMETHING IN THE AIR Thunderclap Newman (1969)
US No 37/UK No 1

The group were assembled and produced by Pete Townshend, consisting of John 'Speedy' Keen on drums and vocals, Andy Newman on keyboards and Jimmy McCulloch on guitar (who later joined Paul McCartney in Wings). Using the pseudonym Bijou Drains, Townshend played bass on this record, and this was the only time that a member of The Who was involved with a number-one hit single. The song was originally titled 'Revolution' but it was decided to change it to 'Something In the Air', as The Beatles had also just recorded a song called 'Revolution'.

14. YOU GOT SOUL Johnny Nash (1968) *US No 58/UK No 6*

Johnny Nash, an African-American, born in Houston, Texas, recorded several hits in Jamaica in 1968. During this time he recorded 'Hold Me Tight', accompanied by Byron Lee & The Dragonaires, and 'You Got Soul' was the follow-up. While in Jamaica he met a struggling band called The Wailers, who included Peter Tosh and Rita and Bob Marley. Hoping to break the rock-steady sound in America, Nash signed them up and financed their early recordings but none were successful. However, both Johnny and Marley went on to bigger and better things.

15. SEARCHIN' The Hollies (1963) *UK No 12*

A cover of the 1957 top-40 hit by The Coasters and the first single by The Hollies to make the top 20. Childhood friends Allan Clarke and Graham Nash had been singing together for a number of years as a semi-professional duo under names such as The Guytones, The Two Teens and Ricky and Dane. When Eric Haydock and Don Rathbone joined them, they became The Fourtones and then The Deltas. After Tony Hicks joined them from a band called The Dolphins, they became The Hollies. After the success of 'Searchin', they set about recording their first album. Just at that time Don Rathbone decided to leave to become their road manager and was replaced by Bobby Elliott from Shane Fenton's Fentones.

16. ONLY THE HEARTACHES Houston Wells (1963) *UK No 22*

Northumberland-born Andrew Smith lived for a time in Canada in the late Fifties where he worked as a logger and it was there that he developed his love of Country music. His inspiration as a singer came from the likes of Slim Whitman, Jim Reeves and Johnny Cash. His life in Canada was short-lived and soon he returned to the UK and lived in Essex, where he met up with a local group, The Coasters. The band invited him to become their vocalist and were so impressed with his performances that soon they became known as Andrew Smith & The Coasters. One of their demos found its way to Joe Meek, who agreed to sign Andrew but without the rest of the group. Andrew insisted that he would only record with the rest of the band.

A compromise was reached that Meek would record Andrew and The Coasters but only sign Andrew, who would have to share his earnings with the other guys. Another surprise came when Meek insisted in changing his name to the American-sounding Houston Wells; and because there was already a successful American group named The Coasters, they became The Marksmen. After two failed singles, Meek chose 'Only The Heartaches' as the third release, which gave them their only UK hit.

17. MAKE THE WORLD GO AWAY Eddy Arnold (1966)
US No 6/UK No 8

Originally an American hit in 1963 by Ray Price, this was by far Eddy's biggest hit, both here and America. Achieving 146 American Country hits, including 28 number ones, he was ranked number one in Joel

Whitburn's Top Country Singles book. Nicknamed 'The Tennessee Cowboy', for many years he came under the wing of the legendary Colonel Tom Parker who also managed Elvis Presley. Eddy died on May 8th, 2008, just one week short of his ninetieth birthday.

18. PEPPERMINT TWIST Joey Dee & The Starliters (1962)
US No 1/UK No 33

Born Joseph DiNicola in New Jersey, Joey attended State College with the ambition of becoming a teacher of English and History. However, he decided to give a career in music a shot with the view that, if it didn't work out, he could always return to teaching. Forming his first group, The Thunder Trio, they won second place in a top amateur contest. In 1958 they recorded their first single, 'Lorraine', for the obscure Little label. Through a contact of high school friends, The Shirelles, Joey was introduced to Sceptre Records, where his first single as Joey Dee & The Starliters, 'Face Of An Angel', was released. Their change of fortune and name came about whilst working at a New York nightclub on West 45th Street called The Peppermint Lounge, where they would introduce their audience to modern dance crazes – not least of all, The Twist. Many star names visited the club including Judy Garland, Nat King Cole, Liberace, and even The Beatles came to check them out.

In 1962, Joey Dee & The Starliters signed to Roulette Records on the promise that they would be able to record live at the Peppermint Lounge. Their first single for the label, 'The Peppermint Twist', was released in November 1961 and topped the American charts a few weeks later. As promised, they then went about recording their first album, *Doin' The Twist At The Peppermint Lounge*.

19. HOLD ON I'M COMING Sam & Dave (1965) *US No 21*

'Hold On I'm Coming' was probably one of this group's most well-known songs, so it's surprising to note that it failed to make the UK charts. It was, however, the first single they made together where the higher voice of Sam Moore took the lead vocal on the opening verse and Dave Prater was given the answering role in the second verse, a formula they maintained for most of their future hits. The song came about when Isaac Hayes was trying to compose with his songwriting partner David Porter, who at the time was in another room. He called out to Porter to listen to a melody he had come up with and the response was, 'Hold on man, I'm coming.'

The Small Faces' 'My Mind's Eye' single may have been a top-20 hit for the group, but it was the beginning of the end between them and their record label, Decca

20. MY MIND'S EYE The Small Faces (1966) *UK No 4*

This was the fifth consecutive British top-20 UK hit single for The Small Faces, but was originally intended as an album track. The single was released without the group's knowledge whilst they were in the middle of a tour of England, much to the band's displeasure. Their manager, Don Arden, had an unfinished rough mix of the track 'My Mind's Eye' in his possession and had been keen to release the song as a single earlier and, whilst the boys were not around to complain, convinced their label, Decca, to run with the single. Despite its high chart-placing, this record signalled the beginning of the end of their relationship both with Arden and Decca.

21. DREAMIN' Johnny Burnette (1960) *US No 16/UK No 5*

After leaving school, Johnny tried his hand at becoming a professional boxer; but, after one fight with a $150 purse and a broken nose, he decided to quit the ring. He began performing in local Memphis bars with his brother Dorsey. In 1952 they formed a group, The Rhythm Rangers, with guitarist Paul Burlison. Landing a record deal with the Coral label, they released three unsuccessful singles as The Rock'n'Roll Trio. Travelling to California, they managed to make contact with Ricky Nelson, who recorded and had a hit with one of their songs, 'It's Late'. As The Burnette Brothers, they gained one release on the Imperial label, 'Warm Love', but after that decided to go their own ways, with Johnny being signed to the Freedom label, an offshoot of Liberty. With them he released three singles, none of which were hits, and in 1959 the label was shut down. Johnny was transferred to Liberty itself under the direction of producer Snuff Garrett. The next two singles sold well but not enough to make the charts. It was his third release, 'Dreamin', that turned him into a star.

22. EVE OF DESTRUCTION Barry McGuire (1965)
US No 1/UK No 3

Barry had previously been a member of The New Christie Minstrels before he was signed up by top record producer Lou Adler at the beginning of 1965. One of Adler's writing protégées was P.F. Sloan, who had already written hits for Jan & Dean. He had just completed work on 'Eve Of Destruction', a song inspired by Bob Dylan. Adler liked it but was only considering it for a B-side. After recording it together with a couple of other songs, the tape was left with Jay Lasker, the Vice President of Dunhill Records, who loved the track and gave it to a DJ on a local radio station. Within a few hours the record was on the air, much to the annoyance of Adler as the track hadn't been completed; it was a guide vocal and a rough mix but that was how the record was released – only to be banned by several radio stations on the grounds of its lyrical content.

23. SWEET DREAM Jethro Tull (1969) *UK No 7*

Ian Anderson formed his first band, The Blades, in Blackpool in 1962 and by 1964 had developed them into a seven-piece white soul unit known as The John Evan Band, named after their pianist. By 1967 they had moved to London in search of work. Work proved to be scarce and most of the group quit and went home, leaving Anderson and bassist Glenn Cornick who decided to join forces with guitarist Mick Abrahams and his friend and drummer, Clive Bunker. Still with work thin on the ground, they underwent several more name changes – many suggested by their booking agents. One, a history enthusiast, came up with Jethro Tull after the 18th century agriculturist.

The name stuck mainly because they'd used it for a booking where the club manger liked them enough to offer them a return date. They released their first album in 1968, *This Was*, after which Abrahams left after a falling out with Anderson – largely over music policy – and formed his own band, Blodwyn Pig. He was replaced by Martin Barre, who worked on the group's next and only UK number one album, *Stand Up*, that produced one of their best-known songs, 'Living In The Past'. They achieved further singles successes including this 1969 best seller, 'Sweet Dream'.

24. CRAZY Patsy Cline (1961) *US No 9*

Although the record was first released in 1961, it wasn't until its re-issue in 1990 that it made it into the British top 20, reaching number 14. Written by Willie Nelson, who was a struggling Country singer at the time, this recording gave him his first big break. A few weeks before the recording, Patsy was in a car crash and was thrown through a windscreen. When she turned up for the session, she was unable to hit the high notes due to severe pain from a broken rib, so the musicians recorded the track without her, and a few days later she added her vocals in one take while standing on crutches.

25. WILL YOU LOVE ME TOMORROW The Shirelles (1961)
US No 1/UK No 4

The Shirelles were the very first female group to top the American charts. The girls were all grammar-school friends and formed a group calling themselves The Poquellos, which is Spanish for little birds. One of their classmates, Mary Jane Greenberg, wanted them to audition for her mother, who ran a small independent record label but the girls weren't interested. After much persuasion, Mary Jane convinced them it was the right thing to do. Her mother loved them and signed them up, but hated the group's name. After recording their first single, 'I Met Him On Sunday', they were forced to come up with a new name and they unanimously settled on The Shirelles. Unable to give the record sufficient promotion, it was licensed to the major Decca label and ended up at number 49 on the American charts in 1958. After several further releases, they were played 'Will You Love Me Tomorrow', written by Carole King and Gerry Goffin. They disliked it but were persuaded to record. A new arrangement gave it a new lease of life. Carole King was present at the recording and, unhappy with the drummer, decided to play the drums herself.

26. JIMMY MACK Martha & The Vandellas (1967)
US No 10/UK No 21

Written by the Motown geniuses Holland-Dozier and Holland, 'Jimmy Mack' gave Martha & The Vandellas their final top-20 hit in The States. The track was originally recorded in 1964 but was shelved at the time as it was deemed unsuitable for release due to the continuation of the Vietnam War, as it tells the story of Jimmy Mack's return home. When it was finally issued in 1967, the war had become a highly debated topic in America, thus the song's sentiment took on a different meaning for many listeners, particularly those soldiers stationed abroad. The B-side of 'Jimmy Mack' – 'Third Finger, Left Hand' – also became a Motown classic, and was successfully covered in the UK in 1972 by The Pearls.

27. IN AND OUT OF LOVE Diana Ross & The Supremes (1967)
US No 9/UK No 13

This second single to be credited to Diana Ross & The Supremes was the penultimate Brian Holland, Lamont Dozier and Eddie Holland production and composition. In addition, it was the final Supremes single to feature former lead singer and founder member Florence Ballard. The track was recorded in Los Angeles – an unusual event, as most of Motown's hits came out of the company's main Detroit studios. The writers were at this time becoming unhappy with their position with the label and they staged a work slowdown, turning out virtually no product throughout the year. In 1968, they left the company, resulting in a series of lawsuits that continued for over a decade.

28. WALK LIKE A MAN The Four Seasons (1963)
US No 1/UK No 12

This was their third American number one, topping the charts for three weeks. The Four Seasons were so popular that during the summer of 1963 that a DJ, discussing the British phenomenon of The Beatles, described them as the UK's answer to The Four Seasons. During the recording of the track, the local fire department received an emergency call from the building that housed the studios. As producer Bob Crewe was insisting upon recording the perfect take, smoke and water started to seep into the studio as the group repeated their efforts upon Crewe's insistence: the room directly above the studio was on fire, yet Crewe blocked the studio door and continued recording until firemen used battering rams to pull them all out.

29. LET THE LITTLE GIRL DANCE Billy Bland (1960)
US No 7/UK No 15

The single was recorded for the American independent Old Town Records, whose boss, Hymie Weiss, used to boast to be the 'Payola

King' of New York. He once was quoted as saying, 'Payola was the greatest thing in the world. You didn't have to go out for dinner with someone and kiss their ass, just pay them, 'Here's the money, just play the record'. One beneficiary of Weiss's shenanigans was Billy Bland, who started his own group, The Four Bees, in 1954. They were brought to New Orleans by Fats Domino's producer and co-writer, Dave Bartholomew, who gave them a song he'd written called 'Toy Bell', that later was turned into 'My Ding-A-Ling'. Bland's hit, 'Let The Little Girl Dance', was recorded towards the end of 1959 and became a hit the following year. The Miller Sisters sang the backing vocals and the band included Buddy Lucas on sax, Mickey Baker on guitar and Rod Porter on drums. This was his only major hit, and in the mid Seventies he retired from the music business. It's rumoured that, at one stage, he went on to run a soul food restaurant in Harlem.

30. GUANTANAMERA The Sandpipers (1966) *US No 9/UK No 7*

Pete Seeger adapted the song from a poem by the Cuban writer Jose Marti. The Sandpipers were a trio from California. Founder members Jim Brady, Michael Piano and Richard Shoff met whilst singing with The Mitchell Boys Choir and decided to go it alone. They called themselves The Four Seasons before someone quickly pointed out that a New York group of that name already existed, so they settled on The Grads. They came to the attention of trumpet-playing record boss Herb Alpert of A&M records, who signed them to the label. After a couple of failed singles, they agreed to change their name to The Sandpipers and added female singer Pamela Ramcier to their line-up. This was their first and biggest hit together and, after a few further less successful singles and a number of popular albums, they finally called it a day in 1975.

31. THE ONION SONG Marvin Gaye & Tammi Terrell (1969)
UK No 9

Surprisingly, this was only a minor hit in The States where it peaked at number 50. The story that most of us have heard was that Tammi was too ill when it came to recording the track, so songwriter Valerie Simpson added her own voice. Although she was uneasy about pretending to be another singer, she agreed to go ahead when she was informed that the record royalties would go towards Terrell's medical costs. In recent years, however, Simpson has denied ever doubling for the singer, leaving us with yet another Motown mystery.

32. WALKING THE DOG The Dennisons (1964) *UK No 36*

In 1963, the Dennisons had minor success with their single, 'Be My Girl'. Their follow-up, 'Walking the Dog', was to be their only UK top-40 hit. They were, however, a very popular Liverpudlian group and it was once claimed they made the biggest impression on Merseyside since The Beatles. Several record labels tried to sign them and Decca won the contract. The 'B' side of this Rufus Thomas song was 'You Don't Know What Love Is', written for them by Ben E King while they were touring with him. They released one final single in November 1964, 'Nobody Like My Baby', but it failed to chart and the group finally broke up in 1966. Their drummer, Clive Hornby, turned his attention to acting and won himself a part in the long-running TV soap *Emmerdale Farm*, playing the part of Jack Sugden.

33. SPEAK TO ME PRETTY Brenda Lee (1962) *UK No 3*

Brenda had dozens of hits in The States but this wasn't one of them. She was born Brenda Mae Tarpley in Atlanta, Georgia, weighing four pounds and 11 ounces. She was fascinated by the family radio at a very

The New Musical Express, welcoming Brenda Lee to the UK

early age and, after hearing a song once, could whistle the complete tune. She would earn a few coins or a bag of sweets by singing when her mother stood her on the counter of their local store. At the age of six, she won a local talent contest. Her father had died by the time she'd turned 10, and she became the family's main breadwinner by singing at events and on local radio and television. Her big break came when she was spotted by country singer and TV personality Red Foley on a TV show in Atlanta. Foley put her in front of a live audience that erupted in applause after her appearance and wouldn't let her leave the stage until she performed a further three songs. She was 11 years old and well under five feet tall. Two months later, she was offered a record deal with Decca, and the rest is history.

34. TAKE THESE CHAINS FROM MY HEART Ray Charles (1963)
US No 8/UK No 5

The roots of Ray Charles's backing vocal group, the Raelettes, lie in another girl group, the Cookies, who formed in Brooklyn in 1954, with vocalists Earl Jean McCrea, Margie Hendrix and Pat Lyles. After making their debut by taking top honours at the famed Apollo Theater's Amateur Night, the Cookies signed to Atlantic Records, backing Lavern Baker, Big Joe Turner and Ruth Brown. In addition, they recorded in their own right as The Cookies, scoring an R&B top-10 hit in 1956 with 'In Paradise'. In the meantime, Charles recruited vocalist Mary Ann Fisher to join him on duets, and when Atlantic session producer Jesse Stone introduced him to the Cookies, the singer simply added Fisher to their line-up and renamed the group The Raelettes. As The Cookies, they will probably be best remembered for their original version of the Carole King and Gerry Goffin song, 'Chains'.

35. STRANGERS IN THE NIGHT Frank Sinatra (1966)
US No 1/UK No 1

On the day of the recording session, Glen Campbell was brought in at the last moment to play guitar. Unfortunately, he was unfamiliar with the song and busked his way round the first take. Sinatra always wanted to get a song completed in one take so when he was told they'd have to do it again, he yelled at Campbell, 'Is that guy with us or is he having a sleep?' Nevertheless, it was Glen who came up with the familiar guitar phrase that helped make it a hit, giving Frank his first and only number one on his own Reprise label – an achievement matched a few months earlier by his daughter, Nancy.

36. IT'S A MAN'S MAN'S MAN'S WORLD James Brown (1966)
US No 8/UK No 13

Written by James with Betty Jean Newsome, who wrote the lyrics based on her own observations of the relationships between men and women. The song itself was a play on the 1963 comedy movie *It's A Mad, Mad, Mad, Mad World*. Brown's backing group, The Famous Flames, were not used on the recording but were credited on the label, and female backing vocals were recorded but left out of the final mix. The song itself evolved over a period of several years. In 1963, Tammy Montgomery, later known as Tammi Terrell, recorded a soundalike song, 'I Cried', and the following year Brown himself recorded a demo version with the title 'It's A Man's World'.

37. TREAT HER RIGHT Roy Head (1965) *US No 2/UK No 30*

Head's only UK hit and by far his biggest success Stateside, 'Treat Her Right' was produced by maverick music executive Huey Meaux, who had just enjoyed success with the Sir Douglas Quintet hit, 'She's About A Mover'. Head had been recording since the late Fifties and had grown up in Crystal City, Texas, near the Mexican border. His mother was a full-blooded Indian from Oklahoma who slaved at a spinach factory in Crystal City, the spinach capital of the world. In 1957, Head formed The Traits and spent the next few years playing low-life clubs, many of which were protected by chicken wire. In 1965, they recorded 'Treat Her Right'. It had originally been a double entendre blues song called 'Talkin' 'Bout A Cow' that they often performed on stage, but the song was re-written to appeal to the masses.

38. WHEN YOU WALK IN THE ROOM The Searchers (1964)
US No 35/UK No 3

When British group The Searchers heard Jackie de Shannon's original recording of 'Needles And Pins', they set about recording their own version. They also achieved major success with another of Jackie's songs – 'When You Walk In The Room'. After the success of 'Sweets For My Sweet', its producer, Tony Hatch, presented the group with 'Sugar And Spice' as a potential follow-up, telling them it had been written by a guy named Fred Nightingale (who in fact turned out to be a pseudonym for Hatch himself who didn't want the group to feel obliged to record his song). Hatch also had considerable success writing under another name, Mark Anthony – with one of his most notable songs being Bobby Rydell's 'Forget Him'.

39. HERE COMES THE NIGHT Them (1965) *UK No 2*
'Here Comes The Night' was written by Bert Burns and featured Jimmy Page on guitar and Phil Coulter on piano (Coulter went on to write a string of hits with Bill Martin, including two of the best-remembered UK entries into the Eurovision Song Contest – winning it for the first time in 1967 with Sandie Shaw's 'Puppet On A String' as runners-up the following year with Cliff Richard's 'Congratulations'). They went on to write and produce hits for many top Seventies' acts including The Bay City Rollers, Slik and Kenny. Prior to this later run of success, they were also responsible for 'Thanks', a huge hit in Germany for J Vincent Edwards.

40. LITTLE CHILDREN Billy J Kramer & The Dakotas (1964)
US No 7/UK No 1
'Little Children' (written by written by Mort Shuman who had composed hits for dozens of artists, including Elvis Presley and Marty Wilde) became Billy J Kramer & The Dakotas' first hit of the year in 1964. Billy's manager, Brian Epstein, was against the release of the single but was finally persuaded otherwise by the group, who were sure they had a hit with the song. They were proved right when it became their biggest selling single and second number one. At the same time, having been released as a double A-side with 'Bad To Me' in the US, it fulfilled their American dream when the record climbed to number seven in their charts. This also made them the only British act, apart from The Beatles, to ever put both sides of the same single into the American top 10.

41. CONCRETE AND CLAY Unit 4 + 2 (1965) *US No 28/UK No 1*
This track was written by group members Tommy Moeller and Brian Parker, who had both previously been members of Adam Faith's backing band, The Roulettes. After reaching number one in the UK, their record label, Decca, insisted that they hastily put together an album, also entitled *Concrete and Clay*, to capitalise on the success; but none of the material was as strong as their hit. Nevertheless, the

next single to be released, 'You've Never been in Love Like This Before', reached the Top 20 in the UK. 'Concrete And Clay' would probably have been a bigger hit in America had it not been for a direct cover by one-hit wonder Eddie Rambeau; and although his version only reached number 35, it would have split both sales and airplay.

42. FLOWERS ON THE WALL The Statler Brothers (1965)
US No 4/UK No 38

Written by founder member Lew DeWitt, the Statler Brothers were travelling with The Johnny Cash Show (as back-up singers) at the time of release of this single. It wasn't until they were reading through a music magazine and saw the American charts that they realised they had a hit on their hands. The group, from Staunton, Virginia, were originally named The Four Stars before changing to The Kingsmen. However, with the success of the song 'Louie Louie' in 1963 by another group with the same name, they became The Statler Brothers, even though only two of them were brothers and neither named Statler.

43. WALK ON BY Dionne Warwick (1964) *US No 6/UK No 9*

This was first released in America as the B-side to Warwick's single 'Any Old Time Of The Day', at which point she had issued several singles that failed to make the grade, and this was the last shot her label, Sceptre, were going to give her before releasing her from her contract. DJ Murray the K, whose show on radio station WINS was the top-rated programme in New York, refused to play it claiming the B-side was far superior. No matter how many people called and pleaded with him, he continued to play the B-side instead because he knew that was the tune with potential. Warwick's record company were less than happy with his decision, but listeners agreed with Murray. 'Walk On By' became the hit and Dionne's recording contract was renewed.

44. TELL ME WHEN The Applejacks (1964) *UK No 7*

The group hailed from Solihull in Warwickshire and began life as a skiffle group called The Crestas. As they progressed and their line-up swelled, in 1961 they changed names to Jaguars, playing mostly instrumentals in the style of The Shadows and The Tornados. By mid-1962, instrumentals were on the wane so they enlisted vocalist Al Jackson and became The Applejacks. Signed to Decca in 1964, they went into the studios and

The Applejacks get stuck into their toffee apples on the cover of 'Tell Me When', which was to be their biggest hit

recorded a song called 'Baby Jane' but this was duly scrapped in favour of 'Tell Me When' (written by Les Reed and Geoff Stephens), which became the group's debut release and biggest hit.

45. BERNADETTE The Four Tops (1967) *US No 4/UK No 8*

As with many of The Four Tops hits, the song was written by Brian Holland, Lamont Dozier and Edward Holland Jnr. When they wrote the song, Brian was going out with a girl whose middle name was Bernadette and, coincidentally, Edward had a different date with the same name, unbeknown to the other two composers. It also transpired that Lamont had a crush on a beautiful Italian girl named Bernadette who had eyes for somebody else. He never told her, but used her as inspiration for writing many songs. Each of the three girls, though, thought the song was exclusively about them. Motown boss Berry Gordy Jnr, who had a reputation for his criticism, took a dislike to the song, hated the false ending and couldn't stand the section where the backing singers went 'ahhhh'. He told the writers that it should have stopped and started on the beat, but they refused to change it on the grounds they wanted to throw the listener off course and give them something to think about.

46. FOOTSTEPS Steve Lawrence (1960) *US No 7/UK No 4*

Steve signed to the mighty ABC Paramount in America in 1959 after previously recording for Coral. His first major hit for his new label was the original version of 'Pretty Blue Eyes', successfully covered in the UK by Craig Douglas. As his version climbed the American charts, he was halfway through a two-year tour of duty with the army and was unable to exploit the record apart from his capacity as the official vocalist with the US Army band at Fort Meyer, Virginia. His follow-up was also covered in the UK, this time by Ronnie Carroll, whose version reached number 36; but it was the original 'Footsteps' that won through.

47. GUITAR MAN Elvis Presley (1968) *UK No 19*

The song was featured in his movie *Clambake* and only managed a low placing of number 43 in the American Hot 100. The song was written by Jerry Reed under the name of Jerry Hubbard and when Presley came to Nashville in 1967 to record some new tracks, he decided he wanted to cover 'Guitar Man' that Jerry himself had recorded some months earlier. The recording didn't go as well as planned as Elvis was unhappy with the guitar sound on the track, so producer Felton Jarvis called Reed who was on a fishing holiday to ask him how he'd got the sound on his own recording. His response was, 'If you want it to sound like mine, then you'd better book me to play it'. Jarvis hired Reed and all was well.

48. NORTH TO ALASKA Johnny Horton (1961) *US No 4/UK No 23*

This was the title song to the movie starring John Wayne and Stewart Granger. In the past, Horton had sung several popular movie tie-in songs but this was the first one that was sung over the opening titles. Soon after recording this track, Horton was killed in a head-on collision with a drunk driver while returning home from a performance in Austin, Texas. An unfounded rumour suggested that on the night of the crash, he was on his way to Dallas to meet actor Ward Bond, star of the Western TV series, *Wagon Train* about a part in the series. Ironically, Bond was attending a football game and died of a heart attack, hours after Horton's fatal crash. Another Horton appeared in *Wagon Train*. Robert and one of his sisters confirmed the story to be true.

49. VALLERI The Monkees (1968) *UK No 12*

Written by Tommy Boyce and Bobby Hart who supplied many of the songs for the group's popular TV series. Don Kirshner, who was musical advisor to the show, knew he required two new songs every week for inclusion and was always keen on having titles that included girls' names. Boyce had an outline of a song he had been working on and told Kirshner that he and Hart had a great song with a girl's name that he'd like to play for him. Boyce got Hart out of bed after the conversation and explained that he'd told a lie and that they had to finish the song as he'd made an appointment to play it. As they were driving to Kirshner's home, they were shouting possible names to each other for the title until they settled on 'Valleri'.

50. (WHAT A) WONDERFUL WORLD Sam Cooke (1960)
US No 12/UK No 27

The song started out as a composition by record producers Lou Adler and Herb Alpert, but neither were that keen on it until they played it to Sam Cooke, who wanted to record it. Not convinced the song was totally right, Sam asked permission to make some changes before finally recording it as an afterthought at the end of one of his sessions. No one thought of releasing it until a year after Sam had left his label Keen and signed to RCA. After it became a hit, RCA purchased the rights to much of Cooke's back catalogue to avoid more of this earlier material being released.

51. GROOVIN' The Young Rascals (1967) *US No 1/UK No 8*

'Groovin'' was the second of three American number-one hits for the group founded by Felix Cavaliere, who was once a member of Joey Dee's Starliters with Eddie Brigati and Gene Cornish. They all decided to leave The Starliters to form The Young Rascals with drummer Dino Danelli. In 1965, they were signed to the Atlantic label and their first release, 'I Ain't Gonna Eat My Heart Out Anymore', made the Billboard Hot 100, but it was their 1966 release, 'Good Lovin'', that gave them their first American number one. They followed with two more top-20 hits before topping the charts again in 1966 with 'Groovin'', after which they decided to drop the 'Young' from their name.

52. HE'S SO FINE The Chiffons (1963) *US No 1/UK No 16*

This single topped the American charts for four weeks. It was written by Ronald Mack, who became the group's manager after overhearing them sing in their school dining room. Mack succeeded in getting Bright Tunes, a company owned by The Tokens, interested in the girls and recorded 'He's So Fine' with The Tokens themselves playing on the backing track. The finished product was taken to Capitol Records, who turned it down on the grounds it was too simple and too trite. The record was taken to 10 other labels before being placed with the Laurie label in the States.

53. IF I ONLY HAD TIME **John Rowles (1968)** *UK No 3*

Born in Kawerau, New Zealand, John Rowles became the country's first international pop star. His love for music began with an obsession to imitate Elvis whilst still at school and won first prize in a talent contest singing 'All Shook Up'. At 17, he headed for Australia and joined singer Eddie Low. Forming a duo, they wore red jackets and played a local nightclub, The Riverside Inn in Melbourne, for $10 a night. When the contract expired, John moved to Sydney and joined a group called The Dingdongers, who changed their name to The Sundowners. By 1966, he decided to go solo. Changing his hairstyle and wearing mod clothes, he secured a place on the Australian TV version of the talent show *New Faces*. This led to several offers, including a recording contract that resulted in two singles being released Down Under. In 1967, he travelled to England where he met up with record producer Mike Leander and together they began forming a plan to launch him in the UK. His first release 'If I Only Had Time' hit the spot right away, reaching number three on the British charts.

54. LOVE LETTERS **Ketty Lester (1962)** *US No 5/UK No 4*

Originally a big American hit in 1945 for Dick Haymes, this was the title song to the movie of the same name starring Jennifer Jones. Ketty Lester, whose real name was Revoyda Frierson, was born in Arkansas. After a residency at The Purple Onion Club in San Francisco in the early Fifties, she joined Cab Calloway's Orchestra for a European tour. After a brief stint in an off-Broadway production of *Cabin In The Sky*, she recorded her only top-40 hit in a garage studio in Los Angeles, and added her vocals in a bathroom in order to get the required echo on her voice.

55. LAY LADY LAY **Bob Dylan (1969)** *UK No 5*

Dylan's final hit of the Sixties was taken from his multi-million selling album *Nashville Skyline* and originally written for the soundtrack of the movie *Midnight Cowboy*, but was submitted too late for inclusion. Like many of the tracks on the album, Dylan's voice is warmer and relatively low-sounding compared to the more abrasive nasal singing style with which he had become famous. Dylan attributed his 'new' voice to having quit smoking before recording the album, but some unreleased bootleg recordings from the early 1960s reveal that Dylan had used this softer singing style in the early days.

56. SHE'D RATHER BE WITH ME The Turtles (1967)
US No 3/UK No 4

This gave the group their fifth American top-40 hit and their second of three top-20 hits in the UK. Although 1967 was probably the most successful year in the history of the group, it was also fraught with problems. At the start of the year, drummer Don Murray and then bassist Chuck Portz quit the group, being replaced by Joel Larson and then John Barbata on drums, and by Chip Douglas on bass. Chip also became the group's music arranger. Impressed by Chip's studio work, Monkee Michael Nesmith approached him to become the Monkees' new producer, as that band wanted to break out of their 'manufactured' studio mould. Chip accepted, left the Turtles and was replaced by bassist and singer Jim Pons.

57. TIN SOLDIER The Small Faces (1967) *UK No 9*

Written by group members Steve Marriott and Ronnie Lane, 'Tin Soldier' gave The Small Faces their eighth UK top-20 hit. The song had originally been written for P. P. Arnold, one of the group's label mates on Immediate, but when the group realised the song's potential, they decided to keep it for themselves and watched it climb to number nine at the end of 1967. Arnold forgave them and ended up singing backing vocals on the record. When the top brass at the BBC heard the disc, they informed the group that the last line of the song needed to be removed before they could play it, believing that Marriott sang 'sleep with you', when in fact the words were 'sit with you'.

58. THE LAST TIME The Rolling Stones (1965) *US No 9/UK No 1*

The group's third number one, but this was the first to have been written by Keith and Mick. The song is believed to have been inspired by a 1955 gospel song recorded by The Staple Singers, 'This May Be The Last Time'

Bucanneers of rock'n'roll's high seas: Johnny Kidd and the Pirates

and also by James Brown's 1964 single 'Maybe The Last Time', which was also based on the gospel song. The Stones' track was recorded in Los Angeles in a day during a stopover on their way to Australia. Despite their gruelling schedule, they wanted to keep releasing singles to capitalize on their growing popularity, and therefore continually recorded between shows.

59. I'LL NEVER GET OVER YOU
Johnny Kidd & The Pirates (1963) *UK No 4*

At the beginning of 1963, the group recorded a version of the Ritchie Barrett song, 'Some Other Guy', a song that was popular amongst the up-and-coming Liverpool groups. Although Johnny was the first to record it, his label, EMI, decided not to release it – only to see The Big Three begin to climb the charts with their version. Depressed by the decision, Kidd and The Pirates decided to cut the song 'I'll Never Get Over You' (written and previously recorded by their manager Gordon Mills and his group, The Viscounts). Although initially unsure about the song's potential, after several takes at slightly different tempos, they were finally satisfied with a somewhat slower version that became the single.

60. HOLY COW Lee Dorsey (1966) *US No 23/UK No 6*

Not only was this Lee Dorsey's biggest UK hit, it was also to be his last in the UK. As with most of his hits, the song was written by Allan Toussaint, with whom he had formed a strong working relationship – thanks largely to Marshall Sehorn, one of the most influential behind-the-scenes men in the history of New Orleans Rhythm and Blues. Sehorn had first signed Dorsey to the small Fury label before it collapsed. Two years later in 1965, Toussaint and Sehorn formed their own partnership and their first priority was to work with Dorsey after acquiring him a record deal with Bell's subsidiary, Amy. From thereon in, the hits kept coming. In 1979, Dorsey suffered two broken legs in a motorbike accident but still managed to appear that year at the New Orleans Jazz and Heritage Festival, performing from a wheelchair. On December 1st, 1986, just before his sixtieth birthday, he died of emphysema.

61. OUT OF TIME Chris Farlowe (1966) *UK No 1*

Born John Henry Deighton in Islington, North London, this artist taught himself to play the guitar before focusing more on his singing abilities. He then decided to change his name to Chris Farlowe, the surname being taken from American jazz guitarist, Tal Farlow; and 'Chris' because it sounded right. He then formed the first of what would be countless line-ups for his group, The Thunderbirds. In 1962, he secured a one-off record deal with Decca, releasing his debut, 'Air Travel', that went almost unnoticed. The following year he signed a five-year deal with EMI's Columbia imprint, for whom he would release five unsuccessful singles. During this time, he cheekily recorded another single for Decca, 'The Blue Beat', under the name of The Beazers, although everyone on the club scene knew their true identity. His final EMI release came out in 1965, 'Buzz With The Fuzz'. His next release, 'Stormy Monday Blues,' was issued on the Sue label as Little Joe Cook. In 1965, he became one of the first artists to be signed to Andrew Oldham's Immediate label and, after a couple of releases, found himself in the top 40 in 1966 with the Keith Richards and Mick Jagger song 'Think', a cover from The Stones' *Aftermath* album, before finally cracking it big time with another of their songs, 'Out Of Time'.

62. 98.6 Keith (1967) *US No 7/UK No 24*

The backing vocals on this single were provided by hit vocal group The Tokens. Barry James Keefer, who recorded under the name of Keith, told his girlfriend soon after recording the song that he couldn't believe that he'd just made a song with a number relating to the average human's body temperature. He first recorded with a group called The Admirations when he was originally called Keif, but changed his name to Keith when it was pointed out to him that that Keif was too close to the Moroccan word for cannabis.

63. HARBOUR LIGHTS The Platters (1960) *US No 8/UK No 11*

Although they had many big hit records in the Fifties, this was the Platters' only UK chart success in the Sixties and indeed their final chart entry. Written by Hugh Williams and Jimmy Kennedy, the theme was first used as background music in the 1940 movie *The Long Voyage Home*, starring John Ford and John Wayne, and later became an American number-one hit in 1950 for Sammy Kaye and his orchestra with vocals by Don Cornell. The Platters' version was released there as a double A-side with another standard, 'Sleepy Lagoon'.

64. LET THERE BE LOVE Nat King Cole (1962) *UK No 11*

This song was written by Lionel Rand (with lyrics by Ian Grant) around 1939. It was believed to have been initially recorded by Van Alexander and His Orchestra in that year, although a version by Sammy Kaye in 1940 is often credited as the first. Nat King Cole's 1961 version featured backing by The George Shearing Quintet, with strings arranged and conducted by Ralph Carmichael. There have subsequently been many cover versions recorded by other artists over the years, including Peggy Lee, Tony Bennett and Shirley Bassey.

65. RAG DOLL The Four Seasons (1964) *US No 1/UK No 2*

The record reached number one in America, a hard feat to achieve at the time with The Beatles dominating the top 20. Producer and writer Bob Gaudio came up with the idea for the song when he was stopped at a red light on his way to the studios and a young poorly dressed girl appeared in front of his car and washed his windscreen. He fished around for some coins to give her but could only find a five-dollar bill to give her. The astonished look on her face led him to remember her when he came to writing the song.

66. ALL I REALLY WANT TO DO Cher (1965) *UK No 9*

It was pure coincidence that both Cher and The Byrds decided to cover 'All I Really Want To Do' at the same time. The Byrds had just enjoyed a number-one hit with Bob Dylan's 'Mr Tambourine Man' and were looking for a follow-up, and Sonny was in search of songs to launch Cher's solo career with both parties exploring the songs on 'Another Side Of Bob Dylan', his third album release. In America, The Byrds version reached the top 40 whilst Cher made the top 20, but in the UK

The Byrds made the top five and Cher had to be content with making the top 10 but decided to make it the title of her debut solo album.

67. GET AWAY Georgie Fame & The Blue Flames (1966) UK No 1

After topping the charts in 1965 with 'Yeah Yeah', Georgie Fame & The Blue Flames had a few further much smaller hits, but the feeling was that they were unable to follow such a successful record but Fame wasn't concerned, he just wanted to record material that sounded good. In 1966, he was invited to write some music for a TV commercial for petrol and the result was 'Get Away'. Not only receive massive radio play, the ad was never off the television screens and Georgie found his second number one.

68. SI TU DOIR PARTIR Fairport Convention (1969) UK No 21

So why did they record 'If You Gotta Go, Go Now' in French? Well, apparently Fairport Convention were playing a gig and one night thought it would be fun to do a Bob Dylan song in French Cajun style, so the band called for volunteers from the audience to help with the translation. A small number of people offered their help so it was really written by committee, and consequently ended up not very Cajun, French or Dylan'. This version was first released as a single and was included on the group's album, *Unhalfbricking*. Dave Swarbrick played the violin, Trevor Lucas triangle and Richard Thompson accordion. The 'percussion' crash towards the end of the song is the sound of a pile of chairs falling over.

69. GIMME LITTLE SIGN Brenton (1967) US No 9/UK No 8

Written by Jerry Winn, Joseph Hooven and Brenton Wood under his real name, Alfred Smith. In 1967 he was signed to the American Double Shot Records, where that year he had a top 40 hit with 'The Oogum Boogum Song'. His biggest hit came in September of the same year with the follow-up, 'Gimme Little Sign'. It's interesting to note that the title line of the song never features, instead the chorus repeats 'Give Me Some Kind of Sign Girl'.

70. LOVE IS ALL Malcolm Roberts (1969) UK No 12

Written by Les Reed and Barry Mason, this made the charts one year after Malcolm's previous hit, 'May I Have The Next Dream With You' which entered the top 40 in October, 1968, and spent over three months in the charts – eventually reaching number eight. Three further singles followed before Malcolm released 'Love Is All', the song with which he represented Great Britain in the Rio de Janeiro Song Festival and won. The record was also a smash hit in South America and remained on their charts for over six months.

71. WE'VE GOTTA GET OUT OF THIS PLACE **The Animals (1965)**
US No 13/UK No 2

Written by husband and wife Barry Mann and Cynthia Weil, who recorded the original demo themselves with the view of offering it to The Righteous Brothers having written their classic, 'You've Lost That Lovin' Feelin'. Mann was then offered a recording contract himself and his label wanted him to release his own version. Meanwhile, showbusiness manager Alan Klein got to hear the song and sneaked a copy to Mickey Most, the producer of The Animals who was looking for new material for them. Loving the song, he rushed them into the studios and had a finished record before Mann's signature was dry on his new contract. When their record was released in America by MGM, EMI mistakenly shipped an outtake version which ended up being released. The lyric that gives away which version is which is the first line of the second verse: Eric Burdon sings 'watch my daddy in bed a dyin', but on the American release he sings 'see my daddy in bed'.

72. TRAVELIN' MAN **Ricky Nelson (1961)** *US No 1/UK No 2*

A double A-side with 'Hello Mary Lou', written by Gene Pitney, 'Travelin' Man' was composed by Jerry Fuller and became Ricky's biggest hit single. Fuller wrote the song while he was waiting to meet his wife in a park; he happened to have an atlas with him and picked out various locations around the world to write about. He first offered it to Sam Cooke via his manager, who simply threw the demo into the wastepaper basket. But Joe Osbourne, Nelson's bass player, rescued it from the litter and played it to Ricky.

73. THE WAY YOU LOOK TONIGHT **The Lettermen (1961)**
US No 13/UK No 36

The group's debut American hit was recorded in eight takes and is a song written by Jerome Kern, with lyrics by Dorothy Fields, that was first recorded by Fred Astaire from his movie, *Swing Time*, and won the Academy Award for Best Original Song in 1936. Fields later remarked,

'The first time Jerry played that melody for me I went out and started to cry'. The Lettermen's Bob Engemann had a brother, Karl, who was an executive at Warner Brothers records and secured the group a contract under which they released two unsuccessful singles. Karl then took a senior job at Capitol, bringing the group with him, where they achieved their first international hit.

74. WHERE DID OUR LOVE GO The Supremes (1964)
US No 1/UK No 3

This was a major breakthrough record for The Supremes, giving them their first taste of the UK charts – as well as their first American number one. The track had been recorded in a key to suit The Marvelettes lead singer, Gladys Horton, but the group had turned the song down. When The Supremes were reluctantly persuaded to record it instead, Diana Ross constantly complained that it was in the wrong key and too low for her, which of course it was. All the girls had a bad attitude in the studio, a fact that co-composer Lamont Dozier believed was exactly what the song needed. When the girls then refused to learn the intricate backing vocal parts, they were told to just sing, 'baby, baby, baby' to get the record finished. Their attitude actually worked to their advantage.

75. ELOISE Barry Ryan (1968) *UK No 2*

The son of pop singer Marion Ryan and Fred Sapherson, Barry began to perform at the age of 15 with his twin brother Paul. In 1965 they signed a recording contract with Decca, for whom they achieved a number of hit singles. When Paul was unable to cope any longer with all the stress of showbusiness, they decided that he would write the songs and Barry would then interpret as a solo artist. Their first effort was this single for MGM – 'Eloise'. Barry himself stopped performing in the early Seventies amidst rumours that he had had an accident in the recording studio. Supposedly he suffered serious burn wounds in the face and could no longer appear in public. However, he made a comeback in the late Nineties and was also part of the UK's 'Solid Silver 60s Tour' in 2003, singing 'Eloise' backed by The Dakotas.

76. CINDERELLA ROCKAFELLA Esther & Abi Ofarim (1968) *UK No 1*

The song was written by guitarist and singer Mason Williams and Nancy Ames as a novelty song to be performed on The Smothers Brothers'

TV Show. Esther and Abi got to hear it and included it on their 1967 album *Two In Three*, consisting of 13 songs in eight different languages recorded in three separate cities – London, Paris and Munich. When asked to appear on the Eamonn Andrews Sunday-night TV show, they chose to perform the song and the response was so great that their record label, Philips rushed it out as a single.

77. EL PASO **Marty Robbins** (1960) *US No 1/UK No 19*

This record managed a number of firsts, being the first single to top the American charts in the Sixties, the first country song to win a Grammy and the longest song (clocking-in at four minutes and 38 seconds) to top the charts in the US. Marty's record label originally rejected the song for a single but agreed it could be included on his album, *Gunfighter Ballads and Trail Songs*. After the album had been released for four weeks, requests for 'El Paso' became so strong that Columbia records executives were forced to relent and released it as a single, despite its long running-time.

78. NATURAL BORN BUGIE **Humble Pie** (1969) *UK No 4*

Written by Steve Marriott, the title of the song was often misspelt as 'Boogie'; it was the debut single and only hit for one of Britiain's first supergroups. Unusually, it does not include its title in the lyrics, but 'natural born woman' instead. In the autumn of 1971, Peter Frampton left the band to pursue a solo career, resulting in his Frampton Comes Alive album of 1976 – selling over 16 million copies worldwide and till one of the best-selling live albums of all time. Momentary, Steve Marriott was under discussion as the replacement for guitarist Mick Taylor, who left The Rolling Stones in 1976. But Mick Jagger blocked the move, because he knew that Marriott would not put up with being in the background.

79. I SAW LINDA YESTERDAY **Doug Sheldon** (1963) *UK No 36*

Sheldon was born in Stepney, London, and as a child attended a stage school where he studied acting. By the time he was 15, he moved to Skegness with his family where he worked in his father's fairground as a barker and bingo caller and, after completing his National Service in the Army, he landed a small part as an extra in the 1961 movie, *The Guns of Navarone*. As a struggling actor, he shared a flat with Michael Caine and Terence Stamp and picked up a few minor roles in TV dramas.

In one of them he was spotted singing by manager Bunny Lewis, who secured him a contract with Decca. His first release made little impact, but at the end of 1961 he covered Dion's 'Runaround Sue', giving him his first top-40 hit. His follow-up, another cover, was of Kenny Dino's 'Your Ma Said You Cried In Your Sleep Last Night' – this became his biggest hit. Several less successful releases followed throughout 1962, then the following year he achieved his final top-40 hit with yet another cover of an American top-20 hit: Dickie Lee's 'I Saw Linda Yesterday'.

80. WHAT IN THE WORLD'S COME OVER YOU Jack Scott (1960)
US No 5/UK No 11

Singer and songwriter Jack Scott was born Giovanni Dominico Scafone Jr in Ontario, Canada. He has been hailed by many of his countrymen as the greatest Canadian rock'n'roll singer of all time. As a teenager he began his singing career and in 1954 formed The Southern Drifters, changing his name to Jack Scott. Three years later, he left the band and signed a record deal as a solo artist. In 1958 he achieved his first hit with the million-selling double A-side of 'Leroy' and 'My True Love'. He served in the United States Army through 1959 and at the beginning of 1960 he signed with the Top Rank label, where he achieved one of his biggest hits with 'What In The World's Come Over You'.

81. MAMA Dave Berry (1966) *UK No 5*

A cover of an original American top-40 hit by BJ Thomas, this was the final UK hit for Dave Berry. Despite having achieved seven top-40 hits, two of them in 1965, his record label, Decca, refrained from releasing an album by him that year despite a busy recording schedule. Then the following year, two came along in quick succession. 'The Special Sound Of Dave Berry' was released in September, 1966, followed by 'One Dozen Berrys' in time for Christmas. Berry thought it was because they didn't know what to do with him; he could sing so many different styles of material.

82. ALL THE LOVE IN THE WORLD Consortium (1969) *UK No 22*

Singer and guitarist Geoff Simpson took the decision to leave Dave Ellis & The Sonnets in 1964 to join another band, Group 66, who mainly performed cover versions of recent hits. It was only when they decided to sing The Four Seasons' 'Rag Doll' in their act that they discovered how well their voices blended together. By 1965, the name Group

66 didn't seem so ahead of its time, so they changed it to the rather unusual Xit and Geoff began writing original material. Sending some of his demos to Tony Macaulay, who had just joined Pye Records as a junior producer, he called them for a meeting that led to the recording their first single, 'Some Other Someday' as West Coast Consortium. Several more singles followed to little success and in 1968, they began working on demos for a possible album but the project ran out of steam. In 1968, under the supervision of producer Jack Dorsey they recorded another of Geoff's songs 'All The Love In The World'. The head of Pye's production team, Cyril Stapleton, hated the recording but loved the song. He took the group back into the studios and remade the track to his own taste. Released in January, 1969 under the truncated name of Consortium, they achieved their one and only UK hit.

83. TWENTY-FOUR HOURS FROM TULSA Gene Pitney (1963)
US No 17/UK No 5

Written by Burt Bacharach and Hal David, this became Gene's tenth American Hot 100 hit. At the time the record was released in the UK, Gene was able to promote it by a fluke: he happened by chance to be visiting our

Gene Pitney launched his career in England with a relentless onslaught of interviews and appearances

shores as someone in New York had arranged for Gene to perform at some of the Mecca ballrooms. When he arrived in the UK, he discovered no one at his record company was that interested in him or his tour of the clubs, so he cancelled all the engagements. With time on his hands, he began to have second thoughts and agreed to promote his new American single by doing every TV and radio show, press interview and anything else his label asked of him. It resulted in the single becoming his first major hit in the UK.

84. PURPLE HAZE The Jimi Hendrix Experience (1967) *UK No 3*

Hendrix once claimed that the song was inspired by a dream in which he was walking under the sea. In the dream, he said, a purple haze surrounded him, engulfed him and got him lost. The song also contains one of the most misheard lyrics of a pop song: 'Scuse Me While I Kiss The Sky' has often been interpreted as 'Scuse Me While I Kiss This Guy'. To add confusion to the situation, from time to time Hendrix would sing it that way and point to one of his band. A month before Hendrix died, he opened a recording studio in New York's Greenwich Village called Electric Lady. One of the studios there was known as 'Purple Haze' and contained a purple mixing board.

85. SOMETHING HERE IN MY HEART (KEEPS A-TELLIN' ME NO) The Paper Dolls (1968) *UK No 11*

The three girls of The Paper Dolls – lead vocalist Susie 'Tiger' Mathis, Pauline 'Spyder' Bennett and Sue 'Copper' Marshall – were signed to Pye Records in 1968 and achieved just one solitary hit with 'Something Here in My Heart (Keeps A-Tellin' Me No)'. Their debut single, it was written by Tony Macaulay and John Macleod. Several strong follow-ups, notably 'My Life (Is In Your Hands)' and 'Someday', failed to chart. They suffered a great disappointment when they were due to record another Macaulay composition, 'Build Me Up Buttercup' later that year. Due to a mix-up with the dates, the girls never turned up for the session and, instead, The Foundations were rushed in to add their voices, giving them a top-five hit.

86. CAPTAIN OF YOUR SHIP Reparata & The Delrons (1968) *UK No 13*

This group were originally formed as The Delrons at high school in Brooklyn. After their first single, 1964's 'Your Big Mistake', made very little impact, they decided a hookier name was needed. Lead singer Mary O' Leary suggested Reparata, after the nun who'd presided at her confirmation. The change appeared to bring them luck and their follow-up single 'Whenever A Teenager Cries' was a regional American hit. Despite touring extensively in the US and becoming well-established, they never managed a major breakthrough into the singles chart. In the UK, 'Captain Of Your Ship' became their only hit. Reparata left the group in 1970 and had a 1975 top-10 hit in South Africa and number 43 in UK with 'Shoes'. She later left pop and became a teacher. The Delrons changed their name to Lady Flash and became Barry Manilow's backing group.

87. DA DOO RON RON The Crystals (1963) *US No 3/UK No 5*
Songwriters Jeff Barry and Ellie Greenwich hadn't quite finished writing this song and stuck in the words, 'Da Doo Ron Ron' until they sorted out something better. When it came to record it, they still hadn't found new words for the phrase, so 'Da Doo Ron Ron' it remained. Darlene Love had previously sung lead vocals on The Crystals records but after adding her vocal to this track, she decided she wanted a solo career. Her voice was quickly removed and replaced by Dolores 'La La' Brooks, although Darlene still sang along with the backing vocals.

88. GOOD VIBRATIONS The Beach Boys (1966) *US No 1/UK No 1*
This became the third American number one for The Beach Boys but the first of only two in the UK. Brian Wilson had set his mind to recording a classic album that would receive the same critical acclaim as The Beatles' *Rubber Soul* and *Revolver*, resulting in The Beach Boys' album *Pet Sounds*. On completion, he set his mind to create the perfect single, spending six months in four different studios to complete 'Good Vibrations,' at a cost of around the equivalent of £12,000, making it the most expensive number-one recorded in the Sixties. Over 30 takes were recorded with a number of different arrangements before Brian was finally satisfied he'd completed what he'd set out to achieve. 'Good Vibrations' was nominated for a Grammy for The Best Contemporary Rock'n'roll Recording of the year but lost out to the song that knocked it off number one in America, 'Winchester Cathedral' by The New Vaudeville Band.

89. IT'S A MAN'S MAN'S MAN'S WORLD James Brown (1966)
US No 8/UK No 13
Written by James Brown with Betty Jean Newsome, who came up with the lyrics based on her own observations of the relationships

between men and women. The title itself was a play on the name of the 1963 comedy movie *It's A Mad, Mad, Mad, Mad, World*. Brown's backing group, The Famous Flames, were not used on the recording but were credited on the label and female backing vocals were recorded but left out of the final mix. The song itself evolved over a period of several years: in 1963 Tammy Montgomery, later known as Tammi Terrell, recorded a soundalike song called 'I Cried' and the following year Brown himself recorded a demo version with the title 'It's A Man's World'.

90. TURN, TURN, TURN The Byrds (1965) *UK No 26*

After achieving two top-five hits with Bob Dylan songs, The Byrds decided to turn their attention to the work of Pete Seeger, who in 1959 had adapted the song from the words of the Book of Ecclesiastes in the Bible (with the exception of the last line). Pete Seeger had waited until 1962 to record it, releasing the song on his album *The Bitter and The Sweet*. The song first appeared in a recording several months before the Seeger version, on an album by the folk group The Limeliters called *Folk Matinee*, under the title 'To Everything There Is a Season'. One of their backing musicians was Roger McGuinn, who of course would later appear on The Byrds' hit single.

91. GOOD TIMIN' Jimmy Jones (1960) *US No 3/UK No 1*

In July 1960 Jimmy Jones moved up the charts from number two to number one, replacing 'Three Steps To Heaven' by Eddie Cochran. This

With 'Good Timin', Jimmy Jones became the first black artist to sell a million singles in the UK

was Jones' follow-up to 'Handy Man' written by Fred Tobias and Clint Ballard Jnr and, like its predecessor, was produced by Otis Blackwell. Topping the charts here led to Jones touring the UK but, unfortunately, he failed to match the quality of his first two hits and his appearances in the charts were soon a thing of the past. It was practically 12 years to the day before Jones's record label, MGM, managed to gain another UK number one with Donny Osmond's 'Puppy Love'.

92. MOVE IN A LITTLE CLOSER Harmony Grass (1969) UK No 24

After making many great records as Tony Rivers & the Castaways which mystifyingly failed to chart, some of that band's members moved to RCA Records with Tony Rivers and became Harmony Grass. This became the group's only hit, although they did release one album for the company titled *This Is Us* and they played a number of London concerts before breaking up in 1970. Rivers found a long and successful career as a backing vocalist for many top stars, including Cliff Richard.

93. YOU ALWAYS HURT THE ONE YOU LOVE
Clarence 'Frogman' Henry (1961) US No 12/UK No 6

This was the second and final top-20 hit in the UK and the last of three in America for Henry following in the footsteps of 'But I Do'. Henry was born in New Orleans and was heavily influenced by Fats Domino and Professor Longhair. His 'frogman' nickname came about after he included frog-like sounds on his first American hit, 'Ain't Got No Home'. In 1964, he opened 18 concerts for The Beatles across the US and Canada. 'You Always Hurt The One You Love' had been first made famous in 1944 by The Mills Brothers.

94. CALIFORNIA HERE I COME Freddy Cannon (1960) UK No 33

After the success in the US of Freddy's debut hit, 'Tallahassee Lassie', his record company set him the task of recording his first album, *The Explosive Freddy Cannon*. His label, Swan, came up with the idea of making it a concept album of songs relating to cities or states across America. The songs included his hit, 'Way Down Yonder In New Orleans', 'Kansas City' and 'Deep In The Heart of Texas', as well as this UK hit that we don't believe ever got a single release in the US.

95. EVEN THE BAD TIMES ARE GOOD The Tremeloes (1967)
US No 36/UK No 4

Written by Mitch Murray and Peter Callander, this became The Tremeloes' third consecutive top-10 hit after the departure of Brian Poole and the follow-up to their chart-topping, 'Silence Is Golden'. This continued their run of hits throughout the Sixties but, by the end of the decade, they decided they wanted to break away from the happy-go-lucky songs provided by other composers and write their own. Their first attempt, '(Call Me) Number One' was an instant hit but then they announced they were going 'heavy' and in a moment of madness they alienated their pop audience in the music press by dismissing their earlier record-buying fans as 'morons'. Despite this, they managed one further top-20 hit in 1970 with 'Me And My Life'.

96. JUST AS MUCH AS EVER Nat King Cole (1960) *UK No 18*

During the Spring of 1960, Nat King Cole visited the UK for the first time in six years on a very tight schedule, during which time he played one concert in London, headed the bill on the top TV show, *Sunday Night At The London Palladium* and recorded his own TV special. Whilst he was in the country, his record label, Capitol thought it wise for him to have a new record on sale. They dug deep in their vaults and came up with a recording from 1958, 'Just As Much As Ever', that had been an American hit in 1959 for Bob Beckham. Nat recorded it and it became a UK hit for the visiting star.

97. WALK AWAY RENEE The Four Tops (1967) *US No 14/UK No 3*

The song was originally a top-five hit in the US in 1966 for The Left Banke, so it was surprising that The Four Tops' version was released so soon after – and even more of a surprise that it became such a big US hit. The Left Banke's bass guitarist Tom Finn brought his girlfriend to the studio one day when the group had assembled for a practice session. Keyboard player Mike Brown was infatuated with her the instant he saw her. Her name was Renee Fladen and although there was never anything between them, Mike wrote the song about her. As for Renee, she moved to Boston with her family shortly after the Left Banke recorded the song; no one in the group ever saw her again.

98. DOMINIQUE The Singing Nun (1963) *US No 1/UK No 7*

In December, 1963, Soeur Sourire (Sister Smile) – better known as The

Singing Nun – knocked 'I'm Leaving It Up To You' by Dale and Grace off the number-one spot in the US after its two-week run. 'Dominique' remained at number one for four weeks, before giving way to Bobby Vinton's recording of 'There I've Said It Again'.

The record came about when two nuns arrived at the Brussels branch of Philips records and asked if they could pay to have a few hundred copies of some of their songs pressed up to give away as presents. It was the busy Christmas period and a company executive politely sent them on their way. Three months later, they were back and this time Philips agreed to give them a few hours of studio time in which they recorded over a dozen songs. The company executives were so impressed with the result that they decided to manufacture thousands of albums and released it throughout Europe. Some months later they decided on 'Dominique' as a single, which became an international hit.

99. IT'S GETTING BETTER Mama Cass (1969) *US No 30/UK No 8*

Written by Barry Mann and Cynthia Weil, the song was first recorded in 1968 by Bobby Rydell, the same year The Will-O-Bees, a New York-based trio, also brought out a version as a single. 'It's Getting Better' was recorded by Cass Elliott for her album *Bubblegum, Lemonade and Something For Mama* and was produced by Steve Barri with an arrangement by Jimmie Haskell. The end result pleased everyone so much it was decided to release it as the second single from the collection, following her version of 'Move In A Little Closer'.

100. WALK RIGHT IN The Rooftop Singers (1963)
US No 1/UK No 10

The Rooftop Singers came together after Erik Darling decided to leave The Weavers, after over four years of service with them, to pursue a solo career on the emerging coffee-house folk circuit in New York. Meanwhile an old childhood friend of his, Bill Svanoe, was back in town toting a rare old 12-string guitar, re-strung so he could play it left-handed. During one of their jamming sessions, Darling suggested they learned to play an old folk-blues song he knew that had been recorded in 1929 by Gus Cannon's Jug Stompers. That song was 'Walk Right In'. Adding singer, Lynne Taylor, they recorded it as The Rooftop Singers.

BEATLES COVERS

Here you'll find a selection of covers of songs by The Beatles – written by John Lennon and Paul McCartney or George Harrison. No apologies for more than one version of some of the titles!

1. PLEASE PLEASE ME **The Score (1966)**

A psychedelic approach to The Beatles' hit by a group who were experimenting with new sounds at the time. This single on Decca was their sole release and has become a big collectors' item, but they were never heard of again.

2. OB-LA-DI, OB-LA-DA **The Bedrocks (1968)** *UK No 20*

It was Marmalade's cover that went to number one but this version gave them a good run for their money. The Bedrocks were a West Indian band from Leeds and this was their only hit. John Lennon always hated the song, saying he found it irritating and irrelevant. McCartney was later sued by a Nigerian percussionist named Jimmy Scott, from whom McCartney had first heard the phrase 'Ob-La-Di, Ob-La-Da'. However, it was a common saying of the Yoruba tribe, apparently meaning life goes on. Matters were settled after McCartney footed the legal bill for Scott after Scott received a prison sentence for failure to make some alimony payments.

3. SOUR MILK SEA **Jackie Lomax (1968)**

Written by George Harrison, this was Jackie's debut single for the Apple label and was one of the first four singles released by the label. They were all put out on the same day and alongside 'Sour Milk Sea' were 'Those Were The Days' by Mary Hopkin', 'Thingumybob' by The Black Dyke Mills Band and, of course, the Beatles own single, 'Hey Jude'. Jackie had been the lead vocalist with Liverpool band The Undertakers and had played all the German hot spots that were also frequented by The Beatles and The Searchers.

4. CAN'T BUY ME LOVE **The Jaybirds (1964)**

This was released on Woolworths' Embassy label, which would copy all the current hits and put two on one single, selling for less than one of the original recordings – a tactic that earned it a high level of interest from the record-buying public. This note-for-note cover by The Jaybirds was backed on the other side by Del Martin singing the Jim Reeves hit 'I Love You Because'.

5. COLD TURKEY The Plastic Ono Band

This became the second hit for John and Yoko's Plastic Ono Band, formed just before the dissolution of The Beatles. Various members of the band included Eric Clapton, George Harrison, Ringo Starr, Keith Moon, future Yes drummer Alan White and old friend of The Beatles, Klaus Voormann. 'Cold Turkey' was written by Lennon and relates to his brief addiction to hard drugs.

6. DRIVE MY CAR The Bo Street Runners (1966)

They took their name from Britain's first professional police constables, the Bow Street Runners, an institution founded in 1749, but removed a 'w' – perhaps in honour of Bo Diddley, who was one of their biggest influences. The group were hugely popular around the R&B clubs but, although they released several singles, they never managed to make the charts. Their line-up over the years included Mick Fleetwood and vocalist John Dominic, who left in 1966. He was replaced by Mike Patto, who sang lead vocals on this, their final single for the Columbia label.

7. AND I LOVE HIM Esther Phillips (1965)

The Beatles song 'And I Love Her' was issued as a single in America and reached number 12 in 1964, at about the time that Esther Phillips recorded her version. She sang it right at the very end of a long recording session; Atlantic records still decided to release it as a single, as it was a very different take on the song, resulting in her most successful disc for the label. Hailed as one of the first female superstars of R&B, Phillips was, at the time, the youngest singer to top the R&B charts. She died from liver failure in 1984 aged just 48.

8. THINGS WE SAID TODAY The Sandpipers (1966)

The song was written for the movie *A Hard Day's Night* and appeared on the B-side of The Beatles' version of the title track. Paul McCartney came up with the idea for the song whilst on a Caribbean cruise in May 1964 on board a yacht called Happy Days. It has been claimed it was about his relationship, at the time, with Jane Asher and the impossibility of spending a lot of time together, owing to their work commitments. The Sandpipers' version appeared on their album *Guantanamera*.

9. GET BACK Anonymously Yours (1969)
A reggae cover version of The Beatles' 1969 number one: Anonymously Yours was a vehicle for the almost-as-anonymous Bart SanFilipo, the man credited as producer, about whom little more is known than his name.

10. STRAWBERRY FIELDS FOREVER Plastic Penny (1968)
The group came together when three members of a group called The Universals joined forces with guitarist Mick Grabham and drummer Nigel Olsson to record for Larry Page's recently formed label Page One. Their debut single and only hit was a cover of a Box Tops original, 'Everything I Am', and after several failed releases the lead singer, Brian Keith, quit the band before the completion of their first and only album *Two Sides Of A Penny*. This track is taken from it and features keyboard player Paul Raymond on lead vocals.

11. RUN FOR YOUR LIFE Nancy Sinatra (1966)
Taken from her hit album *Boots*, this cover of one of the tracks from The Beatles *Rubber Soul* LP, was a 1966 release. Nancy was one of the first artists to be signed to her father Frank's Reprise label, but she had to wait five years for her first hit, after teaming up with producer and songwriter, Lee Hazelwood.

12. FROM ME TO YOU Del Shannon (1963)
Although it only reached number 77 on the American Hot 100, it was enough to win Del Shannon, of 'Runaway' fame, the distinction of being the first artist to make the US charts with a cover of a John Lennon-Paul McCartney song.

13. TICKET TO RIDE Cathy Berberian (1967)
The classically trained American mezzo-sopranon Cathy Berberian was married to Italian composer, Luciano Berio who wrote works of music especially for her (as did Igor Stravinsky). She admitted to a keen interest in opera, dance and musicals. During one of her classical recital encores, she stunned and sent shockwaves through the audience by performing Beatles songs in her operatic style.

14. A HARD DAYS NIGHT **Peter Sellers (1965)** *UK No 14*

Produced by George Martin, this novelty single matched The Beatles with Shakespeare as Sellers recited the lyrics of the song in the style of Sir Laurence Olivier in the movie version of *Richard III*. Sellers also performed the song in full Shakespearian costume for a TV sketch.

15. HEY JUDE **Bing Crosby (1969)**

Bing Crosby was aware that The Beatles admired him and it is thought that perhaps he wanted to repay the compliment. Although a telegram would have sufficed, the great crooner decided to go one better and attack one of their classic songs for his album *Hey Jude!/Hey Bing!*, which also included covers of 'Little Green Apples', 'It's All In The Game' and 'Those Were The Days'. Bing's version of 'Hey Jude' has also appeared on a compilation entitled *Celebrities Butcher The Beatles*.

16. LITTLE CHILD **Jackie Lynton (1964)**

Born John Bertram Lynton, he began singing in his school church choir in Walton-on-Thames and by his late teens he was hooked on pop music. In the early Sixties, Jackie was booked by Larry Parnes to appear on his one-nighters alongside such acts as Billy Fury, Terry Dene, John Leyton and Lance Fortune. With his group The Midnighters, he recorded BBC radio sessions for *Saturday Club* and *Music With A Beat*, and landed a recording contract with Pye, his first disc being produced by Tony Hatch reviving the classic, 'Over The Rainbow'. After several failed singles, he released his version of 'Little Child', a Lennon and McCartney song from the *With The Beatles* album. This was a choice made by his label, despite his own protests.

17. I CALL YOUR NAME **Donnie Brooks (1966)**

Singer Donnie Brooks remains best known in America for his 1960 top-10 pop smash 'Mission Bell', although he is also remembered in rockabilly fan circles for the cult classic 'Bertha Lou', recorded under the name Johnny Faire. His version of 'I Call Your Name' was issued as a single in America in 1966. John Lennon had first begun working on the song in 1957 but it wasn't until 1964 that he finished it off, when Billy J Kramer & The Dakotas were looking for new material. It then ended up on the B-side of their hit, 'Bad To Me', before Brooks gave it a go.

18. MAXWELL'S SILVER HAMMER The Good Ship Lollipop (1969)

The British independent label Ember released this cover from The Beatles' Abbey Road album, the only release by North Devon group, The Good Ship Lollipop. 'Maxwell's Silver Hammer' concerns medical student Maxwell Edison, who uses his silver hammer to murder first his girlfriend Joan, then his teacher, and finally the judge during his murder trial. Despite the grim subject matter, the song is bouncy and upbeat.

19. NORWEGIAN WOOD Jan & Dean (1966)

Jan and Dean achieved 15 top-40 hits in the States between 1958 and 1966. Jan Berry and Dean Torrence formed The Barons whilst at high school with their friend Arnie Ginsburg. The three of them recorded a song called 'Jennie Lee' in Jan's garage and released it as Jan and Arnie, reaching number eight in the US. Their version of 'Norwegian Wood' was originally ditched as a single in favour of a song called 'Batman' but earmarked as the follow up. By the time it came to release it, there was another change of heart and a remixed version of a 1963 album track, 'Popsicle' was issued with 'Norwegian Wood', downgraded to the B-side.

20. HEY JUDE Wilson Pickett (1969) *US No 23/UK No 16*

Wilson Pickett moved to Detroit from Alabama in the late Fifties and made his professional debut as lead singer with the group The Violinaires before joining The Falcons in 1961. In 1964 he signed with the legendary Atlantic label, recording in the Stax studios in Memphis alongside Booker T Jones and Steve Cropper, who were co-writers of Pickett's early hits, 'In The Midnight Hour' and 'Don't Fight It'. Following a string of hits, in 1969 he decided to record a cover of 'Hey Jude' just months after The Beatles had topped the charts with the song. Featuring a guitar solo by Duane Allman, the cover gave him another international hit.

21. HERE, THERE AND EVERYWHERE Episode Six (1966)

This Beatles cover, with lead vocals by Ian Gillan, was given massive airplay by the pirate radio stations of the time and was voted a hit on TV's Juke Box Jury. Despite all the exposure, the record just didn't sell enough to chart.

22. DRIVE MY CAR Bob Kuban & The In-Men (1966)

'Drive My Car' was a cover of the John Lennon and Paul McCartney song featured on The Beatles' Rubber Soul album. Probably best remembered for

Otis Redding, one of the all-time great soul singers, sang a very funky version of 'Day Tripper' in 1966

their American top-20 hit 'The Cheater', Bob Kuban & The In-Men had three singles in the Billboard Hot 100. This was their third and final: it stalled at number 93. Lead singer Walter Scott disappeared from his home in 1983 and his ex-wife and her new husband were charged with his murder after his body turned up three years later with a gunshot wound in his back.

23. DAY TRIPPER Otis Redding (1966)
This cover by the great Otis Redding was released in 1966. It's a little-known fact that in March 1966, Brian Epstein visited the Stax offices in Memphis to investigate the possibility of The Beatles recording their next album there. However, due to security worries, the plan was shelved. There was a notion of rearranging a session at a later date, but it never happened.

24. YESTERDAY Frank Sinatra (1969)
Rivalled only by 'White Christmas', the Lennon-McCartney song 'Yesterday' is one of the most recorded songs in the world. Alongside over 200 different recordings of the song, this Sinatra attempt must be among the versions the Beatles were most proud of. Frank Sinatra recorded his interpretation in Hollywood on February 20, 1969, with a musical arrangement by the mighty Don Costa.

25. STRAWBERRY FIELDS FOREVER Tomorrow (1968)
This band, formed by Keith West, originated from an R&B group from North London called Four Plus One, who were a popular fixture on the local music circuit. In 1965 they were signed to Parlophone and

recorded a version of 'Time Is On My Side' before changing their name to The In-Crowd releasing 'That's How Strong My Love Is', three months later, guitarist Les Jones left the group to be replaced by Steve Howe. Over the coming months the group changed wardrobe, musical direction and outlets emerging as Tomorrow in March 1967.

26. IF I NEEDED SOMEONE The Hollies (1965) *UK No 20*

A cover from The Beatles Rubber Soul album that was written by George Harrison – the only one of his songs that The Beatles performed on their tours. A huge fan of The Byrds, Harrison was very influenced by them in writing this song. He once expressed his dislike of The Hollies' version.

27. IN MY LIFE Judy Collins (1967)

The album of the same name was a departure for Judy Collins, featuring dramatic arrangements by Joshua Rifkin of songs written by Leonard Cohen, Donovan, Bob Dylan and, of course, John Lennon and Paul McCartney. Most of the lyrics of 'In My Life' were written by Lennon, and it is thought to be autobiographical. George Harrison performed the song at one of his concerts in 1974, adding some of his own words and allegedly upsetting the rest of The Beatles.

28. THE FOOL ON THE HILL Sergio Mendes & Brazil '66 (1968) *US No 6*

The song first appeared in The Beatles TV special *Magical Mystery Tour*. The song was prompted by an encounter Paul had while walking his dog, Martha. As he watched the sun rise, he noticed she'd gone missing. While looking for her, he spotted a well-dressed man who appeared to be standing on the top of a hill. He knew the man hadn't been there a few moments earlier as he'd looked in that direction for Martha. Paul walked up to the stranger and exchanged a few comments about the beautiful view from the top of the hill that overlooked London. A few seconds later, Paul looked around again and the man had vanished. Alistair Taylor, a friend of Paul's, was with him at the time and reported the strange incident in his book, *Yesterday*.

Sergio Mendes and Brazil '66 covered it on their fourth album. The original line-up of Brazil '66 was Mendes (piano), vocalists Lani Hall and Janis Hansen, Bob Matthews (bass), Jose Soares (percussion) and Joao Palma (drums). John Pisano guested as guitarist. This line-up recorded three albums between 1966 and 1968 but changed for *The Fool On The Hill.*

29. GIRL **The Truth (1966)** *UK No 27*

This is one of two cover versions of 'Girl' to make the UK top 40; the other being by the UK group St Louis Union (and a slightly bigger hit). 'Girl' was the last song to be recorded by The Beatles for the *Rubber Soul* album, and is believed to have been one of John Lennon's favourite Beatles tracks. Written by him about his dream girl, his then wife Cynthia thought at the time it might have been about her. Paul McCartney claimed that the song was co-written by him during one of his visits to John's house in Kenwood.

30. SHE CAME IN THROUGH THE BATHROOM WINDOW **Joe Cocker (1969)**

After the success of his first hit single, a cover of The Beatles' 'With A Little Help From My Friends', he named his first album after the hit and included another Lennon/McCartney song amongst the tracks. 'She Came In Through the Bathroom Window' was taken from The Beatles album *Abbey Road* and was written by Paul after a fan broke into his house by putting a ladder up against the wall and climbing in through his bathroom window.

31. DON'T LET ME DOWN **Marcia Griffiths (1969)**

Marcia started singing professionally as a vocalist in 1964, for Byron Lee and the Dragonaires. She later teamed up with Bob Andy and, as Bob and Marcia, the pair achieved two top-20 hits in the early Seventies with 'Young, Gifted And Black' and 'The Pied Piper'. She is still one of the leading female artists on the scene. The Beatles released their version on the B-side of 'Get Back' and was a song that John Lennon wrote to Yoko. The song was originally planned for The *Let It Be* album but after the tapes were handed over to producer Phil Spector, he decided not to include it.

32. BACK IN THE U.S.S.R **Cliff Bennett (1968)**

A cover from The Beatles *White Album* (aka *The Beatles*)and the fifth and final single to be released by Cliff. Originally recording under the name Cliff Bennett & The Rebel Rousers, by this time he had altered the billing to The Cliff Bennett Band, by which time several of the original members had departed and the line-up included Mick Green and Frank Farley, who had previously been members of Johnny Kidd & the Pirates.

33. BABY'S IN BLACK The Hi-Fi's (1965)

The song first appeared on The Beatles album Beatles For Sale and is believed to be about Astrid Kirchherr, a German photographer who tended to dress in black. It's Astrid who is generally credited for having styled The Beatles' famous mop top haircuts; during their time in Hamburg, she had a romantic relationship with Stu Sutcliffe, the group's first bass player, who later died of a brain haemorrhage. The Hi-Fis were a London based group who tried for years to achieve a hit record on several labels including Pye and Piccadilly, for whom this single was released. They remained hitless and in 1966 they, like The Beatles, headed off to Hamburg where they recorded more tracks with, sadly, no more success.

34. WE CAN WORK IT OUT Twice As Much (1966)

Twice As Much were former public schoolboy David Skinner and fellow singer, Andrew Rose. Taking their name from a headline in a magazine, the harmony-singing duo signed to Andrew Oldham's Immediate label. Their first single, written by Mick Jagger and Keith Richards, made the top 40. They then set about recording their debut album, 'Own Up', with no expense spared – using up day after day of studio time and the services of the top session musicians in the business, including Big Jim Sullivan, Jimmy Page and Nicky Hopkins. The album featured two Lennon and McCartney covers – 'Help' and 'We Can Work It Out'.

35. STEP INSIDE LOVE Madeline Bell (1969)

Taken from Bell's album *Doin' Things*, this song by John Lennon and Paul McCartney was originally a top-10 hit in 1968 for Cilla Black. It was a bold move on Madeline's part to cover a song so recently in the public's consciousness but, with Cilla's version not having registered in America, her record label, Philips, decided to release Madeline's version as a single. Bell sang backing vocals on several Rolling Stones and Serge Gainsbourg songs, and later went on to join the band Blue Mink.

36. FROM A WINDOW Chad & Jeremy (1965)

'From A Window' was a cover of the song John and Paul wrote for Billy J Kramer & The Dakotas, which reached number 10 in 1964. Chad and Jeremy covered it on their first album, *Yesterday's Gone*. Former drama students Chad Stuart and Jeremy Clyde spent their early days as musicians playing in coffee houses and folk clubs in London until they were given a helping hand by famed movie composer John Barry, with whom they recorded a number of American hits including 'Yesterday's Gone', 'Summer Song' and 'Willow Weep For Me'. They were quickly snapped up by Hollywood appearing as themselves in TV programmes including *The Dick Van Dyke Show* and *Batman*.

37. I FEEL FINE John Smith (1964)

You've probably never heard of John Smith but if you bought records in the Sixties, the chances are you will have one he sang on. John was one of several singers who turned out six-track discs for Pye Records' 'Top Six' series. Pye's band of singers, which also included Tony Stevens, Laura Lee, Danny Street and Ray Merrill, would go into the studios and recreate the hits of the day. They would record all the songs in one three-hour session with musical director Johnny Harris.

38. LIKE DREAMERS DO The Applejacks (1964) *UK No 20*

The Applejacks' follow-up to their debut top-10 hit, 'Tell Me When' was written by John Lennon and Paul McCartney. It was one of the 15 songs that The Beatles performed at their audition for Decca Records on January 1, 1961. The Applejacks formed in Solihull in 1961 and were originally known as The Crestas before changing their name to The Jaguars. At that time, the band were without a lead singer and performed mainly covers of instrumental hits until vocalist Al Jackson joined the line-up in 1962. The following year, they were signed to Decca and in 1964 achieved their first hit single.

39. I'M A LOSER Marianne Faithfull (1964)

Taken from her second album, *Marianne Faithfull*, this was a cover of a track from The Beatles album *Beatles For Sale* and at one time was considered as a single by the Fab Four. Written mainly by John whilst on a plane during a Beatles tour of America with Jackie De Shannon, this has all the hallmarks of Lennon's Bob Dylan- influenced period.

40. YOU'VE GOT TO HIDE YOUR LOVE AWAY
Dino, Desi & Billy (1966)

This trio were born into showbusiness. Dino was the son of Dean Martin; Desi's parents were Lucille Ball and Desi Arnez; and their Beverly Hills schoolmate Billy (William Hinssche) was the son of a businessman who made his fortune selling real estate to the other two lads' fathers. Frank Sinatra heard the three of them rehearsing in an upstairs bedroom when he went to visit Dean Martin. Impressed with what he heard, he signed them to his Reprise label. This cover of the Dylan-inspired Beatles song appears on the trio's album *Our Time's Coming*.

41. THIS BOY The Swinging Blue Jeans (1963)

This Beatles cover by Swinging Blue Jeans was left in the EMI vaults until 2008. The Jeans were a Merseybeat group best known for the hits 'Hippy Hippy Shake' and 'Good Golly Miss Molly'. 'This Boy' was originally the B-side of The Beatles single, 'I Want To Hold Your Hand'. An instrumental version was used for Ringo Starr's big scene in the movie *A Hard Days Night* and retitled 'Ringo's Theme'.

42. EIGHT DAYS A WEEK Alma Cogan (1965)

Alma Cogan gained her success in the Fifties with several novelty songs but was canny enough to embrace new musical trends in the Sixties, counting many of the new wave of pop musicians and singers among her friends. She used to hold big showbusiness parties at her Kensington flat; DJ Alan Freeman was once quoted as saying, 'You name them, they would have rung her doorbell'. In October 1965, Cogan went into the famous Abbey Road studios to begin work on a new album, which was intended to be an entire LP of Lennon and McCartney songs. The project never materialised but she did record five of their songs, including this great arrangement of 'Eight Days A Week'.

43. HEY BULLDOG The Gods (1969)

The precociously named Gods were founded in 1965 and their line-up included Mick Taylor, who later went on to join The Rolling Stones, and Brian and John Glascock of Jethro Tull. They had all been at school together in Hatfield and played together, both as The Strangers and The Juniors. They signed to EMI's Columbia label in 1964 and released their first single, 'There's A Pretty Girl'. The following year they changed their name to The Gods and in 1966 they opened for Cream at the Starlite Ballroom in Wembley. In 1967 Taylor left to join John Mayall's Blues Band and the rest of the group secured a residency at London's famous Marquee Club (succeeding The Rolling Stones' tenure there); John Glascock, who had left the grou,p was asked to return. They then recorded a couple of progressive rock albums and a handful of singles, including the Lennon and McCartney song 'Hey Bulldog'. Originally titled 'You Can Talk To Me', 'Hey Bulldog' was a tough R&B number that appeared on The Beatles movie soundtrack album *Yellow Submarine.*

44. YOUR MOTHER SHOULD KNOW Mike Batt (1969)

Mike Batt's arrangement of The Beatles' song shows early signs of what was to come some five years later, in the shape of The Wombles. Batt had begun his career at the age of 18 when he signed to Liberty Records as an artist, having answered an advertisement placed in the *New Musical Express* by the label, searching for talent. Elton John answered the very same ad. Batt subsequently became head of A&R for Liberty.

45. SHE SAID, SHE SAID Grand Union (1968)

This one-off single by Grand Union was recorded under the heavy influence of Vanilla Fudge after they achieved chart success in 1967 with a psychedelic cover of The Supremes' 'You Keep Me Hanging On'. 'She Said, She Said' is believed to have been written by John Lennon about one of his first experiences with the drug, LSD and was the last track recorded for The Beatles *Revolver* LP. The Fab Four were told they were a song short to complete the album; it took nine hours to rehearse and record the song, complete with overdubs. When they had finished, George Martin, is reported to have said told the group: 'all right, boys, I'm just going for a lie-down'.

46. YOU'VE GOT TO HIDE YOUR LOVE AWAY The Silkie (1965)
US No 10/UK No 28

The Silkie were a group of students from Hull University and their first single for Fontana was called 'Blood Red River', which they quickly followed with a cover of a track from The Beatles soundtrack album for the movie *Help!*. Managed by Brian Epstein, The Silkie's Beatles cover was produced by John Lennon with Paul McCartney on guitar and George Harrison even helped out by playing tambourine. The Silkie then released their own LP, *The Silkie Sing The Songs Of Bob Dylan* and the following year they managed two more singles before they called it a day.

47. MICHELLE Andy Williams (1966)

Taken from Andy's album *The Shadow Of Your Smile*, the song first appeared on The Beatles' *Rubber Soul* LP. John Lennon recalled that, back when they were schoolboys and French culture was trendy, Paul would sometimes pretend to be French at parties and play a little tune. But he only knew a few French words so he made the rest of them up. John remembered the ditty and suggested he work it up into a real song for Rubber Soul: so he asked his friend Ivan Vaughan, whose wife was a French teacher, for a French name and some words to rhyme with it. The result was 'Michelle, ma belle'. Paul came up with the next line, 'these are words that go together well' and he was taught the literal translation 'sont des mots qui vont tres bien ensemble', which he included in the song. They have been misinterpreted more than once as 'Sunday monkey won't play piano song'. It should be pointed out that Paul did send Ivan's wife a cheque for an undisclosed amount for her help.

48. DAY TRIPPER The Spiders (1966)

Now for something truly dreadful. A seven-piece Japanese band, The Spiders dressed in *Sgt Pepper*-style red jackets for their stage performances and amazingly, managed to get onto TV's *Ready Steady Go!* in 1966. As it happens, The Beatles were said to have been less than satisfied with their own version of the song: apparently the

Japan's biggest Beatles fans? The Spiders – all seven of them – got their 'Day Tripper' cover version onto Ready Steady Go

record company had been putting pressure on the group to come up with a new single to follow 'Help!' and they felt they hadn't been given enough time to make the right record.

49. SHE'S A WOMAN Noel Harrison (1966)

Three years before Noel Harrison had an international hit with the big theme song from the movie *The Thomas Crown Affair*, 'The Windmills Of Your Mind', he recorded an album for Decca. Very few people knew about it until it was reissued on CD by Rev-Ola Records: it contained songs written by Bob Dylan, Charles Aznavour, Billie Holliday and a bizarre cover of the John Lennon and Paul McCartney composition 'She's a Woman'.

50. YOU'RE GONNA LOSE THAT GIRL
Five Man Electrical Band (1969)

Hailing from Ottawa in Canada, for six years the group were known as The Staccatos. In 1965, they signed to the Capitol label, producing their first album Initially. They continued to release singles and in 1967 they achieved their biggest hit thus far with a track called 'Half Past Midnight', reaching number 10 on the Canadian charts. Their success led to them playing alongside some of the biggest rock acts of the time including Jefferson Airplane, The Beach Boys and The Young Rascals. In 1969, vocalist and the group's main songwriter, Les Emmerson came up with a song for their new album called 'Five Man Electrical Band', inspiring them to make a name change. 'You're Gonna Lose that Girl', a song that appeared on The Beatles' *Help!* album, is one of the few covers recorded by the group.

51. DON'T LET ME DOWN Dillard & Clark (1969)

In the late-Sixties, Doug Dillard teamed up with ex-Byrds lead singer, Gene Clark to record four pioneering country-rock albums, mixing traditional and modern country with pop and rock. An unlikely song they'd earmarked for this treatment was 'Don't Let Me Down', originally tucked away on the B-side of The Beatles' single, 'Get Back'. The result became one of the more intriguing covers of a Lennon-McCartney song.

52. THE CONTINUING STORY OF BUNGALOW BILL
Young Blood (1969)

There is little known about the Midlands group known as Young Blood, apart from the fact that Cozy Powell (of the Jeff Beck Group,

Whitesnake and many others) was once their drummer. Powell is believed to have played on this track, a cover of a *White Album* song. It was made available again on a double CD released by Sanctuary records in 2006 called *Brumbeat – the Story Of the 60s Midlands Sound*.

53. GOOD DAY SUNSHINE Roy Redmond (1967)

There's very little known about soul singer Roy Redmond, who recorded a handful of tracks for Warner Brothers' soul subsidiary label, Loma. He was one of the many acts to be produced by the talented Jerry Ragavoy, who arranged this track and also wrote several of Roy's other songs. This Lennon and McCartney composition first appeared on The Beatles' album *Revolver*.

54. ALL MY LOVING The Trends (1964)

Another group from Merseyside, The Trends were led by vocalist Freddy Ryder; their records were mainly cover versions. Having attempted this Lennon and McCartney song, from The Beatles second album *With The Beatles*, they then went on to record a couple of Motown classics.

55. THE FOOL ON THE HILL Bobbie Gentry (1968)

There is a lot more to Bobbie Gentry than her best-known song, 'Ode to Billie Joe', which many listeners know simply as 'Tallahatchie Bridge'. She recorded several albums and this Beatles cover was featured on her 1968 album, *Local Gentry*, which also included her interpretations of two other Lennon and McCartney compositions, 'Here, There And Everywhere', and 'Eleanor Rigby'. The original version of 'Fool On The Hill' first appeared on The Beatles' soundtrack to *The Magical Mystery Tour*.

56. ELEANOR RIGBY Frankie Valli (1968)

Timeless was the first actual solo album recorded by Frankie Valli, despite his previous release being entitled *Solo*. The latter was made up mainly of songs originally recorded as singles whilst he was still involved with The Four Seasons. It was on *Timeless* that Valli covered 'Eleanor Rigby'. Written mainly by Paul McCartney, with his first attempt at the lyric apparently referring to 'Father McCartney' (rather than 'Father Mackenzie') – Paul decided he didn't want to freak out his dad and picked out a name from the telephone directory instead. He picked the name Eleanor after actress Eleanor Bron, while Rigby was the name of a store.

57. IT'S FOR YOU **Three Dog Night (1968)**

Taken from their eponymous debut album, Three Dog Night's version of the Lennon and McCartney song runs for a mere 94 seconds. It was produced by Gabriel Mekler who would go on to produce Janis Joplin, Etta James and Steppenwolf among others. The group were signed to Dunhill Records, the label launched by record producer Lou Adler and their album consisted entirely of songs by outside writers. But considerable effort was expended into making their versions of the songs unique to the style of the group. 'It's For You' had previously been a top-10 hit in 1964 for Cilla Black.

58. SHE LOVES YOU **Homer & Jethro (1964)**

The Tennessee duo were Henry 'Homer' Haynes and Kenneth 'Jethro' Burns who made a reputation by performing parodies of popular songs. Back in 1953 when many DJs were reluctant to play the Patti Page's sugary 'How Much Is That Doggie In The Window', they were delighted to give a spin or two to the duo's 'How Much Is That Hound Dog In The Window'. Over the years they sent up dozens of hit songs and in 1964 tackled Beatlemania with a single: the A-side was 'I Want To Hold Your Hand' with of 'She Loves You' on the flip. Hayes suffered a fatal heart attack and died in 1971 aged just 51; Burns left this world 18 years later in 1989.

59. MISERY **Kenny Lynch (1963)**

This is believed to be the first cover of a Beatles song to be released in the UK. John and Paul had written 'Misery' in 1963, in the hopes that Helen Shapiro, the artist who was top of the bill of a tour the Beatles were a supporting act on, would record it. Shapiro's record producer, Norrie Paramor turned it down. But Kenny Lynch, who had been on the same bill as the Beatles in early 1963, on their first British tour took the composition. He gave it a much more pop-oriented arrangement than the Beatles would use when they recorded 'Misery' themselves when they were short of material for their debut album *Please Please Me*.

CLASSICALLY POP

Here we have a selection of records that were based on classical music themes – some instantly familiar, some a little more obscure.

1. ASIA MINOR Kokomo (1961) *US No 8/UK No 35*

This became the one and only hit for Kokomo, a mysterious entity that never granted an interview or gave a public performance to help promote his 'Asia Minor' track. The artist in question turned out to be pianist and arranger Jimmy Wisner, who later explained that he used the pseudonym because 'Asia Minor' was a rock record and he only wanted to be recognised as a jazz musician. He had the notion to record the melody from Grieg's 'Piano Concerto In A Minor' with a rollicking beat, so he bought an old upright piano for $50 and painted the hammers with shellac to produce a sound that was a cross between piano and harpsichord. The title of the piece came about when one of the musicians on the session asked what key it was in, to which he replied 'Asia Minor'.

2. LIKE I DO Maureen Evans (1962) *UK No 3*

Maureen Evans scored a UK top five hit with a melody based on the classical piece 'Dance Of The Hours' from the 1876 opera *La Gioconda* by Ponchielli. Maureen began her recording career as a session singer performing cover versions of big hits of the day for Woolworths' budget label, Embassy, before transferring to their full-price sister label, Oriole, on which she had a number of successful releases including this disc, which climbed all the way to number three.

3. HELLO MUDDAH, HELLO FADDUH Allan Sherman (1963)
US No 2/UK No 14

The melody for this novelty hit was also adapted from Ponchielli's 'Dance Of The Hours'. The single won a Grammy for 'Best Comedy Performance' and the following year, Allan recorded a sequel to the single using the same title and melody but different lyrics. He then wrote a third version for an American TV commercial, in which he appeared advertising a board game about Camp Granada.

4. ALONE AT LAST Jackie Wilson (1960) **US No 8**

Jack Leroy Wilson Jr was born in Detroit, Michigan, the only son of Jack

Sr and Eliza Mae Wilson. Growing up in the rough Detroit area of North End, Jackie, who was also called 'Sonny' by friends, grew up rough, joining a gang called the Shakers and often getting in trouble. Wilson became a major influence in the transition from R&B into soul, after he became a member of the vocal group The Dominoes, before going solo in 1957. He went on to record over 50 hit singles in America, taking in a variety of musical styles. In 1975, he collapsed on stage during a charity concert and lapsed into a coma. By the time of his death in 1984, he was recognized as one of the leading soul artists of his generation. Just missing out on making the UK top 40 (it peaked at number 50), this song was based on Tchaikovsky's 'Piano Concerto No.1' in B flat.

5. PILTDOWN RIDES AGAIN The Piltdown Men (1961) UK No 14

Having achieved far more success in the UK than in their native America, this was their second of three top 20 UK hits. This time they rocked-up Rossini's 'William Tell Overture'. The group were the brainchild of Ed Cobb, a founder member of a doo-wop and Tin Pan Alley vocal quartet called The Four Preps, and Lincoln Mayorga, who became The Preps pianist and arranger. They persuaded their label Capitol to give them some studio time to record some instrumentals. In search of a dirty saxophone sound, they found mean-sounding session musician Scott Gordon to share duties with fellow sax-man Jackie Kelso for their first session, resulting in an imaginative version of the old nursery rhyme 'Old MacDonald', which they called 'MacDonald's Cave'. The Rossini-inspired follow-up, 'Piltdown Rides Again', features a full horn section sequestered from the LA Philharmonic Orchestra.

6. REFLECTIONS OF CHARLES BROWN Rupert's People (1967)

This record was credited to a band that didn't exist. Their whole history is enormously complicated. The band went through three separate line-ups but their story begins with an even more obscure band, Sweet Feeling. Their manager, Howard Condor, asked the group's guitarist to rewrite a song called 'Charles Brown', which they had previously recorded as a B-side. The result, now titled 'Reflections of Charles Brown', was quite different to its original with a melody based on Bach's 'Air on a G String'. Conder then recruited another band, Les Fleur de Lys, who had released a few records of their own, to record the song, together with a B-side, 'Hold On'. But they decided not to work with

Conder after the tracks were finished. The single was released anyway, under the band name Rupert's People and has become a sought-after collector's item. Conder's plan was to release the record by getting Sweet Feeling to promote it under the Rupert's People moniker. But the group refused and Conder enlisted a group of musicians from the Merseybeats, Screaming Lord Sutch's Savages and The Knack to be the band. This didn't last long. Eventually, a few members of Sweet Feeling reconsidered and joined Rupert's People, releasing a couple more singles between 1967 and 1968.

7. PAST, PRESENT AND FUTURE The Shangri-Las (1966)

The group were formed whilst they were at high school in Queens, New York, and consisted of two sets of sisters: Mary and Elizabeth Weiss and identical twins Marge and Mary Ann Ganser. They gained their first recording contract in 1963 with the Kama Sutra label before signing with Red Bird the following year. Their biggest hits were 'Leader Of The Pack' and '(Remember) Walking In The Sand'. Then, in 1966, they recorded 'Past, Present And Future' with a melody based on Beethoven's 'Moonlight Sonata', with the lyrics spoken rather than sung by the girls.

The Shangri-Las, from Queens, New York, were regarded as being the 'tough girl group'

8. PRELUDE IN C SHARP MINOR OPUS 3
Ian Menzies & The Clyde Valley Stompers (1960)

This is Ian Menzies' own jazz arrangement of a classical piece by Sergei Rachmaninov. The Clyde Valley Stompers were formed in Glasgow, in 1952 and soon found a local following. When leader and bass player Jim McHarg emigrated to Canada in 1954, Ian Menzies took over control of the band and helped extend their popularity throughout the UK during the Fifties trad jazz boom. They achieved a UK top-40 hit in 1962 with 'Peter And The Wolf' but although they appeared on numerous television shows, the days of trad jazz were fast coming to an end. The group disbanded in 1963, although they occasionally re-formed for the odd performance, including some 1981 recording sessions, on which several of the founder members appeared once again under Menzies leadership.

9. A LOVERS CONCERTO **The Toys (1965)** *US No 2/UK No 5*

The melody for this one was adapted from 'Minuet In G', a composition written by the composer Christian Petzold but which is often thought to have been written by Johann Sebastian Bach, because it was included in a book of sheet music kept by his wife Anna Magdalena. After a few more releases, The Toys called it a day in 1968.

10. TCHAIKOVSKY ONE **The Second City Sound (1966)** *UK No 22*

This group made their name by rocking up the classics, although this was their only hit. It is based on the beginning of the first movement of Tchaikovsky's famous Piano Concerto number one, after which they went on to mash-up 'Lizst's Hungarian Rhapsody', naming it 'Shopping List' before moving onto 'Greig's Piano Concerto' in 1967, naming that 'Grieg One'.

11. NO NEED TO EXPLAIN **Flamma Sherman (1968)**

Flamma Sherman was the first act signed to Simon Napier-Bell's SNB label. They were four sisters from Liberia who were brought to Simon's attention by their mother, who happened to be the wife of the Liberian ambassador in London, George Flamma Sherman. This was their self-written debut single that owed a little to Bach's 'Air On A G String', given an arrangement by Ian Green (an arranger for Cilla Black, Don McLean and Rosetta Hightower). In the week of release, it received several plays on Radio 1 but then the network had a strike and was practically off the air for two weeks. By the time normal service was resumed, many important new records were stacked up waiting to be played an da lot of the previous records, including Flamma Sherman's, fell by the wayside. The record fizzled out, and although they made a couple more singles, none had the same appeal as their first.

12. MOONLIGHT LOVER **Doris Day (1963)**

Based on Beethoven's 'Moonlight Sonata', this song was recorded at the Columbia Studios in Hollywood. It was due to be part of an album to be called *Love Him*, containing a collection of ballads with a more contemporary feel, following her previous LP of show tunes. Tommy Oliver was brought in to arrange and conduct the orchestra and Doris' son, Terry Melcher, who had co-written one of his mother's biggest hits, 'Move Over Darling' a few months earlier, was brought in to produce. One of the songs recorded but not included at the time was 'Moonlight Lover', as it was intended to be a single, but the idea was shelved. It wasn't until 1995, when the album was reissued on CD that it was finally included in the running order.

13. IT'S NOW OR NEVER **Elvis Presley (1960)** *US No 1/UK No1*

This well-known Elvis hit topped the American charts for five weeks and in the UK it remained at number one for an amazing eight weeks. As soon as Elvis left the army in 1960, he was rushed into the studios in Nashville to record some new songs, including 'Are You Lonesome Tonight' and 'It's Now Or Never'. The latter was intended to be his first post-army release but was held up in the UK over copyright problems, due to the song being based on the 1899 Italian song, 'O Sole Mio'. However, no such problem arose in America, where the song became the King's biggest hit of his career, after Aaron Schroeder and Wally Gold were commissioned to write English lyrics to Eduardo di Capua's classic song.

14. SATURDAY NIGHT AT THE DUCKPOND **The Cougars (1963)** *UK No 33*

The Cougars came from Bristol and were discovered by Cliff Richard's producer, Norrie Paramor, who was judging a West Country talent contest that they won. They were then signed to Parlophone and recorded three singles and a six-track EP. Among the singles was this, based on the main theme from Tchaikovsky's ballet, 'Swan Lake'.

15. BUMBLE BOOGIE B. **Bumble & The Stingers (1961)** *US No 21*

When the Mercury label was formed just after World War I, one of its first releases was a jazzed-up version of Rimsky Korsakov's 'Flight Of The Bumble Bee' by pianist Jack Fina. In the spring of 1961 the small American Rendezvous label that had just enjoyed a big smash with the Ernie Fields Orchestra's version of 'In The Mood' were in search of another instrumental hit and plans were set in motion to record a new version of 'Bumble Boogie' with a small combo.

Just as the recording was being set up, label boss Leon Rene was paid a visit by a young hustler named Kim Fowley, who was touting his off-the-wall ideas to local independent labels. The two hit it off immediately and Fowler was given the task of producing the record. Arranger Ernie Freeman recorded two piano tracks and guitarist Tommy Tedesco was brought in to play guitar, creating a similar sound to his contribution to The Piltdown Men's records. They decided to call the group B. Bumble and The Stingers, and the result was an American top-30 hit.

16. THE DYING SWAN **Chris McLure (1966)**

Scotsman Chris McLure was a member of the pop group The Fireflies in 1965. The following year he decided on a solo career and signed to Decca, for whom he released 'The Dying Swan', based on Tchaikovsky's 'Swan Lake'. He then signed to Polydor and released a couple of further singles before forming The Chris McLure Set then, in 1969, returning as The Chris McLure Section. Under this name, he worked well into the Seventies, after which he continued playing the local Scottish club circuit as a solo act under the name of Christian.

17. WILLIAM TELL TWIST **Ricky Brown & The Hi-Lites (1963)**

In the early Sixties the Twist was always a useful source of dance material. More than once pop act figured that the 'The William Tell Overture' was a prime target to be given the big-beat treatment. One such release was by Sounds Incorporated and was called just 'William Tell'. This other version by Ricky Brown and The Hi Lites was released under the more descriptive title of 'The William Tell Twist'.

18. SABRE DANCE **Love Sculpture (1968)** *UK No 5*

The band were formed in Cardiff in 1966 by Dave Edmunds from the remnants of another local group, The Human Beans. Love Sculpture based their act mostly on blues standards and their first album *Blues Helping* included their arrangement of George Gershwin's 'Summertime'. Their treatment of Aram Khachaturian's classical piece, 'Sabre Dance' gave them their only hit single; it became a success following enthusiastic support from John Peel.

19. NATURE BOY Bobby Darin (1961) *US No 40/UK No 24*

This song, written by Eden Ahbez, was originally the theme for the 1948 movie *The Boy With Green Hair*, starring Dean Stockwell and sung by an uncredited choir. The same year it became a hit for Nat King Cole. Songwriter Herman Yablokoff alleged that the melody to 'Nature Boy' came from one of his songs, 'Be Still My Heart', but further research shows that the melody has more than a passing resembelence to passages from Antonín Dvorák's Opus 81, his 1887 'Piano Quintet No 2 in A'.

20. RAIN AND TEARS Aphrodite's Child (1968) *UK No 30*

The psychedelic rock act led by Demis Roussos signed their first recording contract with Mercury Records in Paris after the group were stuck there on their way to London from Greece. They went into the studio and recorded this, their debut single. 'Rain And Tears' was based on Pachelbel's famous 'Canon In D' and went on

Aphrodite's Child: the psychedelic prog-rockers preceded Demis Roussos' reign as the king of Seventies smoochy balladry

to sell over a million copies around Europe, where they became an overnight success.

21. EMERALD CITY The Seekers (1967)

The composer credits to this song were given as Kim Fowley and John Martin, the latter later being discovered to be a pseudonym for The Seekers' own Keith Potger, a fact the group revealed on their 1993 reunion tour. The melody was based on 'Lied An Die Freude' (Ode To Joy) from Beethoven's 'Ninth Symphony'.

22. BECAUSE The Beatles (1969)

John Lennon once claimed that the musical resemblance to Ludwig van Beethoven's 'Piano Sonata No.14', better known as the 'Moonlight Sonata' came about when he heard Yoko Ono playing the piece on the piano. Lennon asked her if she could turn the music upside down and play the chords backwards. When she carried out his request, he wrote the lyrics to 'Because' around what she was playing and the song was included on The Beatles' *Abbey Road* album.

23. STRANGER IN PARADISE Matt Monro (1967)

The song comes from the 1953 musical *Kismet* and although credited to Robert Wright and George Forrest as composers, the melody was taken from the music of Alexander Borodin's 'Dance Of The Maidens' that featured in his opera, *Prince Egor*. It was from this work that most of the score of the musical originated. 'Stranger In Paradise' became an international hit for Tony Bennett, topping the UK charts in 1955. Since when there have been dozens of other recordings by artists, including Engelbert Humperdinck, Johnny Mathis, Jack Jones and this 1967 version by Matt Monro, featured on his album *Invitation To Broadway*.

24. JUANITA BANANA The Peels (1966)

The Peels were a studio group assembled by writers and producers Tash Howard and Murray Kenton. The musical source of this minor American novelty hit from 1966 dates back to 1851; its melody during the chorus being borrowed from part of Guiseppe Verdi's 'Caro Nome' from his opera *Rigoletto*. The song tells of a Mexican banana grower's daughter who yearns to become an opera singer.

Despite significant regional play in America, it slipped off their charts after reaching number 59.

25. SHE WEARS MY RING Solomon King (1968) *UK No 3*

The song began life as 'La Golondrina', meaning 'The Swallow' in Spanish, and was written in 1862 by Mexican composer Narciso Serradell Sevilla and first recorded in 1906 by Senor Carl Francisco. In later years it was adapted by the songwriters Felice and Boudleaux Bryant as 'She Wears My Ring', first recorded under that title in 1960 by Jimmy Bell. It then became a massive hit in 1968 for another of music-mogul Gordon Mills' big-voiced protégés, Solomon King. There have since been versions by many other artists including Elvis Presley and Roy Orbison.

26. DAT'S LOVE The Vernons Girls (1962)

This song was included on their four-track EP *Lover Please* and was based on Bizet's 'Habanera' from his opera *Carmen* that was later turned into 'Dat's Love' when lyrics were added by Oscar Hammerstein for the musical *Carmen Jones*. He translated the libretto from the opera from French into English but pretty much left the original music intact. The Vernons Girls first came to the public's attention through their regular appearances on the TV show *Oh Boy*.

27. MOZART VS THE REST Episode Six (1969)

Just before Christmas 1969, Episode Six, a rock group from Harrow, were booked for a Radio 1 Club session and the producer asked them to come up with a couple of lively numbers. They responded with 'Mozart Vs The Rest', a tune based on Mozart's 'Rondo A La Turk' arranged by guitarist Tony Lander. After the show, the BBC were swamped with requests for the track so Episode Six rushed into the studio and recorded it in double-quick time. Which may account for the sound of Ian Gillan (later of Deep Purple) surfacing for breath half way through what would become the band's final single release.

28. TONIGHT IS SO RIGHT FOR LOVE Elvis Presley (1960)

The song 'Tonight Is So Right For Love' was adapted from a barcarolle composed by Jacques Offenbach. It was due to be included on the soundtrack album of Elvis's movie *G.I. Blues*. However, copyright issues ensued and European copies of the album featured a substitute song with a similar title, 'Tonight's All Right For Love', adapted from a melody composed by 19th century waltz king, Johann Strauss II. The original song remained as opening track for the American album.

29. TAKE ME TONIGHT Gene Pitney (1961)

This Gene Pitney track from 1961, 'Take Me Tonight', is based on Tchaikovsky's 'Pathétique' and included on his album, *The Many Sides Of Gene Pitney*. The American singer-songwriter had 16 top-40 hits in the US and 22 in the UK in total and was the writer behind classic hits such as 'He's a Rebel' by The Crystals and Ricky Nelson's 'Hello Mary Lou'.

30. NIGHT Jackie Wilson (1960) *US No 4*

This became Jackie's fourth American top-10 hit and was the third to have been based on a classical piece. In 1960 he reached number four with 'Night', based on the aria 'Mon Cœur S'Ouvre à ta Voix' (My Heart Opens At Thy Sweet Voice) from the opera *Samson and Delilah* by Camille Saint-Saëns, with lyrics by Johnny Lehmann. Then, later the same year, he found himself at number nine with 'Alone At Last' based on Tchaikovsky's 'Piano Concerto in B Flat'. In 1961 his recording of 'My Empty Arms', based on 'Vesti La Giubba' from Ruggero Leoncavallo's 1892 opera *Pagliacci*, reached number nine.

31. ENTRY OF THE GLADIATORS Nero & The Gladiators (1961) *UK No 37*

If you visit almost any circus or traditional fairground, you might well eventually hear Czech-born Julius Fucik's 1897 military march, 'Entrance Of The Gladiators', being played. Its musical symbolism conjures up images of clowns, tumblers and galloping horses. The piece was originally titled 'Grande Marche Chromatique' relying, as it does, heavily on the use of chromatic scales. In 1961, Nero & The Gladiators decided to jazz up this classical piece, turning it into a slinky shuffle akin to a Teddy Boy swinging his chain on a street corner. This, in conjunction with the violent intimations of its title, gave the BBC sufficient reason to restrict the plays for 'Entry Of The Gladiators'.

32. MY MIND'S EYE The Small Faces (1966) *UK No 4*

This became the group's fifth consecutive UK top-20 hit. Originally intended just to be an album track, it ended up being released as a single without the band's knowledge or consent whilst they were on tour in the north of England. The song was written by Ronnie Lane and Stevie Marriott who once admitted to taking as inspiration part of the popular Christmas hymn 'Gloria In Excelsis Deo' (also known as the 'Greater Doxology') for the melody and chorus.

33. NIGHT OF FEAR The Move (1967) *UK No 2*
Written by Roy Wood, 'Night Of Fear' became The Move's debut single, its main riff being based on Tchaikovsky's '1812 Overture'. It was originally planned to be the B-side of another of Roy's songs, 'Disturbance' but in the end the general consensus was that 'Night Of Fear' was the stronger song. The decision was taken to reverse the sides, which made both record company and group happy as it features all four members of the band singing a four-part harmony.

34. SWAN LAKE The Cats (1969)
This 1969 release was a somewhat bizarre rocksteady recording by one of the first British ska bands to achieve any sort of hit when they reached number 48 with their reggae-ish adaptation of the music from Act 2 Scene 10 of Tchaikovsky's 'Scene' from his ballet, 'Swan Lake'. The Cats hailed from Mile End in London and were previously known as The Hustlin' Kind until they changed their name in the summer of 1968. The group Madness recorded a version of the same piece of music for inclusion on their 1979 debut album *One Step Beyond*.

35. SO DEEP IS THE NIGHT Ken Dodd (1964) *UK No 31*
This became the TV entertainer's seventh UK top-40 hit and the one before he hit the number-one spot with 'Tears'. 'So Deep Is The Night' has an English lyric by Sunny Miller and is one of several songs based on Chopin's 'Etude' (Opus 10, No.9). An early version by Webster Booth and Ann Ziegler was featured in the 1946 British comedy film, *Demobbed* and Jo Stafford's 1950 hit 'No Other Love' was also derived from the same melody.

37. WHISPER WONDERFUL WORDS Christine Quaite (1963)
Christine was born in Leeds and began singing when she entered a local talent contest in Bridlington, Yorkshire aged eight. She went on

to enter countless other competitions, one of which was in Manchester where, at the age of 13, she won second place. This led to a recording contract with Oriole, for whom in 1962 her first release was 'Oh My'. She followed that with one of numerous cover versions that have been made of Johnny Crawford's American hit 'Your Nose Is Gonna Grow'. But it's her third release that's of interest here. 'Whisper Wonderful Words' borrowed the melody of the classical piece 'Habanera' from Bizet's opera *Carmen*.

38. RHAPSODY IN THE RAIN Lou Christie (1966) *UK No 37*

Written by Lou Christie with his songwriting collaborator Twyla Herbert (a former concert pianist and self-described clairvoyant who believed she could psychically predict which of their songs would become hits), this was the follow up to his international hit 'Lightning Strikes'. The song became Christie's fourth million-seller despite a number of American radio stations banning it, because they felt some of the lyrics were too suggestive. The line that caused the objections was 'we were making out in the rain'. So Lou changed it to 'we fell in love in the rain' and all was well. The one we recommend, however, is the 'X-rated' version that we feel our readers can handle. The way, the melody was based on part of Tchaikovsky's 'Romeo And Juliet' theme.

39. PETER AND THE WOLF Harpers Bizarre (1967)

Taken from Harpers Bizarre's debut album, *Feelin' Groovy*, this was an adaptation from part of Sergei Prokofiev's symphony for children, *Peter And The Wolf*, in which each character of the work is represented by an instrument of the orchestra'. Musician, composer and producer, Ron Elliott, best known as lead guitarist of rock band The Beau Brummels added some lyrics to the theme played by the strings representing the story's boy-hero, Peter.

40. THE STORY OF THREE LOVES Duane Eddy (1963)

Duane Eddy playing Marty Paich's arrangement of Rachmaninoff's adaptation of his 18th variation of *Rapsody on a Theme of Paganini*. Phew! Got that? 'The Story Of Three Loves' was originally released as the B-side to Eddy's single, 'The Son Of Rebel Rouser'.

Double A-sides

Back when the 7-inch single was king, from time to time record companies or artists weren't able to decide between two songs – which one to release as the A-side. So they took the easy way out and issued them as a double A-side. It wasn't always a good idea, as it sometimes split airplay and stopped a record from climbing higher in the charts. Here are just a few examples.

1. UNDER MY THUMB/THE LAST TIME The Who (1967)
UK No 44

The Who recorded this as a gesture of support after the songs' two composers were imprisoned on drug charges, and to help them cover the cost of bail. Jagger was sentenced to three months in prison for possession of amphetamine tablets he had legally purchased in Italy and Richards received a heavy-handed one-year confinement for allowing his Sussex home to be used for illegal smoking of drugs.

'Under My Thumb' and 'The Last Time' were two of The Who's favourite Jagger and Richards songs. So the decision was taken to release both Rolling Stones covers as a double A-side. Pete Townshend played bass on this session as John Entwistle was away on his honeymoon. The Who stated an initial intention to continue recording Stones songs for as long as they were in jail, but they were released before The Who cut any further tracks. Although fans of both groups appreciated the gesture, the record failed to reach any higher than number 44 on the UK charts.

2. WE LOVE YOU/ DANDELION The Rolling Stones (1967)
US No 50/UK No 8

The drugs convictions received by Mick Jagger and Keith Richards were quashed on 31 July, 1967. The Rolling Stones appeared to make light of the incident when they released 'We Love You': it featured sound effects of slamming prison doors and rattling chains.

The record was released as a double A-side with 'Dandelion', becoming that became a 'flower power' anthem with vocal harmonies not a million miles away from the style of The Beach Boys. 'Dandelion' was also the name that Keith and his partner, Anita Pallenberg would later give to their daughter.

The Who in 1967 (left to right): Keith Moon, Pete Townshend, John Entwistle and Roger Daltrey

3. MAN OF MYSTERY/ THE STRANGER The Shadows (1960)
UK No 5

This piece was composed by Michael Carr for a series of B-movie Edgar Wallace mysteries (hence the title) that were shown in cinemas for many years. The Shadows had their doubts about recording it, given it was quite a departure from the style of 'Apache', their previous (number-one) hit. It was probably because of the group's reluctance that it was released as a double A-side, the flip being composed by Bill Crompton and Morgan Jones. Perhaps this was the record company's way of keeping everyone happy. At the time, they preferred 'The Stranger'. But after the success of 'Man of Mystery', The Shadows began to appreciate the value in trying out different musical approaches.

4. POP GOES THE WEASEL/ BEE BOM Anthony Newley (1961)
UK No 12

After the success of his previous single, 'And The Heavens Cried', Anthony Newley publicly announced in May, 1961 his desire to become a movie director. He formed his own company, New Voyage Productions and, having received interest from financial backers, contacted songwriter Lesley Bricusse. Together they came up with an adaptation of *The Pilgrim's Progress* entitled 'Boy On A Wall'. The money men where not impressed and the project was aborted. The following month his album *Tony* was released and a single from it, 'Pop Goes The Weasel' was simultaneously released using his own arrangement. The track became a firm favourite with the younger audience, giving him another smash hit.

It was backed by 'Bee Bom', written by Johnny Worth under his pseudonym of Les Vandyke, and was later covered by Sammy Davis Jnr. in 1964, who was a big fan of Newley and would often perform the song in his live stage shows.

5. JUMBO/ THE SINGER SANG HIS SONG The Bee Gees (1968)
UK No 25

Following four top-20 hits, The Bee Gees were not in harmony with their record label and management team concerning their next release. The group wanted to put out a song called 'Jumbo' about an imaginary elephant, while Robert Stigwood (their manager) wanted to release 'The Singer Sang His Song'. On this occasion, The Bee Gees were given their own way.

However, although the group won out, few radio stations wanted to play the record, so the single was immediately deemed a double A-side, and picked up a few plays for 'The Singer sang His Song'. But by this time it was too late and the disc stalled at number 25. Until 2001, 'Jumbo' had been a much sought-after track, as it was only ever released as a vinyl single; finally, it appeared as a bonus track on a Bee Gees greatest hits CD.

6. REACH FOR THE STARS/ CLIMB EV'RY MOUNTAIN
Shirley Bassey (1961) *UK No 1*

This double A-side release gave Shirley Bassey her ninth UK top-40 hit and her second and final number one. 'Reach For The Stars' was written by Austrian singer and songwriter Udo Jurgens with English lyrics by Norman Newell, who also produced the record. The other side of this double A-side was written by Richard Rodgers and Oscar Hammerstein for their 1959 musical *The Sound Of Music*. In the original stage production, the Mother Abbess sang the song at the end of the first act but when Ernest Lehman wrote the screenplay for the movie version, he moved the scene so that the song would be the first major piece of music in the second act.

7. HELLO MARY LOU/ TRAVELIN' MAN Ricky Nelson (1961)
US No 9/UK No 2

Written by Gene Pitney, who recorded his own version, this song gave Ricky Nelson his biggest UK hit. In America the airplay for the two sides was completely split, resulting in both tracks making the top 10. The track features an influential guitar solo by the legendary James Burton, often cited by modern guitarists as one of the all-time great players. 'Travelin' Man' was written by Jerry Fuller while he was waiting to meet his wife in a park. He happened to have an atlas with him and picked out various locations around the world to write about. On completion, he first offered it to Sam Cooke, via his manager, who simply threw the demo into the waste-paper basket. But Joe Osborn, Nelson's bass player rescued it from the litter and suggested to Ricky that he record it.

8. DO WHAT YOU GOTTA DO/ AIN'T GOT NO – I GOT LIFE
Nina Simone (1968) *UK No 2*

Written by Jim Webb, 'Do What you Gotta Do' was recorded for

Simone's third album *Nuff Said* for RCA Records. Simone had been with the Philips label since 1964 but when her contract came to an end, she thought it was time for a new beginning. RCA wanted to help her gain popularity with the younger audience and encouraged her to record material by modern composers. This was the closing track from the album but has been rather eclipsed by the other side of the single, 'Ain't Got No – I Got Life'.

It was recorded at the New York Westbury Music Fair Concert in April 1968, just three days after the murder of Martin Luther King, and the entire concert was dedicated to his memory. The song comes from the musical *Hair*, with lyrics by James Rado and Gerome Ragni and music provided by the Canadian-American composer Galt MacDermot. The hippy ideals in the lyrics took on a different complexion in Nina Simone's version, and it suddenly becoming a Civil Rights protest song.

9. EVIL HEARTED YOU/ STILL I'M SAD The Yardbirds (1965)
UK No 3

Written by Graham Gouldman, this became the group's biggest UK hit single and made an early use of the fuzz-box (guitar distortion pedal) by guitarist, Jeff Beck. Although it is Beck that plays on the song, when the track received a brief American release, it mistakenly had a picture sleeve showing Eric Clapton as part of the line-up.

This was only a double A-side in the UK: for the American market, 'Still I'm Sad' was only the B-side of the single, 'I'm A Man', a Bo Diddley cover that reached number 17 on their charts.

10. CABARET/WHAT A WONDERFUL WORLD
Louis Armstrong (1968) *UK No 1*

With Louis Armstrong so associated with trad jazz, his record label in the UK were worried that by releasing 'What A Wonderful World' – which had very little to do with jazz – his fans might avoid purchasing the disc. So the decision was taken to release it as a double A-side, featuring his very jazzy interpretation of the title song from the musical *Cabaret*. Although it picked up a few plays, it was the other side that the DJs really got behind.

'What a Wonderful World' was originally offered to Tony Bennett, who turned it down. After the first few days of the single's release, Armstrong's record label realised that most of the attention was being given to 'What A Wonderful World', and they decided to concentrate all their efforts on promoting that track. They pushed it all the way to the top, making Louis the oldest person to have topped the UK charts.

Neither side became a hit in America until 1988 when 'What A Wonderful World' climbed to number 32, following its use in the movie *Good Morning Vietnam*. Actress Sandra Bullock named her adopted son Louis because every time she looked at him it reminded her of 'What A Wonderful World'.

11. ROCK-A-HULA BABY/ CAN'T HELP FALLING IN LOVE

Elvis Presley (1962) *US No 1 (Billboard Easy Listening chart)/UK No 1*

Both songs on this double A-sided single came from the movie *Blue Hawaii*. 'Rock-A-Hula Baby' was written by Ben Weisman and Fred Wise with newcomer Dolores Fuller, who went on to compose a dozen further songs for Elvis. 'Can't Help Falling in Love' was inspired by the French melody 'Plasir D'Amour' by Jean Paul Martini from his opera *Annette et Lubin*. Elvis recorded the song in 1961 but it wasn't until the following year that his fans got to hear it when it was included in the movie soundtrack. In 2005, along with all his number one hits, both sides were reissued and the record went to number three in the UK.

12. ONCE THERE WAS A TIME/ NOT RESPONSIBLE

Tom Jones (1966) *UK No 18*

After the success of 'It's Not Unusual', which topped the charts in 1965, Tom Jones and his manager had real trouble finding a song that would match the success of his debut hit. He achieved two further top-20 hits with his version of 'With These Hands' and the title song to the movie *What's New Pussycat*. For his next release, they were undecided as to whether to go with a ballad or an upbeat song, so they chose one of each and issued the two songs as a double A-side. 'Once Upon A Time' was an Italian song, written by Mario Del with English lyrics by Peter Callander, while 'Not Responsible' was the uptempo track, written by Tom's manager, Gordon Mills and given an arrangement by Johnny Harris. Although it wasn't a massive hit, it performed better than his next release, 'This And That', which failed to even make the top 40. He needn't have worried though, because later in the year he'd have the Christmas number one with 'Green Green Grass of Home'.

13. BLUE BAYOU/MEAN WOMAN BLUES Roy Orbison (1963)
US No 29/UK No 3 US No 5/UK No 3

Written by Roy with Joe Melson, the song was featured on Roy's album, *In Dreams*, and was later revived in 1977 by Linda Ronstadt, who had a top five hit with the song in America. The other side was interesting – essentially a cover of Elvis Presley song. It was written by African-American songwriter Claude Demetrius, who had composed songs for artists including Louis Armstrong and Jimmy Witherspoon. He got a big break when he was signed to Gladys Music, a company that owned the exclusive publishing rights to the music of Elvis Presley. In 1957, he composed 'Mean Woman Blues' for Presley's movie, *Loving You*, which the 'Big O' managed to make his own for this 1963 hit.

14. MICHAEL ROW THE BOAT ASHORE/LUMBERED
Lonnie Donegan (1961) *UK No 6*

The song started life as a 19th-century spiritual and under the title of 'Michael' became a number-one hit both in the UK and the US for The Highwaymen. When Lonnie heard their soft folk approach to the song, he decided to give it his famous skiffle treatment, but because the American version was already beginning to sell, it was decided to release the record as a double A-side. Written by Leslie Bricusse and Anthony Newley, the other song came from the pair's musical *Stop The World I Want To Get Off*, in which Newley played the character Littlechap.

Skiffle star Lonnie Donegan had a double-A-sided hit with an old 19th-centry spiritual

15. BABY ROO/ WHERE THE BOYS ARE **Connie Francis** (1961) *UK No 5*

Written by Neil Sedaka

and Howard Greenfield, this became Connie's fifteenth UK top-20 hit in 1961. In the same year, she starred in her own American TV special sponsored by a well-known gent's hair cream, in which she sang and acted with Tab Hunter and Art Carney. She had also made more appearances on *The Ed Sullivan Show* than any other singer. 'Where the Boys Are' was the title song to a movie starring George Hamilton, and was the big-screen debut of Connie herself as an actress. This song was also written by Sedaka and Greenfield but it was another case where the UK didn't follow the US: in the States, 'Where The Boys Are' was a double A-side but paired with a song called 'No One'.

16. SERENATA/LET'S **Sarah Vaughan (1960)** *UK No 37*

1960 was a very important year in the life of Sarah Vaughan. Having been with Mercury Records since 1953, she signed a long-term recording contract with Morris Levy's recently formed Roulette label. It was a big-budget deal, with what amounted to a blank cheque to cover recording sessions in Hollywood and New York with top arrangers including Quincy Jones and Billy May. For this, she had to deliver a minimum of 16 album releases over the term of the contract. Three key producers were assigned to her various projects, with musical director Joe Reisman taking care of the arrangements for her singles. One of the first releases was 'Serenata'. Originally written in 1947 by Leroy Anderson as an instrumental, Anderson's favoured lyricist, Michael Parrish, added words three years later. Roulette's output in the UK went through EMI's Columbia's label and when the tapes of 'Serenata' arrived, they were not convinced it was the right song for the British market. The American B-side, with its brief title, 'Let's' was deemed more suitable but with pressure from the US to release 'Serenata' as the lead track, a compromise was reached and the single became a double A-side.

17. CHAIN OF FOOLS/SATISFACTION **Aretha Franklin (1967)**
UK No 37

Joe South played the guitar solo on the track and when songwriter Ellie Greenwich heard a rough mix, she suggested another harmony part should be added. Singing it to Jerry Wexler at Atlantic records, he whisked her into the studio and added the extra part. 'Chain of Fools' was paired with Aretha's cover of the Rolling Stones hit '(I Can't get No) Satisfaction)', which she entitled just 'Satisfaction'. Aretha's record label, Atlantic, soon discovered that the radio stations and the record buying public were asking for Stones cover, and the decision was taken to re-promote the single but pushing the Jagger and Richard song, resulting in a top-40 hit. In America, the track was a straightforward A-side release and contained a different song, 'Prove It', as the B.

18. I'M LOOKING OUT THE WINDOW/DO YOU WANNA DANCE
Cliff Richard (1962) *UK No 2*

Cliff's seventeenth consecutive single to reach the top 20, a run which included five number ones, was this double A-side. Although this was his first official double A-side single, the B-sides of two of his previous hits, 'Mean Streak' and 'Travelling Light', had in fact made the charts – 'Never Mind' and 'Dynamite' respectively.

Having topped the charts for six weeks with his previous release, the upbeat title song from the movie, *The Young Ones*, there was a worry that a ballad might not have the same impact and although everyone believed in the strength of 'I'm Looking Out The Window', it was decided to release it as a double A-side with the rocking revival of Bobby Freeman's 1958 American top-10 hit, 'Do You Wanna Dance'. Who knows, if they'd put their faith in just one of the songs, it might have managed to climb that one position higher to the top spot...

19. HEADLINE NEWS/STOP HER ON SIGHT (S.O.S)
Edwin Starr (1968) *UK No 11*

First released in 1966, when it reached number 39, at the end of 1968 Tamla Motown decided to try again with this Edwin Starr track. The label was having a huge amount of success with reissuing their back catalogue, and the Starr song was made a double A-side with 'Stop Her On Sight (S.O.S)' – a song that was also from 1966. Their plan worked and the record climbed to number 11. Interestingly, neither track was actually recorded for Motown. In 1966, Starr was signed to the American Ric Tic label that was released through Polydor in the UK. 'Stop Her On Sight' originally had reached number 35 but when he signed to Motown, they bought the rights to some of his earlier tracks.

20. LOVER PLEASE/YOU KNOW WHAT I MEAN
The Vernons Girls (1962) *UK No 16*

Written by Billy Swan, this was a cover of the biggest American solo hit for ex-Drifters singer, Clyde McPhatter. The Vernons Girls version entered the charts in May 1962 and as soon as it started its descent down the top 20, their label, Decca decided to re-promote it as a double A-side with the Liverpudlian accented song, 'You Know What I Mean', receiving so much exposure that it kept the record in the best sellers for a further seven weeks. Assembled from employees of Vernons Pools, the original 70-piece choir were slimmed down to a more manageable 16-piece act for the TV show *Six-Five Special*' and *Oh Boy*. By 1962, they were just a trio of Maureen Kennedy, Francis Lee and Jean Owen. DJs took a fancy to what started out as the B-side of 'Lover Please' and 'You Know What I Mean', written by Trevor Peacock, began to climb the charts in its own right.

21. YOU ONLY LIVE TWICE/JACKSON Nancy Sinatra (1967)

US No 14/UK No 11
Written by John Barry and Leslie Bricusse, this was the title song to the fifth James Bond movie, starring Sean Connery. There are two very different versions of the song by Nancy – this version, which was released as a single in 1967 and the grander wistful version featured

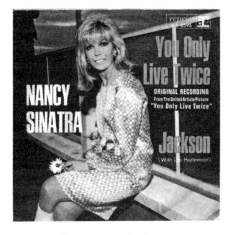

in the film's opening sequence and on the soundtrack album.

The James Bond theme song was less of a hit in America, where it was also a double A-side: 'Jackson' had a greater appeal to the US market. The song was written by Jerry Leiber and Billy Ed Wheeler, who came up with the original idea and took it to Leiber – who hated most of the lyrics. He suggested scrapping the majority of them and beginning the song with what was then the last verse. Despite protests about starting a song with the climax, Jerry helped re-write the words and Billy Ed Wheeler recorded the song on his first album with Joan Sommer taking the female part, which was copied by Johnny Cash and June Carter in their version, before Nancy and Lee decided try a version.

22. VALLEY OF TEARS/YOU'RE SO SQUARE (BABY I DON'T CARE)
Buddy Holly (1961) *UK No 12*

Fats Domino, who wrote the song with Dave Bartholomew, had a hit with it in the Fifties. But it was Buddy Holly who made it a double A-side with 'Baby I Don't Care', both songs originally recorded for his self-titled 1958 album. Released as a single in the UK in 1961, it became a top-20 hit. Buddy Holly and The Crickets visited the UK in March, 1958 for a month-long tour to promote the album and by the time they left England, they had no less than four of their singles in the charts.

On the other side of the single was the groovily titled 'You're So Square (Baby I Don't Care)', written by Jerry Leiber and Mike Stoller for Elvis Presley's 1957 movie *Jailhouse Rock*. Word has it that the composers were late delivering four songs for the movie so their publisher tracked them down at a Hollywood hotel, where they were enjoying breakfast together; he pushed a sofa up against the door of one of their rooms and went to sleep until the songs were completed.

23. WHO AM I/ THIS IS IT **Adam Faith (1961)** *UK No 5*

This was Adam's second double A-side release, as the previous year he'd issued the pairing of 'When Johnny Comes Marching Home' with 'Made You'. On this occasion Les Vandyke (or Johnny Worth to his friends), wrote the two songs and the combined timing of both tracks was less than four minutes.

The single was his seventh consecutive top five hit. All in all, Faith achieved 23 top 40 singles of which 11

made the UK top 10, including his two number ones. Ten of the 11 singles that made the top 10 also made the top five.

25. PENNY LANE/ STRAWBERRY FIELDS FOREVER
The Beatles (1967) *US No 8 UK No 2*

Both sides of this single were recorded at the same time. The Beatles were in the process of completing their *Sgt. Pepper* album and both were considered for inclusion but were left off the final running order. As a result of EMI and Brian Epstein putting pressure on the group for a new single, the two tracks were issued on the one single. The producer, George Martin, has stated that he believed that the pairing of the two titles probably resulted in the greatest single released by the group – despite it being the first of many a release by them not to make number one.

The working title of 'Strawberry Fields Forever' was 'It's Not Too Bad' and the song took 45 hours to record over a five-week period. The Beatles recorded three very different arrangements of 'Strawberry Fields Forever', the first of which began with the verse (beginning with 'living is easy') instead of the chorus ('let me take you down'). The final single version of the song consisted of parts of two takes being spliced together to make the full song.

26. HIGH VOLTAGE/OLD SMOKIE Johnny & The Hurricanes
(1961) *UK No 24*

This double A-sided single became the last top-40 hit for Johnny & The Hurricanes in the UK. Disappointingly, neither track charted in America. The group developed a following in Europe and in 1962 played the Star Club in Hamburg with the then-almost-unknown Beatles serving as their opening act.

Johnny & The Hurricanes were known for taking old songs and giving them a rock'n'roll treatment and this was their adaptation of a round-the-campfire folk song classic. Johnny Paris and The Hurricanes continued to tour Europe and America until his death in 2006.

INSTRUMENTALS

Every week on Sounds Of The Sixties on BBC Radio 2, we play an instrumental track just before Saturday's 9am news. Here you'll find 100 of the many that have been featured over the years.

1. THE LONELY SURFER Jack Nitzsche (1963) *US No 39*

Jack Nitzsche was born and educated in Chicago but moved to Los Angeles, where he found a job copying music for Sonny Bono, who was a talent scout for Specialty records. This job resulted in him becoming an arranger for Lee Hazelwood. He then went to work for Phil Spector and was largely responsible for the arrangements on many of Phil's big hits. It was during this period he signed an artist deal for himself with Frank Sinatra's Reprise label and recorded four albums, the first of which featured 'The Lonely Surfer'. Nitzsche then went on to compose music for several major Hollywood movies including *An Officer And A Gentleman*, *One Flew Over The Cuckoo's Nest* and, with Ry Cooder and Mick Jagger, *Performance*.

2. GIRL FROM MILL VALLEY Jeff Beck (1969)

Taken from his album *Beck-Ola*, this was recorded after Beck's departure from The Yardbirds. The album was made in haste by a put-together band who didn't get on too well and producer, Mickey Most, who didn't have a lot of sympathy for Beck's musical selection. The album turned into, essentially, a jam session featuring original songs, a couple of re-arranged Elvis covers and this soulful instrumental written by keyboard player Nicky Hopkins, dedicated to his then girlfriend, who came from Mill Valley.

3. WADE IN THE WATER Ramsey Lewis Trio (1966)
US No 19/UK No 31

The R&B pianist was born in Chicago in 1935 and his trio including Eldee Young on bass and Isaac 'Red' Holt on drums. They disbanded in 1965, with Young and Holt forming the successful (albeit unimaginatively named) Young-Holt trio whilst Ramsey Lewis re-formed his trio with Cleveland Eaton on bass and future Earth, Wind & Fire player Maurice White on drums. 'Wade In The Water' was based on a pre-American Civil War slave song and only became a hit in Britain when it was reissued by Chess in 1972.

4. ON THE REBOUND **Floyd Cramer (1961)** *US No 4/UK No 1*

Cramer was born in Louisiana and, as a pianist in the Sixties, became an integral part of the Nashville session scene, where there was a great shortage of keyboard players. His work can be heard on many hit singles including those by Elvis Presley, Jim Reeves and Hank Locklin. Ironically his biggest American hit was called 'Last Date' and reached number two, only to be held off the top spot by Elvis's 'Are You Lonesome Tonight' on which he played piano. Cramer was reluctant to tour as an artist due to his lucrative work as a session man, a field in which he continued working right up to the time of his death in 1997.

5. TAKE ME TO MY LOVER **Les Reed & His Orchestra (1968)**

A 1968 British cult film inspired by the glamour of two- wheeled transport sported a soundtrack composed by one of Britain's leading songwriters, Les Reed. The movie in question was 'Girl On A Motorcycle' starring Marianne Faithful and the legendarily stylish French actor Alain Delon.

6. THE PINK PANTHER THEME **Brother Jack McDuff (1964)**

Written by, and originally recorded by, Henry Mancini & His Orchestra, the popular TV theme got a salacious jazz-blues interpretation by legendary organist Brother Jack McDuff in 1964. McDuff actually began his musical career playing bass. After taking up the organ, he started his own band which featured a young George Benson on guitar.

7. THE PIED PIPER **Steve Race & His Orchestra (1963)** *UK No 29*

Steve Race's first job was as a pianist with Harry Leader's band, and he went on to play with the bands of Lew Stone and Cyril Stapleton, and to arrange for both the Ted Heath band and Judy Garland. In 1962 and 1963 he won awards for his commercial jingles for ITV, with the most lucrative being for Birds Eye frozen peas: 'Sweet as the moment when the pod went pop'. He also won an Ivor Novello Award for his composition 'Nicola', named after his daughter. Race's radio and television programmes included *Jazz In Perspective, Music Now, Many A Slip, My Music* and *With Great Pleasure.* For many years in the Sixties he was a neighbour of Phil Swern – author of this book – and helped him start his collection by frequently giving him batches of singles he no longer required.

8. LOVE AT FIRST SIGHT Sounds Nice (1969) *UK No 18*

With Jane Birkin and Serge Gainsbourg's single 'Je T'Aime...Moi Non Plus', heading towards number one, almost all the radio stations banned the single on the grounds that it was too raunchy with all the heavy breathing. Organist and arranger Tim Mycroft had the idea of getting together session musicians including Clem Cattini, Herbie Flowers and Chris Spedding to record and rush-release an instrumental version without all the grunts and groans. His plan paid off, as his record began picking up airplay and sales but no doubt enhancing the demand for the original.

9. KICK OFF Bert Weedon (1964)

Bert Weedon had wanted to play the guitar from his very early childhood. When he was just 12 years old he persuaded his father to buy him a rather battered guitar off a stall in London's famous Petticoat Lane Street Market, for exactly 75p. And so began the career of one of Britain's most accomplished instrumental stars. His technique has influenced hundreds of today's top guitarists; he was probably the only British instrumentalist to rival Duane Eddy. This instrumental was composed by bandleader Jack Parnell and originally recorded by his big band.

10. SPANISH FLEA Herb Alpert & The Tijuana Brass (1965)
US No 27/UK No 3

Herb Alpert is a lot more than just a trumpeter. In the US alone, Herb Alpert's achievements include three number one hits, 28 albums on the Billboard charts, eight Grammy awards, 14 platinum and 15 gold albums. He has sold in excess of 80 million albums worldwide. He is the 'A' in A&M records – founded in 1962 alongside the 'M', his partner Jerry Moss – which was sold to Polygram in 1989 for a reported $500 million. 'Spanish Flea' is probably one of the best-known instrumental tunes to have ever hit the charts. A vocal version of it was released in 1966 by blonde bombshell Kathy Kirby, who first found chart success in 1963 adding lyrics to The Shadows' number one hit, 'Dance On'.

11. A SWINGIN' SAFARI Bert Kaempfert & His Orchestra (1962)

Bert Kaempfert had a huge following in Germany, selling millions of albums, and he wrote many successful songs. Most memorable are

'Spanish Eyes' for Al Martino and 'Wooden Heart' for Elvis Presley. He also wrote a song that was originally recorded as part of the score to the 1965 movie *A Man Could Get Killed* – 'Strangers In The Night', starring James Garner and Sandra Dee. It became a number-one hit for Frank Sinatra.

12. GONZO **James Booker (1960)**

James Booker was a flamboyant, one-eyed keyboard player from New Orleans. His father was a minister at a local church, and he encouraged his son to learn an instrument. He grew up to become one of the city's central music figures during the Fifties and Sixties. In 1954, he cut his first record under the supervision of Fats Domino's co-writer and producer, Dave Bartholomew. In 1960 he had a US hit in the form of 'Gonzo', which became his nickname. Despite being out of character for the wild man, it nevertheless reached number 43 on the Hot 100. Booker was also a top session player, touring with Fats Domino, Dr John, Lloyd Price and many others. In the late-Sixties he went through various drug-related illnesses; he died in 1983.

13. AMERICA **The Nice (1968)** *UK No 21*

In the early part of 1967, the trio of Keith Emerson (keyboards), David O' List (guitar) and Lee Jackson (bass) backed powerful soul singer PP Arnold in concert. Before she went on stage, they would play a few numbers themselves to an enthusiastic response from the audience. A few months later, they formed The Nice, adding drummer Brian

Flamboyant New Orleans boogie and soul pianist James Booker

Davison and became a successful concert band across Europe almost overnight. Their mix of psychedelia, jazz, rock and adaptations of classical pieces had crowds rocking in the aisles. 'America' was a rocked-up instrumental version of the song from *West Side Story*.

14. THE HORSE Cliff Nobles (1968)

In 1968, Cliff Nobles' single 'The Horse' climbed to number two on the American charts. The only problem for the artist was that he wasn't on the record. He was the singer of the A-side, 'Love Is Alright', while 'The Horse' was in fact the backing track to that song. When a promo copy of the single was sent to a local radio station in Tampa, Florida, the DJs loved it. But unfortunately the record got badly scratched and they began playing the other side, having noticed that the music was the same (only without the vocals) while they waited for a replacement copy. Years later, the rightful A-side, complete with vocal, became a staple of Northern soul clubs in the UK, from where it then spread to lovers of R&B throughout the world.

15. SOUL BOSSA NOVA Quincy Jones (1962)

His full name is Quincy Delight Jones Jnr and, over his five decades in the entertainment industry, he has received 79 Grammy nominations and won 27. He is probably best known for production work on one of the best-selling albums of all time, *Thriller* by Michael Jackson. This track was sampled on the 1991 hit by Dream Warriors, 'My Definition Of A Boombastic Jazz Style', and again on the 2005 single, 'Number One Spot' by Rapper Ludacris.

16. THEME FOR TWIGGY Grapefruit (1969)

After Pete and Geoff Swettenham and John Parry left Tony Rivers and The Castaways with the view of forming their own group, they met Terry Doran, the managing director of The Beatles' Apple music publishing company. He introduced the boys to George Alexander, who became the fourth member of Grapefruit and wrote most of their material including their hit single, 'Dear Delilah', their popular 'Elevator' and this instrumental, 'Theme For Twiggy', which appeared on the B-side of their single 'Someday Soon'.

17. INDIAN BRAVE The Outlaws (1961)

The Outlaws were once Mike Berry's backing group, and this number was written by Joe Meek under the pseudonym of Robert Duke. It appeared on the B-side of their minor hit single 'Ambush'.

18. THE GOOD, THE BAD AND THE UGLY Hugo Montenegro (1968) *UK No 2/UK No 1*

Hugo Montenegro and his Orchestra provided the backing on dozens of American hit singles throughout the Fifties but he is best remembered in the UK for this movie theme that became the first instrumental to top the British charts in over five years.

Hugo himself supplied the grunts and the whistler is Muzzy Marcellino, who did a similar job in 1954 on the original soundtrack of another western, *The High And The Mighty*. It was in the first week of June that Hugo moved up to the number two position, but he only held onto it for just one week. In the UK, however, it was number one for four weeks.

19. MARIA ELENA Los Indios Tabajaris (1963) *US No 6/UK No 5*

First published in 1932, it was written by Spanish composer Lorenzo Barcelata, with English words added later by Bob Russell. The song was dedicated to Maria Elena, the wife of Mexican President Emilio Portes. Jimmy Dorsey and his Orchestra achieved an American number one with it in 1941, with vocals provided by Bob Eberly. This instrumental version was recorded in 1958 but not released until 1962 by Natalico and Antenor Lima, better known as Los Indios Tabajaris.

20. WASHINGTON SQUARE The Village Stompers (1963) *US No 2*

The famous square in New York's Greenwich Village where folk musicians would meet and play their songs, evolved into a potent symbol for their music. It also became the inspiration for this local Dixieland band's hit. After writer Bob Goldstein completed the tune, all he needed was an act to perform it, The eight-piece Village Stompers solved his problem.

Having just released a failed single under the name of Frank Hubbel and The Hubcaps, they changed their name and signed to the Epic label where they were assigned top producer, Joe Sherman to work with them. They came up with this massive hit, which achieved the number two spot during the third week of November but only managed to sustain the position for one week.

21. BEEFEATERS Johnny Dankworth & His Orchestra (1964)

This was used by Tony Blackburn as the theme tune to his daily Radio 1 breakfast show in the Sixties: he had it slowed down to simulate dubbed barks from his imaginary dog, Arnold. The track was also the theme tune of Rediffusion TV's *Search for a Star*.

22. MASHED POTATOES Nat Kendrick & The Swans (1960)

This is a rare recording made in Miami by James Brown's band, recording under a different name due to a dispute Brown was having with his label, King Records. He can be heard playing the piano and shouting the song's title. To prevent Brown's voice from being recognized, his shouted vocals were covered by Carlton 'King' Coleman, a local radio DJ, though Brown's voice remains just about audible in the background. Leadership of the band was officially credited to Nat Kendrick, who was Brown's drummer at the time.

23. WORK OUT The Flintstones (1964)

The Flintstones were originally a six-piece called The Cavaliers, who auditioned for Joe Meek in 1959 and were signed to his Triumph label. In 1960, they were involved with a weird project of Joe's called *I Hear A New World*, for which they were renamed The Blue Men. In 1962, with a change of line-up, they became The Flintstones but, to avoid any confusing associations with the cartoon characters, Meek decided to rechristen them The Stonehenge Men and recorded two tracks with them for HMV. In 1964, with yet another revised line-up, they reverted back to The Flintstones and released this track under the supervision of Mickey Most. Unfortunately the record disappeared without trace and so did the band.

24. LOVE THEME FROM ROMEO AND JULIET
Henry Mancini (1969) *US No 1*

Henry Mancini was America's most prolific movie theme composer, winning more Oscars and Grammy awards than any other recording artist. His scores graced such classics as *Breakfast At Tiffany's*, *The Days Of Wine And Roses* and *The Pink Panther*. Ironically, his only American number one single was from a film score he didn't write himself. One night, after seeing Franco Zeffirelli's *Romeo And Juliet*, starring 17-year-old Leonard Whiting and 16-year-old Olivia Hussey, he was so impressed with Nino Rossi's musical score he tried to obtain the soundtrack, only to find that it had never been released. He decided to arrange his own version of the love theme for inclusion on an album he was in the middle of recording. His record company had already chosen his instrumental version of 'The Windmills Of Your Mind' as a single and Mancini suggested the 'Romeo and Juliet' theme for the B-side. On release, radio stations began flipping the disc, resulting in his biggest hit, topping the US charts in the last week of June where it remained for two weeks before giving way to 'In The year 2525' by Zager and Evans.

25. PENETRATION The Pyramids (1963) *US No 18*

This was the group's second American hit, composed by the group's bassist, Steve Leonard and was originally called 'Eyeballs'. Inspired by The Chantays' hit, 'Pipeline', the track was recorded in Hollywood at a cost of just over $300. The group's guitarist, Willy Glover wasn't featured on the disc as he left the studio to get something to eat before the final take only to return to find they'd made a recording with which they were all satisfied. The band's most memorable gimmick was to arrive on stage wearing Beatles-style wigs and them whip them off during their act to reveal newly close-shorn heads, much to the shock and amusement of the audience.

26. BRISTOL EXPRESS The Eagles (1962)

The group was led by Terry Clarke, who built his own homemade guitar, together with Roderick Meacham on drums, Michael Brice on bass and Johnny Payne on rhythm guitar. They began by playing mainly covers of instrumentals in local Bristol dance halls launching their professional career in 1962 after being spotted by composer, Ron Grainer who used the group to record part of the soundtrack for his movie project, 'Some People', resulting in them being awarded the Duke Of Edinburgh Trophy for their contribution to the film. Soon afterwards, they were signed to Pye Records where they released this, their first single.

27. THEME FROM EXODUS Ferrante & Teicher (1961) *US No 2/UK No 6*

Composed by Ernest Gold, this was the theme from the Otto Preminger movie starring Paul Newman. Arthur Ferrante and Louis Teicher met at the age of six whilst at school and began working as a two-piano classical duo in 1947. For the recording of 'Exodus', arranger Don Costa assembled a 45-piece orchestra and a choir before they added their piano parts. It was in the third week of January, 1961 that the record climbed to its peak position of number two, remaining there for just one week.

28. WONDERLAND BY NIGHT Bert Kaempfert & His Orchestra (1961) *US No 1*

The beginning of 1961 was definitely the time for instrumentals on the American charts. The first week of January that year saw the man who first produced The Beatles, Bert Kaempfert, knock Elvis Presley off his perch, having been at number one for six weeks, 'Wonderland By Night' or 'Wunderland Bei Nacht' was the title theme to a movie that related the darker side of Germany's 'economic miracle'. It remained at the top of the charts for three weeks before being replaced by 'Will You Love Me Tomorrow by The Shirelles, who in turn were knocked off number one by yet another instrumental, 'Calcutta' by Lawrence Welk's Orchestra.

29. LET THERE BE DRUMS Sandy Nelson (1961) *US No 7/UK No 3*

Starting out as a member of the Kip Tyler Band, Sandy appeared at many big rock 'n' roll shows and worked as an in-demand session man playing drums on the million-selling 'To Know Him Is To Love Him' by the Teddy Bears. In 1959, with a little help from his friend Bruce Johnston, he went on to cut his own instrumental single titled 'Teen Beat' that hit gold, making the top 10 in both America and Britain. In 1961 he recorded 'Let There Be Drums', co-composed with Richie Podolor, who went on to successfully produce Three Dog Night and Steppenwolf.

31. THEME FROM THE LEGIONS LAST PATROL
Ken Thorne & His Orchestra (1963) *UK No 4*

This often requested instrumental is quite hard to come by. The piece was originally called 'Concerto Disperato' and was recorded by Italian trumpeter, Nini Rosso before being covered by Ken Thorne and his Orchestra and becoming a hit under the title 'The Theme from 'The Legion's Last Patrol'. Rosso's original was rushed out on the little-known Durium label but was too late to make the British charts. The movie itself was originally called *Marcia o Crepa* (March or Die) but known as *The Legion's Last Patrol* in the UK and *Commando* in America and tells about the Algerian War of Independence.

32. MARCH OF THE MODS Joe Loss & His Orchestra (1964)

UK No 31

Loss formed his first professional band in 1930, a seven-piece that played at the Astor Ballroom in London's Haymarket, and three years later they made their first radio broadcast. Despite the outbreak of World War II, Joe managed to keep going with his musicians and even played to the troops in France. Their popularity continued after the war and they changed styles to pander to the fashions of the time, playing whatever was popular. In the Sixties he made the pop charts with such numbers as 'Wheels Cha-Cha', 'Must be Madison' and 'March Of The Mods'.

33. FISH AND STICKS Eric Delaney & His Big Band (1963)

Eric was born in Acton and came from a musical family, gravitating towards a drum kit at a very early age and giving his first public performance at the age of six. Four years later, he formed his first group, which included his mother on piano and father on banjo. By the time he was 16, he won the title of Britain's best swing drummer and a year later, in 1941, he was touring the UK with the Bert Ambrose Octet with George Shearing on piano. Forming his own band in 1954, he performed at The Royal Variety show two years later. This is one of his own compositions that he recorded in 1963.

34. CLASSICAL GAS Mason Williams (1968) *US No 2/UK No 9*

Originally released in 1968 on the album *The Mason Williams Phonograph Record*, the piece has been recorded and released numerous times since by both Williams and other artists. Williams was the head writer on the hit American comedy TV series *The Smothers Brothers* at the time he recorded the track and premiered it on the show. It was originally supposed to be called 'Classical Gasoline', but the title was mistakenly changed by the copyist of the orchestral arrangement (by Mike Post, who was responsible for many top TV themes including *The Rockford Files*, *The A Team* and *Hill Street Blues*.

35. WHAM Lonnie Mack (1964) *US No 24*

Born Lonnie McIntosh, Mack hailed from Indiana and acquired his first electric guitar at the age of 13 when he began playing with his brother, Alvin before forming his own group. As a session guitarist, he worked with many top acts including James Brown, The Doors and Freddy King. He came to the attention of Fraternity Records boss Harry Carlson and in 1963 had a top five American hit with his workout of Chuck Berry's 'Memphis Tennessee' that he called simply 'Memphis'. 'Wham' was the successful follow-up, claiming the number 24 position in the States.

36. THE RISE AND FALL OF FLINGEL BUNT The Shadows (1964)
UK No 5

This was to be their last instrumental hit of the Sixties to make the top 10, although the following year 'Don't Make My Baby Blue', their first vocal hit, reached number 10. 'The Rise And Fall Of Flingel Bunt', a joint composition by all four members of the group, starting out as nothing more than a spontaneous 12-bar studio jam and developed from there with Hank laying a heavy riff over a throbbing bass line and pounding drums. The weird title came about via a combination of the name of the gangster movie, *The Rise And Fall Of Legs Diamond* and a Shadows in-joke concerning a mythical poltergeist named Flingel Bunt that they blamed for the many mishaps that took place on the film set of their movie with Cliff Richard, *Wonderful Life*.

37. AFRICAN WALTZ Johnny Dankworth & His Orchestra (1961)
UK No 9

In 1961, Dankworth's recording of Galt MacDermot's 'African Waltz' reached the British top 10 and remained in the charts for several months. American altoist Cannonball Adderley sought and received Dankworth's permission to record the arrangement for himself and had a minor hit in the US as a result.

The Shadows in 1964: masters of the twangy guitar instrumental

38. THEME ONE George Martin Orchestra (1967)

When George Martin was asked by The BBC to compose and record the signature tune for their first all-pop radio station to be launched at the end of September 1967, he readily agreed. As is the way with these things, the commission was late, leaving George little time to complete the recording. The brief was that the music had to be very British but very contemporary. He recorded his composition at EMI's Abbey road studios, adding a mighty pipe organ at the Central Hall in Westminster. The BBC were delighted and the station opened every morning and closed every night with 'Theme One' for over two years.

39. SOUL FINGER The Bar-Kays (1967) *US No 17/UK No 33*

Four of the five members of the group were killed in the plane crash that took the life of Otis Redding in 1967. Their bass player, James Alexander, who was not on the plane and later reformed the group with four new members. 'Soul Finger' was written by the original group during a break in a recording studio session. When it came to record the track, they enlisted the help of some neighbourhood children who had been hanging about outside the studios. They were invited in and instructed to shout 'Soul Finger' when one of the group pointed at them. They were paid in soft drinks.

40. THE PAJAMA PARTY Bruce Johnston Trio (1963)

Born Benjamin Baldwin, Bruce Johnston began playing bass and keyboards on many hit records before gathering together a selection of fellow session musicians in 1963 to record this instrumental as The Bruce Johnston Trio. He recorded it whilst working for Del-Fi Records in America, whose product was released on London Records in the UK. The single was considered an odd choice for the British label to issue, as the record had made little impact anywhere else. Two years later, Johnston went on to become a full-time touring replacement for Brian Wilson in The Beach Boys and eventually a studio member of the group.

41. NOLA Judd Proctor (1961)

Although over the years, 'Nola' has become the most popular of Judd Proctor's tracks, most listings suggest that it was originally the B-side of his single 'Palamino'. A guitar hero in the late Fifties, he started off in

The Ray Ellington Quartet and appeared with them on many episodes of *The Goon Show* on BBC radio before becoming a much in-demand session musician. His favourite guitar was the Hofner President and he became known as the fastest left-hand player in the business.

42. MINNESOTA FATS Johnny & The Hurricanes (1962)

One of the most distinctive instrumental groups of the Fifties and Sixties, Johnny & The Hurricanes were formed in Toledo, Ohio and were originally known as The Orbits. After working as a backing group for singer Mack Vickery, they travelled to Detroit in search of similar work with better-known performers, however, in 1959, two music promoters, Harry Balk and Irving Michanik signed them in their own right and recorded their first single, 'Crossfire' that made the US top 30. A string of hits followed and the group continued to work with various different line-ups until November, 2005, just two weeks before leader, Johnny Paris was hospitalised and subsequently died of pneumonia and septic blood, following surgery.

43. BURNING SPEAR The Soulful Strings (1968)

The duo of Chess Records' house arranger, Charles Stepney, and Richard Evans, a musical director who worked mainly for Chess, was given carte blanche to create some interesting instrumental albums for the label. Calling on a number of fellow musicians, they created The Soulful Strings and released seven albums between 1966 and 1971. This track was released as a single in 1968 and culled from the album *Grooving With The Soulful Strings*.

44. DIAMONDS Jet Harris & Tony Meehan (1963) *UK No 1*

After leaving The Shadows, Jet was signed to the Decca label where he achieved a couple of hits on his own before Tony Meehan, another ex-Shadow who was working at Decca as a producer, suggested they team up again for a one-off record. He approached Jerry Lordan, who had composed 'Apache' and 'Wonderful Land' for The Shadows, to come up with something new. The result was 'Diamonds'. Because of its success, they continued to record together, scoring two further hits. When Jet was involved in a serious car accident, their manager insisted Tony appeared on *Ready Steady Go* alone, miming to the track 'Applejack' without Jet by his side. After which the partnership ended.

45. GIBBLE GOBBLE Willie Wright & his Sparklers (1961)

Willie Wright & his Sparklers were from Oklahoma but they travelled to Cincinnati in the hopes of securing a recording contract with the King label. Happily, they succeeded in their goal, although they ended up on the company's subsidiary, Federal, recording 11 tracks in 18 hours on their first session in May 1960. 'Gibble Gobble' was one of the titles they recorded on that day and was released on the B-side of their fourth single, 'Bloodhound'.

46. ORANGE BLOSSOM SPECIAL The Spotnicks (1962) *UK No 29*

Originally named The Phrases, The Spotnicks were from Sweden, and toured England when their single, 'Orange Blossom Special', was climbing the charts. They were guests on *Thank Your Lucky Stars* and *Saturday Club*, on which they were asked to perform the number live in the studio. The producers were unaware that this would be impossible, as the guitar part had been recorded for an album using a slower tempo which had then been speeded up for the single release. Not wishing to miss a booking, they decided to use the same approach for the broadcast by recording another slowed-down version, then hiding the tape deck behind an amplifier. At the correct moment, Bo Winberg, the guitarist, pressed the play button and the rest of the band played live to the tape while Winberg mimed. No-one noticed.

Sweden's Spotnicks: a band that was truly out of this world

47. ON THE REBOUND Floyd Cramer (1961) *US No 4/UK No 1*

Cramer taught himself to play the piano whilst growing up in Louisiana before relocating to Nashville in 1955, where he would become one of the busiest session players on the circuit, playing on hits by artists including Brenda Lee, Roy Orbison, The Everly Brothers and probably most importantly, Elvis Presley. He also released records under his own name and became well known after his hit American single, 'Last Date'. In the UK it was this track that he is best known for.

48. I WAS KAISER BILL'S BATMAN Whistling Jack Smith (1967) *US No 20/UK No 5*

This record was the brainchild of British songwriters Roger Cook and Roger Greenaway, who as the recording duo David and Jonathan had top-20 hits with 'Michelle' and 'Lovers Of The World Unite'. 'I Was Kaiser Bill's Batman' was recorded with an uncredited producer, unknown studio musicians and The Michael Sammes Singers. When the record started to climb the charts and record stores found they couldn't order enough copies to keep up with demand, a singer named Billy Moeller, who recorded for Decca under the name of Corby Wells, was quickly recruited to become Whistling Jack Smith for TV and live appearances. As the record's popularity died down, the nonexistent Mr Smith faded from the scene.

49. PERCOLATOR Billy Joe & The Checkmates (1961) *US No 10*

This instrumental found favour with DJs, who used it as music to talk over when they were heading for a commercial break or a new bulletin. Record-label boss Lew Bedell had the idea for the record after seeing a coffee commercial on TV and together with arranger, Ernie Freeman, came up with 'Percolator'. Taking three trusted session musicians into Conway Recorders, a new studio in Hollywood, the record was engineered by a young British protégé, Shel Talmy. To get the sound of coffee bubbling, Ernie took a chamois cloth and had marimba player Julius Wechter wind it around his mallets before he hitting them.

50. TAURUS Spirit (1968)

American rock band Spirit recorded this instrumental, 'Taurus' for their debut eponymous album. The piece has often been considered to be the recording Jimmy Page got the idea for Led Zeppelin's 'Stairway To

Heaven' from, after hearing them play it when they were their support act on tour. However, a court case in 2016 declared that Led Zep were not guilty of plagiarism.

51. THE SNAKE Maximilian (1961)

Max Crook met Del Shannon in 1959 and was asked to join his band as a keyboard player, with his Musitron organ soon becoming the centrepiece of the combo. During a live performance, Max accidentally hit an unusual chord change on the Musitron that became the basis for the song 'Runaway'. In January, 1961, Crook and Shannon travelled to from Michigan to New York, each to record their own singles. Del cut 'Runaway' and 'Jody' while Max cut 'The Snake' and 'The Wanderer'. When the tapes were sent to England for release, 'The Snake' was accidentally put on the B-side of approximately the first 1000 pressings – and also on the first French Del Shannon EP.

52. GREEN JEANS The Flee-Rekkers (1960)UK No 23

This became the first hit single on Joe Meek's own Triumph label, which was formed at the beginning of 1960. But by July the same year, the company was bankrupt and Meek then had to lease his recordings once again to other labels. The Flee-Rekkers recorded several instrumental tracks for Meek but this was their only chart success, a jazzed-up version of 'Greensleeves'.

53. WIPE OUT The Surfaris (1963) *US No 2/UK No 5*

'Wipe Out' was first released in the US on the group's own Princess label before being picked up by Dot Records. After the success of the single, the label was unable to pick the rights to a follow up. For some inexplicable reason, the group had product available at the time on eight different labels, none of which would agree to licence any of their tracks. It was this situation that probably caused The Surfaris to become another one-hit wonder act when the record climbed to number two in America during the second week of August, 1963.

54. SOUL COAXING Raymond Lefevre & His Orchestra (1968)

Another often requested instrumental by our 'avids', this Michel Polnareff composition is a much sought-after track by Northern soul fans across the country. During the early Fifties, the late Raymond

Lefèvre played piano for Franck Pourcel's Orchestra before signing to the French Barclay label in 1956, recording his debut album in the same year. In the Sixties, his orchestra accompanied many leading French stars including Richard Anthony and Claude François. In 1968, Peggy March recorded a vocal version of 'Soul Coaxing' with English lyrics by Sunny Skylar under the title of 'If You Loved Me'.

55. HIT AND MISS **The John Barry Seven (1960)** *UK No 10*
John Barry first made the UK charts in 1960, when invited to compose a new theme tune to the successful TV programme *Juke Box Jury*. It had previously been introduced for the first six editions with a piece of music called 'Juke Box Fury' by Ozzie Warlock & The Wizards. Barry's composition, 'Hit And Miss' became the new theme in 1960.

56. DANSE A LA MUSIQUE **The French Fries (1968)**
This obscure Northern soul favourite just about qualifies as an instrumental – it has a few chants from the backing singers. 'Danse A La Musique' is in fact a French version of Sly & The Family Stone's hit 'Dance To The Music' by a group calling themselves French Fries, which turned out to be Sly and his band. It is said they recorded the track late one evening after a heavy bout of partying in the recording studios.

57. KING KONG **Terry Lightfoot & His New Orleans Jazzmen (1961)**
This was a traditional jazz arrangement of the theme and title music of a South African opera that had opened in London in 1961. Terry formed his New Orleans Jazzmen in 1955 and as their front man usually dressed in a sober suit and tie and his horn-rimmed glasses. Hailing from Potters Bar in Middlesex, he could have easily passed as your local bank manager. However, he was an accomplished clarinet player and, with trad jazz in full swing in the UK, he and his band made regular appearances on the *Morecambe And Wise* TV show, reaching a huge audience with their music.

58. WALK ON THE WILD SIDE (Pt 2) **Jimmy Smith (1962)**
The single version was released in two parts with a dramatic organ solo featured in the second half. Jimmy Smith, born in Norristown, Pennsylvania, succeeded in popularising the Hammond organ in the commercial market whilst retaining his credibility within jazz circles. After a spell on the Blue

Note label, he was snapped up by Verve under a special arrangement, as his existing contract still had a year to run, and found immediate success when his treatment of this Elmer Bernstein film theme.

59. POET AND PEASANT Peter Jay & The Jaywalkers (1963)

After seeing the group playing in a summer show at London's Windmill theatre, the music impresario Larry Parnes invited Peter Jay & The Jaywalkers to join a tour headlined by Billy Fury, on which they would get their own spot, as well as backing Eden Kane, which led to further backing work with both Georgie Fame and Marty Wilde. The band even came up with the arrangement for Marty's hit version of 'Jezebel' although they didn't get to play on the track. In 1962, The Jaywalkers were offered a recording contract with Decca and under Joe Meek's supervision, achieved their only UK hit with their first record release, 'Can-Can '62'. The follow up, 'Totem Pole', went virtually unnoticed so they returned to the classics for their next release, Rossini's 'Poet And Peasant'. Despite several further releases, their hit-making days were over.

60. PEAK HOUR The Krew Kats (1961)

Big Jim Sullivan, who passed away at the beginning of October 2012, learned a lot of his techniques from the late Eddie Cochran and was the first musician in the UK to own a Gibson guitar (bought for him by Marty Wilde). 'Peak Hour' was written by Big Jim and was the B-side of 'Trambone', the only hit single by The Krew Kats of which he was a

Peter Jay & the Jaywalkers

member alongside Brian Bennett and Brian 'Liquorice' Locking, both of whom went on to join The Shadows.

61. THE SPARTANS Sounds Incorporated (1964) *UK No 30*

Written by Russ Conway, who also recorded his own version, this became the first of Sounds Incorporated's two hits. It was followed by their arrangement of 'Spanish Harlem' and both tracks made the UK top 40 in 1964. Formed in 1961, The Spartans got their break that year when Gene Vincent's band The Blue Caps had been denied work permits for the UK and they were asked to back the singer on tour. This led to further bookings with other visiting Americans including Brenda Lee, Little Richard and Sam Cooke. They released their first record, 'Mogambo', on Parlophone to little interest followed by three releases produced by Joe Meek for Decca that went the same way. In 1963 Brian Epstein signed them to his management company and the following year secured them a more lucrative recording contract with EMI, which found them work as Cilla Black's backing group.

62. NUT ROCKER B. Bumble & The Stingers (1962)
US No 23/UK No 1

The piece is an adaptation of Tchaikovsky's 'Nutcracker Suite'. It was record producer Kim Fowley who had the idea of rocking-up the ballet's main theme; he made a recording of 'Nut Rocker' with session men under the name of Jack B Nimble & The Quicks, pressing up 500 copies for the Del Rio label. The company's boss hated the track and smashed up most of the copies, resulting in Fowley taking his idea to another label, Rendezvous, and repeating the arrangement. This time he called the group B. Bumble & The Stingers. The label bosses wanted to change the title to 'Rickshaw Run' but, after persuading them it was a bad idea, the record was finally released and became a UK number one.

63. ALFIE Eivets Rednow (1968)

One of dozens of cover versions of Bacharach and David's song 'Alfie', this instrumental version is probably one of the most unusual. Stevie Wonder was enjoying a string of hits in his own right but really loved the song. He wanted to record it but didn't want it released under his own name so he simply spelt it backwards. When heard, there's no mistaking his individual style of harmonica playing. His version ended up at number 66 in America.

64. EVENING IN PARIS/THEME FROM THE TRAITORS
The Packabeats (1962)

Produced by the late Joe Meek and widely acknowledged by connoisseurs as one of the best double A-sided instrumentals of the era. 'Evening In Paris' was backed with 'The Theme From The Traitors', from a movie starring Patrick Allen and James Maxwell. It was the second single by The Packabeats, following on from the George Martin-produced 'Gypsy Beat', which gained a fair amount of airplay for the earlier line-up of the group.

65. CONCERTO IN THE STARS **Frank & The Barbarians (1961)**

The record was released in the UK on the Oriole label and was composed by Eric Siday, who had the first percussion synthesizer built for him by Robert Moog. As far as we can make out, the 'Frank' in the band was composer, arranger and conductor Frank Barber.

66. SUMMER HOLIDAY **The Prediktors (1965)**

The Prediktors hailed from various regions of Ohio, where they played local clubs performing covers of recent hits. In the mid-Sixties, Dave Padwin replaced guitarist Harvey Mandel, after which the band located to Chicago for three years, playing in some of the city's leading clubs. In 1965 they released what appears to be their only single, a cover of the Johnny Gibson Trio's song 'Summer Holiday' – and even that failed to get a UK issue.

67. BOIL THE KETTLE **The Projection Company (1967)**

The Projection Company were a group of musicians put together by guitarist Jerry Cole who, over the years, had led a number of outfits including The Generation Gap, T Swift And The Electric Bag and The Stone Canyon Rock Group. Taken from the album *Give Me Some Lovin'*, 'Boil The Kettle' is an instrumental cover of a song originally recorded by another of Jerry's creations, The IDs.

68. TEENSVILLE **Chet Atkins (1960)**

This single by one of the world's most famous guitarists, Chet Atkins, was the title track of a 1960 album. By the late Fifties, Atkins had become so well known that he was asked to design signature model guitars for both Gibson and Gretsch. In 1957 he had become the manager of RCA's Nashville Division where he worked with Elvis Presley, playing on all his sessions recorded in Nashville. By 1968 he was promoted to Vice President of the company and in 1993 was awarded a lifetime achievement Grammy for his contribution to the music industry.

69. SOUL BOSSA NOVA Quincy Jones & His Orchestra (1962)

Probably Quincy Jones's most famous instrumental, this was taken from his 1962 album *Big Band Bossa Nova*. The track appeared on the soundtrack to Sidney Lumet's 1964 movie *The Pawnbroker* and Woody Allen used it in *Take The Money And Run* in 1969. It has been the theme to the *Austin Powers* movies, was used by Alan Freeman as a signature tune during his afternoon show on Radio 1 and in 1991 it was sampled on the top-20 hit by Canadian hip-hop group Dream Warriors, 'My Definition of a Boombastic Jazz Style'. It also introduced the 1998 football World Cup TV coverage.

70. THE EMPEROR OF WYOMING Neil Young (1968)

The opening track to Neil Young's eponymous debut album following his departure from Buffalo Springfield, this was first released in 1968. But the album was quickly withdrawn and remixed for reissue the following year. Young was unhappy with the original sound quality, due to the use of a newly created technology that was intended to make stereo records compatible with mono record players, but which had the unfortunate side-effect of degrading the sound in both stereo and mono.

71. TOKYO MELODY Helmut Zacharias & His Orchestra (1964)
UK No 9

In his homeland of Germany, Helmut Zacharias was a huge star in the world of easy listening music. A top jazz violinist, he sold millions of albums during his career as a bandleader. In 1964, The BBC selected his composition 'Tokyo Melody' as the theme tune for their coverage of that year's Olympic Games, resulting in the record selling something in excess of 12 million copies around the world.

72. GREASE MONKEY
Kenny Burrell with The Brother Jack McDuff Quartet (1963)

In the early Sixties, organist Jack McDuff was one of the most successful musicians signed to the Prestige label. The company never missed an opportunity to get him into the recording studios with a variety of combinations to increase sales of their albums. One of the most exciting pairings was that with Detroit guitarist, Kenny Burrell, whose stylish playing had previously made him partner of choice for Hammond organist Jimmy Smith. 'Grease Monkey' comes from the 1963 album *Crash* and also features Harold Vick on sax, Joe Dukes on drums and Ray Barretto on congas.

73. BOMBORA The Atlantics (1964)

Released on the Oriole label in the UK, The Atlantics were an Australian surf-rock band formed in the early Sixties. 'Bombora' was their most successful release and the title track of their first album. Over the years The Atlantics have re-emerged sporadically and in 2000 they reformed with three of their original members.

74. AND THEN THERE WERE DRUMS Sandy Nelson (1962)

Sandy Nelson began his professional career as a session drummer playing on many of Phil Spector's productions then in 1959 he financed the recording of his own composition, 'Teen Beat' and managed to licence it to the American Imperial label resulting in a top-10 hit both here and in the States. His biggest hit followed in 1961 with 'Let There Be Drums' but after that there appeared to be a lack of interest in further Sandy Nelson drumming records. However, he managed two further top-40 hits, ending 1962 with the less successful but just as well made 'And Then There Were Drums'.

Sandy Nelson: king of the 'Drums' record craze

75. GREEN ONIONS Count Basie & His Orchestra (1967)

Released as a single in December 1967, this was Count Basie's big-band arrangement of the Booker T & The MG's classic instrumental hit, 'Green Onions' that had been recorded in many different versions by artists that included The Ventures, The Shadows, Al Cooper and Mongo Santamaria.

76. HAVE FAITH IN YOUR LOVE Sounds Orchestral (1965)

After the success of their cover of Vince Guaraldi's 'Cast Your Fate To The Wind', Sounds Orchestral suggested to their arranger Johnny Pearson and producer John Schroeder that perhaps the two of them could compose something of their own in the same style as the hit, by way of a follow-up. The result was 'Have Faith In Your Love'. But, pleasant as it was, it lacked the appeal of the Guaraldi hit.

77. BUCKET FULL OF SOUL Trudy Pitts (1968)

New York-born Trudy Pitts trained as a pianist and began working as a music teacher, playing in orchestra pits (no pun intended) for Broadway shows in the evenings. Her husband, drummer Bill Carney, encouraged her to switch to the Hammond organ after he saw how much the audiences enjoyed listening to the instrument when he was working with Shirley Scott's band. Pitts quickly developed her skills and was signed to the Prestige label where she recorded four albums. The third, *A Bucket Full Of Soul*, was the most successful and this is the title track.

78. SOUPY'S THEME (SOUPY'S SHUFFLE)
The Miniature Men (1962)

This track by The Miniature Men was arranged by organist Hank Levine. 'Soupy's Theme (Soupy's Shuffle)' was released in America on the Dolton label. Dolton was hailed as the first rock'n'roll label to emerge from Seattle, the brainchild of Bob Reisdorff, a young record salesman who wanted to produce records rather than sell them, and so had persuaded his boss to allow him to run a label from their company's headquarters. Success followed when they signed The Ventures, The Fleetwoods and Vic Dana, amongst others.

79. JACK THE RIPPER Link Wray & His Ray Men (1963)

This was the title track to the group's 1963 album but had been released as a single late in 1961. Born Frederick Lincoln Wray Jr in North Carolina, he built his career on recreating the distorted electric guitar sound of early blues records, scoring an American top-20 hit in 1958 with 'The Rumble'. In recent years, *Rolling Stone* magazine placed him at number 45 of the 100 greatest guitarists of all time.

80. NIGHT CREATURE The Gigolos (1960)

This record has often been described as 'the best Duane Eddy record he never made'. Recorded in the same studios as Eddy's early hits, it featured most of Duane's backing band, The Rebels, including drummer Bob Taylor, who wrote and produced the track alongside DJ Sonny Knight. For years, fans thought it was Duane masquerading under a pseudonym.

81. THE LONELY MAN THEME Cliff Adams & His Orchestra (1960)
UK No 39

In 1959, the Imperial Tobacco company launched a new brand of cigarette that was promoted by an effective TV commercial, showing an actor in a trench coat and trilby lighting up on a damp, deserted street with a voiceover declaring that 'You're never alone with a Strand'. Composer Cliff Adams composed the music that accompanied this 30-second ad and called it 'The Lonely Man Theme'. The single version managed to get into the lower end of the UK charts. Fortunately for many, the public appeared to associate smoking a Strand as unsociable and the brand was short-lived.

82. CHECKPOINT Dennis Newey (1961)

Dennis Newey was a guitarist who, during the late Fifties and early Sixties, played with the Northern Dance Orchestra before forming his own group, The Numen and gained a three-record deal with the Philips label. It's unclear if his band played on his records or if they were replaced by session men. 'Checkpoint' was the first of the three releases and was written by Dennis with Ken Hawker, Nick Shakespeare (who later became better known as Ken Lewis) and John Carter, who had hits as members of The Ivy League.

83. SATURDAY NIGHT STOMP Eddie 'Bluesman' Kirkland (1962)

Born in Jamaica to a mother who he believed was his sister – she was aged 11 when she gave birth – Kirkland was an American harmonica player as well as a guitarist, singer and songwriter. He became known as 'the gypsy of the blues' due to his rigorous touring schedules, mainly for John Lee Hooker – he became his road manager until 1962 when Hooker decided to work overseas. Kirkland himself recorded for a number of labels including King, Fortune, Volt and Tru-Sound, for whom he recorded the album *It's The Bluesman*. It may not have sold many copies, but it did contain this infectious instrumental, his own 'Saturday Night Stomp'.

84. MUSIC TO WATCH GIRLS BY
The Bob Crewe Generation (1966) *US No 15*

Bob Crewe has enjoyed enormous success as a songwriter, performing artist and record producer. Although he neither read music nor played any musical instruments, he would always surround himself in the studio with a core of regular musicians and in 1966, when he was assembling a team to make a big band album, a friend of his told him there was a piece of music called 'Music To Watch Girls By' being used in a soft drinks commercial and he should consider recording it. Learning that RCA were planning to bring out a version by trumpeter Al Hirt, Crewe contacted arranger Hutch Davie and booked a recording session that very same night, making 80 copies of a single, which were sent by special delivery to the top radio stations. Which enabled Bob and his crew (pun intended!) to beat any competition.

85. TWELFTH STREET RAG **Bobby Summers (1960)**

This was issued on the B-side of Bobby's 1960 single on the Capitol label, which was his arrangement of the Glenn Miller classic 'Little Brown Jug'. 'Twelfth Street Rag' was composed by Euday L Bowman in 1914, after one of his friends declared that he was planning to open a pawn shop on Twelfth Street in New York, whilst the two of them were walking along it. Bowman is believed to have told his friend that if he managed to get rich with such a venture, he'd write a tune on three notes to make himself rich. The result was one of the best selling rags of the ragtime era.

86. PINBALL **The Van Doren-Hawksworth Collection (1965)**

Van Doran was a well-known keyboard player, who recorded a number of singles for HMV whilst Johnny Hawksworth was a successful arranger and composer and met Doran whilst they were both involved in recording library music for Chappell's publishing company. In fact

'Pinball' is likely to have been one of the pieces they recorded together and decided was strong enough to issue as a single.

87. BEAUTIFUL IN THE RAIN Tony Hatch Orchestra (1967)

This was the title track to the 1967 album by The Tony Hatch Sound and features Greg Brown on flugelhorn. It was originally written by Tony Hatch with the singer and actress Jackie Trent as a song but it was decided it worked better as an instrumental and was later released as a single.

88. ZOOM, WIDGE AND WAG Bobby Graham (1965)

Drummer Bobby Graham was one of London's most in-demand session players and became very friendly with future Led Zeppelin guitarist Jimmy Page, who was also working the session circuit. When Bobby was given the opportunity by Fontana Records to cut a solo single, he called on his friend to add some guitar work on 'Zoom, Widge And Wag' which was, in fact, the B-side to 'Skin Deep'. But it was this side that received most of the attention.

89. THE OX The Who (1966)

The Ox was one of the nicknames The Who gave to their bass player John Entwistle and this track first appeared on the B-side of their single, 'The Kids Are Alright', as well as being the closing track on their debut album, 'My Generation'. 'The Ox' was written by way of a jamming session by Entwistle, Keith Moon, Pete Townshend and keyboard player Nicky Hopkins.

90. GROW YOUR OWN The Small Faces (1966)

Released as the B-side of their big hit, 'Sha-La-La-La-Lee', the group were given five minutes at the end of the recording session to come up with an instrumental piece of their own as instructed by their manager, Don Ardon. The Small Faces jammed their way through what was finally titled 'Grow Your Own', getting more satisfaction from this recording than from the hit A-side.

91. FREE FOR ALL King Curtis (1961)

In the early Sixties, the Prestige label was best known for its serious jazz releases. But it set up a subsidiary, Tru-Sound records, for more commercial material probably aimed at the mainstream black market. Although not producing any big-sellers, the label had an interesting

King Curtis: one of America's leading R&B sax players in the Sixties

roster of artists including King Curtis who released a 1961 album called *It's Party Time*, from which 'Free For All' is taken. He became one of America's leading tenor sax players, appearing on dozens of hits for artists that included Aretha Franklin, The Coasters and John Lennon.

92. SANDSTORM The Fatimas (1967)

This is something of a mystery record by a little-known group, The Fatamas, whose instrumental record was originally planned to be a vocal under the title of 'Hoochy Coo' using an all-female group. Sound effects were added to the backing track, resulting in 'Sandstorm', which was considered to be the more commercial option; it was 'Sandstorm that was released as a single.

93. WALTZING TO JAZZ Larry Page Orchestra (1966)

Having successfully managed The Kinks, Larry Page was keen to bring Ray Davies' songwriting talents to the attention of the middle-of-the-road market. Page recorded his own album in 1965 calling it *Kinky Music – The Larry Page Orchestra plays the music of The Kinks*. The following year he released *Music For Night People*, which included this track, 'Waltzing To Jazz'. Released as a single, it found success across Europe. Larry continued to record with his orchestra well into the 1990s.

94. STICKS AND STONES Johnny 'Hammond' Smith (1961)

'Sticks And Stones' was written and originally recorded by Titus Turner, with Johnny 'Hammond' Smith's version being included on his 1961 album *Stimulation*. Born in Louisville, Kentucky, Smith's career took off when he began working as an accompanist to singer Nancy Wilson. He was renowned for playing the Hammond B-3 organ, earning him the nickname that also avoided any confusion between him and jazz guitarist Johnny Smith.

95. LIKE THUNDER The Rialtos (1961)

The label credit reads 'The Rialtos as featuring Freddie Thomas', although the group were founded in 1959 in Tulare, California by Robert Hollister and calling themselves Bobby Hollister and The Rialtos. Freddie Thomas was their lead guitarist and the group often performed at local dances but because they were underage they were not allowed to perform in venues that sold alcohol. They announced that they were about to release a record but it failed to materialise as they had recorded it in one of the band's garage and couldn't afford to have copies pressed. In 1961 they were signed to the small American Pike label where they released two singles, the first of which was 'Like Thunder'.

96. THE BLUE EAGLE PT 1 The Jimmy Rivers Combo (1960)

The saxophone had a major influence on the arrangements of many hit records of the early Sixties, both vocal and instrumental. Saxman Jimmy Rivers from New Orleans played on dozens of other artists' recordings, as well as releasing a number of his own singles and albums including this 1960 disc he made for the American Ric label, 'The Blue Eagle'.

97. THE ASPHALT JUNGLE Duke Ellington & His Orchestra (1961)

The Asphalt Jungle was a 1950 hit movie directed by John Huston with a then-unknown Marilyn Monroe taking on a small but important part (and not even originally included in the cast listings). In 1961, a short-lived spin-off TV series starring Jack Warden managed 13 episodes before it was cancelled, but its saving grace was Duke Ellington's main theme, played by Ellington and his Orchestra.

98. LOVE IN THE OPEN AIR The Tudor Minstrels (1966)

Written by Paul McCartney for the 1966 movie, *The Family Way*, starring father and daughter John and Hayley Mills, it was produced and directed by brothers John and Roy Boulting. The soundtrack recording of 'Love In The Open Air' was arranged and orchestrated by George Martin but credited on the record to The Tudor Minstrels, winning an Ivor Novello Award in 1968 for 'Best Instrumental Theme'.

99. FESTIVAL TIME The San Remo Strings (1967)

First released in 1967, this one passed the record-buying public by until its reissue in 1971 when, thanks to the Northern soul clubs, it climbed to number 39 on the UK charts. The San Remo Strings were an American group made up mainly of master violin players, fronted by Bob Wilson, who first recorded as The San Remo Golden Strings before signing to Motown.

100. ELIJAH ROCKIN' WITH SOUL Hank Jacobs (1967)

Hank Jacobs made his name as a keyboard player with his 1964 release, 'So Far Away', which became an American and UK R&B classic instrumental. His recording output was quite substantial and in 1967 he signed to American DJ Al Scott's Call Me label, for whom he released the biblically inspired 'Elijah Rockin'', written by soul singer Bettye Swan.

JUNIOR CHOICE

A very popular segment of the Sounds Of The Sixties radio show for many weeks was one that looked at some of the memorable records that were constantly being requested on 'Junior Choice' – the BBC pop music programme for children. Here are two dozen of the most popular.

1. THE 'OOTER SONG Sidney James (1961)

The song was written by Les Vandyke, a pseudonym for Johnny Worth, who wrote hits for many artists including Adam Faith, Eden Kane and Jimmy Justice. Sid James made a name for himself as a loveable cockney in the popular radio and TV series *Hancock's Half Hour*, even though he was born several thousand miles away from Bow Bells – in Johannesburg in South Africa. Arriving in the UK in 1946 he notched up dozens of small parts in British movies, landing a major part in 1951 as one-quarter of *The Lavender Hill Mob* for Ealing studios, which also starred Alec Guinness. He became a leading player in the *Carry On* series of films, for 15 years. In 1961, he released this children's favourite that today would be considered distinctly non-PC, 'The 'Ooter Song'.

2. FIREBALL Don Spencer (1963) **UK No 32**

This theme song to the long-running successful puppet series *Fireball XL5* became the only hit for singer Don Spencer, who made a name for himself in his homeland of Australia as a children's entertainer. Coming to England, he performed on three national tours with The Hollies, Rolling Stones, The Four Seasons and Marianne Faithfull. Showing his versatility, Don turned his hand to comedy, appearing in the BBC series *Let's Face It* with Ronnie Barker. After his Sixties heyday, he continued to put on shows for children all over Australia and did an extraordinary amount of charity work, which has earned him the 'Heart of Variety Award' for services to charity.

3. A WINDMILL IN OLD AMSTERDAM Ronnie Hilton (1964)
UK No 23

After a string of hits throughout the Fifties and a minor resurgence in the early Sixties, Ronnie had his final UK chart single with this song. He used The Michael Sammes Singers and sped-up their voices to sound like mice. The song was written by comedy writers Ted Dicks and Miles

Rudge, whose work included the Bernard Cribbins' hits, 'Hole In The Ground' and 'Right Said Fred'.

4. WHITE HORSES Jackie (1968) *UK No 10*

Jackie's full name was Jackie Lee. She was a session singer and songwriter, who performed the English-language version of this theme to the TV series of the same name. The series was a co-production by Yugoslavian and German TV and the German version was sung by Ivon Robic; the UK version was written by Michael Carr and Ben Nesbit. Jackie's jazz-styled album, also called *White Horses*, was also released in 1968, which included contributions from Dudley Moore on piano.

5. BOOM OO YATA-TA-TA Morecambe & Wise (1963)

The track also features Dick Hills and Sid Green, who were Morecambe and Wise's scriptwriters on their first TV series for ATV, *The Two Of Us* between 1961 to 1968. The double-act lasted for just over 43 years and they worked together until Morecambe's death in1984: they were widely considered to be the most successful double act in Britain for generations.

6. PUFF THE MAGIC DRAGON Peter, Paul & Mary (1963) *US No 2*

This song was written by Peter Yarrow and his college friend, Lenny Lipton, whose poem the song was based upon; Lipton had been originally inspired by an Ogden Nash poem, 'Custard The Dragon'. In 1961, Yarrow joined Paul Stookey and Mary Travers to form Peter, Paul & Mary, and the group incorporated the song into their live stage act to great response, prompting them to record it the following year.

8. I'VE BEEN EVERYWHERE Lucky Starr (1962)

An American version of 'I've Been Everywhere' was recorded by country singer Hank Snow, but it was the performance by Australian singer Lucky Starr that was requested more often. Lucky used English place names as opposed to the American cities in Snow's recording. The song was written in 1959 by Geoff Mack and several country artists, including Lynn Anderson and Johnny Cash, went on to record it. Lucky Starr released an EP in his homeland called 'Lucky's Been Everywhere', which contained four different versions naming places in Great Britain, U.S.A., New Zealand, and Australia.

9. ENGLISH COUNTRY GARDEN Jimmie Rodgers (1962) *UK No 5*

By the end of 1958, it seemed that the days of hit singles were over for Jimmie Rodgers, as he faded from British reckoning. Until, that is, some three and a half years later. In mid-1962, his British label outlet, Columbia, decided to release a version of the familiar chestnut, 'English Country Garden', which several months earlier had been buried on the B-side of an American release, 'A Little Dog Cried' (his final US hit on the Roulette label). By the time the single hit the British charts, Jimmie had left Roulette, prompted by the apparent lack of royalties paid to him, and had signed to Dot. Via heavy radio plays and a Junior Choice favourite, the single became his biggest-ever UK hit.

10. GOING TO THE ZOO Julie Felix (1966)

Written by Tom Paxton, this first appeared on an EP called *Songs from The Frost Report*, a TV series presented by David Frost that first brought Julie to the public's attention. When she recorded the song, she thought little more about it other than that is was quite a cute little song. But her record label, Decca, decided to release it as a single and over a period of time it sold more copies than many chart hits. The song became a firm favourite with her younger audience.

11. MY BROTHER Terry Scott (1962)

Written by Terry and Mitch Murray, this song was sung in the persona on a schoolboy character; Scott used to dress up in a school uniform complete with short trousers and cap to perform the song on television. Apparently, many of the requests for this record came from conservative parents trying to curb the amount of pop music on the radio, disapproving of the cacophonous, electric-guitar-based sound that their children loved to have blaring from their Dansette record players.

12. WHERE'S ME SHIRT Ken Dodd (1965)

Ken Dodd took his singing very seriously and achieved 18 top-40 hits between 1960 and 1975. He did from time to time, however, churn out the odd comedy song and one of his many catchphrases resulted in this track – taken from a rare Ken Dodd EP called *Doddy And The Diddy Men*. Co-written by Ken and Max Diamond, it featured a colourful cast list of contributors: Dicky Mint, Mick The Marmalizer, Little Evan, Hamish McDiddy, Nigel Ponsonby Smallpiece, Nicky Nugget and Smarty Arty.

13. RIGHT SAID FRED Bernard Cribbins (1962) *UK No 10*

The second of three top-40 hits for actor Bernard Cribbins. Like his first chart success, 'Hole In The Ground', this was composed by comedy writers Ted Dicks and Miles Rudge. Apart from starring in dozens of British movies, Bernard became an established face on television appearing on *The Val Doonican Show*, *Last Of The Summer Wine*, his own series, *Cribbins*, and not forgetting *Jackanory*. It was Beatles producer George Martin who invited Dicks and Rudge to come up with songs for Cribbins: the Eighties band Right Said Fred took their name from this song.

14. BANGERS AND MASH Peter Sellers & Sophia Loren (1961) *UK No 22*

Following their success with 'Goodness Gracious Me' (which reached number four in the UK), producer George Martin felt a follow-up was required and asked the writers of the hit, David Lee and Herbert Kretzmer, to come up with another song. The result was 'Bangers And Mash'. An album, *Peter and Sophia*, followed containing comedy sketches, solo tracks by the two actors and duets. Sellers once admitted that he had massive crush on Loren.

15. WHO'S AFRAID OF THE BIG BAD WOLF Pinky & Perky (1961)

This song was written by Frank Churchill for the cartoon of the same name and later appeared in an animated short film, *Three Little Pigs*, produced by Walt Disney in 1933 and based on the fairy tale of the same name. The song is sung by the pigs after they ignore the good advice they are given – that they need to build themselves a stronger, wolf-proof home. Pinky & Perky were given their first TV series by the BBC in 1957 and were created by Czechoslovakian immigrants, Jan and Vlasta Dalibor. At the time, the puppets had very limited movements and looked alike. Pinky wore red clothes and Perky blue (a distinction that was of little use in the days of black-and-white TV).

16. DELANEY'S DONKEY Val Doonican (1964)

Two of Val Doonican's records were often heard on Junior Choice, one being 'Paddy McGinty's Goat' and this one, 'Delaney's Donkey'. Val got his big break in 1963 when he was booked to appear on ITV's top variety show *Sunday Night At The London Palladium*. As a result of this performance, he was offered his own show on BBC television, which ran for over 20 years and moved to Saturday as its popularity grew.

17. SEVEN LITTLE GIRLS SITTING IN THE BACK SEAT
The Avons (1959) *UK No 3*

Released towards the end of 1959 but reaching its peak position on the charts in the new year, this was a cover of a big US hit by Paul Evans and The Curls. The Avons were Valerie and Eileen Murtagh, who performed as The Avon sisters at the 1958 Radio Show exhibition at Olympia in London. There they were heard by top record producer Norrie Paramor, who signed them to EMI's Columbia label. They then added Ray Adams and became The Avons, achieving a major hit with this, their first single. After a few more smaller successes, they jointly wrote The Shadows' 1962 number-one hit instrumental, 'Dance On', with a vocal version by Kathy Kirby making the charts the following year.

18. ON TOP OF SPAGHETTI **Tom Glazer & The Children's Chorus** (1963) *US No 14*

Tom Glazer who was one of a group of folk singers, including Lead Belly, Woody Guthrie, Josh White and Burl Ives, who helped popularise folk music in the 1940s with songs such as this parody of the traditional folk song, 'On Top Of Old Smokey'. He hosted his own radio show in America between 1945 and 1947 and also composed the score to the 1957 movie *A Face In The Crowd*, starring Andy Griffith and Walter Matthau. Tom Glazer was self-deprecating about his novelty hit, often

The Avons – a songwriting and performing trio discovered by Norrie Paramor

making light of it. In onstage banter he'd speculate about being asked by St Peter at the Pearly Gates about what he accomplished in music; and having to sheepishly mumble that he wrote 'On Top of Spaghetti'.

19. SUPERCALIFRAGILISTICEXPIALIDOCIOUS
Julie Andrews & Dick Van Dyke (1963)

Written for the movie *Mary Poppins* by brothers Robert and Richard Sherman, the song's title came via a summer camp in the Adirondack Mountains. It was a word that the kids had delight in knowing – one they knew and their parents didn't. An outrageous pun on the title of this song appeared in *The Sun* newspaper in February 2000. A major soccer match in Scotland pitted underdogs Inverness Caledonian Thistle against Celtic, one of the top teams in the country. After Thistle thrashed the favourites by three goals to one, a bright journalist at the paper came up with the magnificent headline 'SUPER CALEY GO BALLISTIC CELTIC ARE ATROCIOUS'.

20. DO-RE-ME Julie Andrews & Children (1965)

The movie version of Rodgers and Hammerstein's musical *The Sound Of Music* was filmed in 1964 by Twentieth Century Fox. The budget was over $8000,000 and shooting took place in Salzburg – around the area of the actual Von Trapp's family villa but not in the actual property. (The Von Trapps were the real-life family about whom the wartime story was based.) Several stars were considered for the female lead of Maria including Doris Day, Mia Farrow and Lesley Ann Warren before they settled on Julie Andrews. The movie was nominated for 10 Academy awards and won five, including Best Picture and Best Director (Robert Wise). The soundtrack album has sold over 10 million copies worldwide and spent a total of 381 weeks on the UK album chart – 70 of which at number one. This song continues to be a children's favourite.

21. THE ANIMAL SONG King Perry (1969)

King Perry (whose real name was.. King Perry) formed the band responsible for 'The Animal Song' in the mid-1940s. They gigged mostly around Perry's hometown of Gary, Indiana as well as in Detroit and Chicago. After moving to Los Angeles, Perry was managed to get his own daily TV show on KTTV in Hollywood but with the arrival of rock'n'roll, his brand of R&B was no longer in vogue and he gave up the

Flanders &
Swann: the
'Hippopotamus
Song' men

music business in favour of a thriving career in real estate, returning
belatedly to the music business in 1967. This track was recorded in the
Fifties but wasn't ever actually made available until 1969.

22. THE HIPPOPOTAMUS SONG Flanders & Swann (1960)

Actor and singer Michael Flanders and composer, pianist and linguist
Donald Swann were a duo who specialised in writing and performing
comedy songs. They first performed and recorded this song at their
long running 'A Drop Of A Hat' review show which opened on New
Year's Eve in December 1956 when the pair hired The New Lindsey
Theatre in London's Notting Hill to perform their material. The show
was so successful that it transferred the next month to the Fortune
Theatre, where it ran for over two years before the pair took it on tour
throughout the UK, America, Canada and Switzerland. In 1963, they
opened a second review, 'At The Drop Of Another Hat' and again
took it around the world before finishing up at The Booth Theatre on
Broadway. This version of 'The Hippopotamus Song' – probably better
known as 'Mud, Mud, Glorious Mud' – was recorded in 1960 and was a
constantly requested record on Junior Choice.

23. MESSING ABOUT ON THE RIVER Josh MacRae (1961)

One of the most requested songs featured on Junior Choice in the
Sixties, 'Messing About on the River' was written and produced by
Tony Hatch, and years later was used in a movie version of *Wind In
The Willows*, the book that had inspired Hatch to write the song. Josh

"FOUR FEATHER FALLS"
(Words & Music by Barry Gray)
MICHAEL HOLLIDAY
with Orchestra conducted by Barry Gray

MacRae was a Scottish folksinger known as much for his music as his activism. He said his first introduction to folk music was watching a film featuring Josh White singing 'The Riddle Song', and he was then completely hooked on folk. One of the first folk singers to emerge from Scotland during the Sixties folk explosion, he was a founding member of The Reivers. He died in the late Seventies.

24. FOUR FEATHER FALLS Michael Holliday (1960)
The first episode of *Four Feather Falls* was transmitted in the UK on Thursday 25 February, 1960, at 5pm and was featured on the front cover of that week's edition of listings magazine the *TV Times*. It was another of Gerry Anderson's puppet-show adventure series for kids, following the hugely successful *Thunderbirds* and *Fireball XL5*. The series had a Wild West setting and had a cowboy hero (voiced by none other than Nicholas Parsons). It was an instant success and programme maker Gerry Anderson (of *Thunderbirds* fame) fully expected ITV to commission a second series. Despite having worked out a concept for the next batch of stories, he was met with stony silence from the network.

NOVELTY RECORDS

An absolute favourite of the Sounds of the Sixties programme, this is a feature in which we play comical or badly made records by well-known comedians and personalities which, in several cases, did not hinder them turning into monster hits.

1. THE OLD PAYOLA ROLL BLUES (Pt 1) **Stan Freberg (1960)**

Stan Freberg was born in California, the son of a Baptist minister. He grew up in Pasadena and at the age of 11 was helping his magician uncle with his stage act. After leaving school, he turned down an offer of a drama scholarship in favour of working with the legendary Mel Blanc, providing the voices for many cartoon characters for major movie studios. In the Fifties he signed a recording deal with Capitol Records and recorded dozens of comedy songs. This track, poking fun at a big payola scandal within the music business in America, raised a few eyebrows. The record featured Billy May's orchestra and singer, Jesse White. Part two of the track, on the other side of the disc, heard the luckless Stan attempting to get radio stations to play the song.

2. ROWDY **Clint Eastwood (1962)**

Clint was making a name for himself playing Rowdy Yates in the TV series *Rawhide*. This record was an oddity released by the Cameo Parkway label better known for the likes of Chubby Checker and Bobby Rydell. Clint actually released an album for the label, entitled *Cowboy Favourites*, which included 'Tumbling Tumbleweeds' and 'San Antonio Rose'.

3. A HARD DAYS NIGHT **Mrs Miller (1966)**

Mrs Miller (Elva Ruby Connes Miller) was born in Missouri and came to California before the end of the depression. An untrained soprano vocalist, she made her mark whilst America was at war in Vietnam, and even travelled there to serenade the soldiers in 1967. Her music fuelled a recording contract with Capitol, landed her on American Radio coast to coast, on the stage at the Hollywood Bowl and roles in a few impossible-to-find cult movies. As a joke, her record label released an album called *Mrs Miller's Greatest Hits*, from which this track is taken. Her voice has been described as possessing a shocking lack of control, with a pitch that never remains the same for very long.

4. WHEN YOU COME TO THE END OF A LOLLIPOP
Max Bygraves (1960)

Max's records received regular airplay on Junior Choice and in particular, his 1959 hit 'You're A Pink Toothbrush'. The following year he surprised television audiences when, in December, he topped the bill on 'Val Parnell's Sunday Night At the London Palladium' and performed 'When You Come To The End Of A Lollipop', a song that had been written by Al Hoffman and Dick Manning.

5. JOLLITY FARM The Bonzo Dog Doo-Dah Band (1967)

Taken from their debut album *Gorilla*, which the Bonzoes said was dedicated to a chap named Kong who must have been a great bloke. In February 1929, the music-hall singer Leslie Sarony – a man known for his comic miserable songs and gloomy subject-matter – sang a cover of a ditty called 'Misery Farm'. A few months later, Sarony wrote his own answer to the song entitled, 'Jollity Farm'. Several decades later, The Bonzo Dog Doo-Dah Band took this music-hall oddity into the psychedelic era with this cover.

6. KOOKIE, KOOKIE (LEND ME YOUR COMB)
Edward Byrnes & Connie Stevens (1960)

Edward Byrnes was born Edward Breitenberger in New York City and was known for playing the part of Kookie in the popular American TV series, 77 *Sunset Strip*, which ran from 1958 until 1963. Connie Stevens, who was born Concetta Ingolia, also appeared in the series and Warner Brothers thought it would be a good idea to team them up to record this novelty song. Connie also had a solo hit in the charts around the same time with 'Sixteen Reasons'.

7. MUCK-ARTY-PARK Soupy Sales (1969)

A most odd single, released by the Motown label, from comedian known as Soupy Sales. Born Milton Supman in Franklinton, North Carolina, 'Soupy' was his childhood nickname. He recorded a couple of LPs for Reprise in the early Sixties and in 1969 he travelled to Detroit where he signed to Motown and recorded one album *A Bag Of Soup*, which must have been one of the most expensive in the label's history. In the course of five months, the label attempted to record 16 songs over 25 recording sessions with numerous remakes and extra overdubs, shelving several tracks. But one that did escape, and which finally ended up as a single was this parody of 'Macarthur Park'.

8. MY BABY'S CRAZY 'BOUT ELVIS **Billy Boyle (1962)**

Billy Boyle was a teen idol from Ireland who came to London in 1961 after being cast for the rock musical *The Scattering*. After being seen on TV by Robert Stigwood, who promptly signed him for management and secured a recording contract with Decca. Although he didn't set the pop world on fire, he had a very successful career on both the stage and in movies. His West End theatre appearances included *Maggie May*, *Hello Dolly* and *Some Like It Hot*, whilst amongst his film credits were *The Hunted*, *Barry Lyndon* and *The Wild Geese*.

9. WE LOVE YOU BEATLES **The Carefrees (1964)**

The song is an adaptation of 'We Love You Conrad', from the musical *Bye Bye Birdie*. Three session singers, Lyn Cornell, Barbara Kay and Betty Prescott were approached by producer Reg Warburton to pose as the Carefrees after he obtained permission from the publishers to change the lyrics of the song in favour of The Beatles. Three male vocalists, Don Riddell, Johnny Evans and Johnny Stevens, helped out with the 'yeah yeah yeahs'. Although the single made little impact in the UK, it reached number 34 in The States and in the wake of its success, they went back into the studio and quickly recorded an entire album called *We Love You All* especially for the American market.

10. JEREMIAH PEABODY'S POLYUNSATURATED QUICK-DIS-SOLVING FAST-ACTING PLEASANT-TASTING GREEN AND PURPLE PILLS **Ray Stevens (1961)** *US No 35*

The first of Ray Stevens' records to reach the American Hot 100, this song tells of sales talk for a patent medicine or snake oil remedy. Stevens describes himself as 'The Comedy King of Music City' – referring to

Nashville, where the country-pop singer-songwriter resides. It was also the longest song title – a total of 13 words – to have made the American charts. Stevens' record company had to use a miniature type face to fit all the words onto the label of a single.

11. JUST COULDN'T RESIST HER WITH HER POCKET TRANSISTOR Alma Cogan (1960)

Although the song was on the B-side of Alma's 1960 Christmas single, 'Must Be Santa', this side of the disc received almost as many radio plays after the end of the Christmas period and became a number one hit for her in Japan where Sony were heavily promoting their newest invention, the 'tranny' radio. Written by Jack Keller, and Larry Kolber, the original version was by American singer, Danny Jordan, but failed to make the US charts.

12. DOWN CAME THE RAIN Mister Murray (1964)

This is still one of the most requested novelty records on *Sounds Of The Sixties*. Mr Murray is in fact songwriter Mitch Murray. He followed up this piece of nonsense with another equally ridiculous song called 'I Drink To Your Memory' and in 1968 recorded a song, 'You're Outta Your Mind' as Mr & Mrs Murray, with his wife.

13. AGE OF CORRUPTION Alan Klein (1965)

Not to be confused with the man that once managed The Beatles and Rolling Stones, this Alan Klein is the one that played a summer season at Butlins holiday camp in Skegness with his rock'n'roll group, The Al Kline Five. In the group was the future Tornados guitarist George Bellamy. The pair became a folk and country-based duo who made several appearances on *Saturday Club*. After their brief spell together, Alan decided to go it alone. After a spell as a bookie's runner, a labourer and cook, he ended up on the dole, whilst he continued to pitch his songs to anyone who was prepared to listen. His change of luck came when, in 1961, Joe Brown decided to record his song, 'What A Crazy World We're Living In', which hit the top 40 in January, 1962. The song caught the attention of theatre producer Gerry Raffles, who suggested Alan write a teenage pop musical based around the song.

The show opened at the Theatre Royal Stratford in October that year.

His music came to the attention of up-and-coming record producer Joe Meek, who produced two singles with Alan for the Oriole label with backing from The Tornados. In 1965 he signed with EMI's Parlophone label and his second single was a controversial but humorous poke at Barry McGuire's 'Eve Of Destruction', but which was mysteriously withdrawn soon after its release. It could have been that the song was credited to Klein as composer and, although he claimed he was careful not to exactly copy McGuire's tune, the two songs were probably too close for comfort.

14. ELEANOR RIGBY Doodles Weaver (1966)

Winstead Sheffield 'Doodles' Weaver was an American comedian – the brother of TV executive Sylvester Weaver and the uncle of actress Sigourney Weaver. In 1946 he was signed as member of Spike Jones' City Slickers, recording and touring the country with Jones. One of his most famous recordings was his satirical take of a horse-race commentator on 'The William Tell Overture', which received huge amounts of airplay. He appeared in more than 90 films, including *The Great Imposter*, Alfred Hitchcock's *The Birds* and *The Nutty Professor*, starring Jerry Lewis. In 1966, Weaver recorded this novelty version of 'Eleanor Rigby' on which he mixes up the words, insulting and interrupting the audience while playing the piano. Sadly, Weaver was a troubled man and he committed suicide in 1983 by shooting himself.

15. THERE'S A HOLE IN MY BUCKET
Harry Belafonte & Odetta (1960)

The origin of this traditional children's song is uncertain, but there are several possibilities. In George Korson's 1949 *Pennsylvania Songs and Legends* there is a song that, translated from the German, goes: 'When the jug has a hole/Dear Henry, dear Henry /When the jug has a hole/ Stupid thing, then stop it up!' This was collected in 1940, and is earlier than any known English-language version, which suggests that it might be a traditional 'Pennsylvania Dutch' (i.e. German) song. Ed McCurdy recorded it in 1958 on *Children's Songs*, then Harry Belafonte recorded it with Odetta in 1960. There are several other sources of German-language, or German-American, versions dating from the 1940s and early Fifties, all of which have Henry as the stupid questioner, and Lisa as the voice of common sense.

16. COME OUTSIDE Mike Sarne (1962) *UK No 1*

The song features former *Are You Being Served?* and *Eastenders* star Wendy Richard, who was a professional model at the time of the record's release. The song was written by Charles Blackwell, the man who arranged many of producer Joe Meek's hits, including John Leyton's number one, 'Johnny Remember Me'. Leyton and Sarne were both managed by Robert Stigwood and both combined their singing career with acting and live performances. Mike later turned his hand to photography providing pictures for both *Vogue* and *Cosmopolitan* before reinventing himself again as a movie director.

17. HERE COMES THE JUDGE Pigmeat Markham (1968)
US No 19/UK No 19

His real name was Dewey Markham, the nickname deriving from a stage routine, in which he declared himself to be 'Sweet Poppa Pigmeat'. 'Here Comes the Judge' was Pigmeat Markham's only hit either in the UK or America, reaching number 19 on both charts. The song's title was inspired by a catchphrase originated by Markham that was constantly used on the popular American comedy series *Rowan And Martin's Laugh In*.

18. WILD THING Senator Bobby (1967) *US No 20*

There have been conflicting reports as to the true identity of Senator Bobby: the most likely is Bill Minkin of a comedy act called The Hardley-Worthit Players, although there is another favourite candidate in James Voight, the brother of actor, John. Either way, the single's vocalist was supposed to be doing an impression of Senator Robert Kennedy. In America, it was one of the last hits for the Cameo Parkway label before it filed for bankruptcy in 1969. Former Beatles and Rolling Stones manager Alan Klein purchased all the tapes belonging to the company and changed its name to Abkco and all the material languished unreleased in the vaults until relatively recently.

19. TOMORROW Ricky Livid & The Tone Deafs (1964)

Ricky Livid was a character created by Hugh Paddick for the BBC radio's comedy series *Beyond Our Ken*, which starred Kenneth Horne and was a forerunner to the more successful *Round The Horne*. Livid was an unsuccessful pop singer who found it difficult to string a sentence together but was always enthusiastic about his work, a sample of which was released on this 1964 single. The B-side was a parody of The Dave Clark Five's 'Bits And Pieces' called 'Nuts And Bolts'.

20. FRANKFURTER SANDWICHES
Joanne & The Streamliners (1965)

Joanne was one Rosemary Squires (born Joan Rosemary Yarrow) from Bristol, who began broadcasting on the BBC's *Children's Hour* on the Home Service in 1940. She sang in various combos and after becoming a professional singer, she was employed by many of the big-band leaders, including Ted Heath, Geraldo and Cyril Stapleton. In 1962, she just failed to make the charts with her version of 'The Gypsy Rover', followed some years later by 'Frankfurter Sandwiches' under the pseudonym of Joanne & The Streamliners. Joanne then revealed herself as singer Rosemary Squires.

21. OLD RIVERS **Walter Brennan (1962)** *US No 5/UK No 38*

Walter Brennan appeared in over 200 movies, which were mainly Westerns. He had the honour of being painted by Norman Rockwell and once had almost all his teeth knocked out when he was kicked in the head by a horse. Many of his characters had weird and wacky names and were toothless old men, including Old Atrocity, JF Thunderbolt Brimstone and Doc Butcher Featherhead. He is probably best remembered as Grandpa Amos McCoy from the TV series, *The Real McCoys*, a forerunner to *The Beverley Hillbillies*. 'Old Rivers' featured backing vocals by The Johnny Mann Singers,

22. MAY THE BIRD OF PARADISE FLY UP YOUR NOSE
Little Jimmy Dickens (1965) *US No 15*

Little Jimmy was so named because he stood less than five-feet tall, something he was perhaps attempting to compensate for with his flamboyant, studded cowboy outfits. He was the thirteenth child of a West Virginian farmer and began performing as Jimmy The Kid whilst studying at the University of West Virginia. By the beginning of the Fifties he started using the name Little Jimmy Dickens, signed his first recording contract with Columbia and released his first single, 'Take An Old Cold Tater And Wait'. Many further recordings followed but it wasn't until 1965 that he found his biggest international hit with the intriguingly titled 'May The Bird Of Paradise Fly Up Your Nose'.

Short of stature but long of song-title, Little Jimmy Dickens was the country singer responsible for 'May the Bird of Paradise Fly up your Nose'

23. MY BOOMERANG WON'T COME BACK
Charlie Drake (1961)
US No 21/UK No 14

Born Charles Edward Springall in London, Charlie adopted his mother's maiden name of Drake when he first took to the stage, beginning his career as a singer before turning to comedy. He teamed up with Jack Edwards and the pair called themselves Jigsaw; they later appearing on children's television as Mick and Montmorency. Drake's first record was a cover of Bobby Darin's 'Splish Splash' and he achieved a higher chart placing than the American. Releasing several more singles, he achieved his biggest-selling single with this story of an Aborigine having trouble with his boomerang; it was a surprise top-40 hit in America.

23. SPEEDY GONZALES **Pat Boone (1962)** *US No 6/UK No 2*
This became Pat's final single to make the top 10 both in the US and UK. The original version of the song about the fastest mouse in Mexico was recorded some months earlier by the unknown David Dante, but Pat rapidly released his cover, featuring the voice Mel Blanc as Speedy and Robin Ward providing the 'la la las'.

24. PURPLE AEROPLANE **Spike Milligan (1966)**
Although the composer credits go to Spike Milligan, it can't go unnoticed that he borrowed more than the odd musical note from Lennon and McCartney's 'Yellow Submarine'. The track was issued as a single in 1966 soon after The Beatles' number one hit. In a BBC poll in August 1999, Spike Milligan was voted the 'funniest person of the last 1000 years'.

25. WHAT A WORLD **Benny Hill (1965)** *UK No 20*

This was the comedian's take on protest songs by folk singers such as Bob Dylan and Donovan. Benny was born Alfred Hawthorne Hill in Southampton. He got his first important showbusiness break as a performer when he was hired as Reg Varney's straight man, beating a then unknown Peter Sellers to the job.

26. THIN CHOW MEIN **Des O'Connor (1962)**

Des has more than once been quoted as saying he takes his singing seriously and would never consider making a comedy record. But unfortunately there are a few of us that have better-than-average memories and remember his parody of Jimmy Dean's 'Big Bad John'. The spoof is very non-PC, poking fun as it does at a poor Chinese person.

27. THE HIGHWAY CODE **The Master Singers (1966)** *UK No 25*

This actually is part of the Highway Code, sung to a psalm chant. It was devised by John Horrex, a schoolmaster at Abingdon School, in the late-Fifties. Over the years it was performed at numerous church socials and charity events as entertainment, using whatever singers were available. When George Martin heard a recording of the song, he decided to record his own version with a group of vocalists he put together, calling them The Master Singers.

28. CALL UP THE GROUPS **The Barron Knights (1964)** *UK No 3*

Formed by guitarist Pete Langford, The Barron Knights were signed to the Fontana label, but dropped after their debut single 'Let's Face It' failed to chart. Shortly afterwards, they landed a contract with EMI and a prestigious support spot to the Beatles on their first UK tour. The Barron Knights' first two EMI releases were flops, too, but in 1964 they came up with the idea of 'Call Up the Groups', sending up some of the UK's top acts. It resulted in a number-three hit, following a sensational appearance on the ITV pop show *Ready Steady Go*.

29. HANDS OFF STOP MUCKING ABOUT **Kenneth Cope (1968)**

Co-written and produced by Tony Hatch under his pseudonym of Mark Anthony for Liverpool-born actor Kenneth Cope who first became prominent in the BBC TV late-night satire show *That Was The Week That Was*, screened between 1962 and 1963. He later revived his career in the mainstream hit series *Randall and Hopkirk Deceased*. This 1963 single features backing vocals by The Breakaways and palpable expectations (that weren't achieved) of following in the footsteps of Mike Sarne's novelty number one, 'Come Outside'.

30. THAT NOISE Anthony Newley (1962) *UK No 34*

A novelty song written by Newley and Leslie Bricusse, this is partly a parody of their own 'What Kind Of Fool Am I', the hit song from their musical *Stop The World, I Want To Get Off*. Newley, uninterested in school life, left at the age of 14 to work as an office boy for an insurance firm.

Answering a newspaper ad for boy actors, he applied only to find they wanted unaffordable fees to enrol. Nevertheless, after an audition, he was offered a job as an errand boy for shillings a week, which included free acting tuition. In 1948 he landed two major movie roles, first as Dick Bultitude in Peter Ustinov's *Vice Versa*, followed by the Artful Dodger in David Lean's *Oliver Twist*. He made a successful transition from child star to top pop crooner in the Sixties.

Anthony Newley, pop crooner, songwriter and stage-show Svengali

31. LOPSIDED OVERLOADED (AND IT WIGGLED WHEN WE RODE IT) Brian Hyland (1961)

After the success of 'Itsy Bitsy Teeny Weeny Yellow Polka Dot Bikini' both here and in America, Brian Hyland's follow-up, 'Four Little Heels' fared less well, only reaching number 29 in the UK. His record label decided he should return to the tried-and-tested formula of the Bikini song and found him this wacky novelty number – which failed to chart altogether. Not long after its release, Brian refused to record any further daft songs and changed labels from Kapp to ABC-Paramount, where he was allowed more say in the song selection process.

32. CLICK CLACK '65 Dicky Doo & The Don'ts (1965)

When singer, songwriter and performer Gerry Granahan wanted to record the novelty song 'Click Clack' back in 1958, he didn't want to release it under his own name but as he was already under contract for his records and not wanting to get into legal battles, he created Dicky Doo & The Don'ts and leased the track to the American Swan label. To everyone's surprise the record climbed to number 28 in the Hot 100 and he had four more charting singles to follow. By the middle of 1959 the hits had dried up. But in 1965 he decided to try again with the first hit and remade it as 'Click Clack '65'. Unfortunately by this time, the wheels had definitely fallen off his career.

33. EL PASO Homer & Jethro (1960)

In the Fifties and early Sixties, Henry D Hayes (Homer) and Kenneth C Burns (Jethro) were the undisputed masters of popular-song parody lampooning hundreds of pop and country hits often to the dismay of the original artists. They met in 1936 during an audition for a Tennessee Radio station and teamed up as Junior and Dude (pronounced 'doodee') but were renamed when WNOX programme director Lowell Blanchard forgot their names and announced them as Homer and Jethro. Signed to RCA in 1949, they began recording parodies and achieved success with 'Baby It's Cold Outside' – though they were only given permission to change the lyrics by its composer on the condition the label carried an apology to Frank Loesser. In 1960, again with permission from Marty Robbins, the pair recorded this re-working of his hit 'El Paso', featuring Floyd Cramer on piano and Chet Atkins on guitar.

34. DON'T JUMP OFF THE ROOF DAD Tommy Cooper (1961)
UK No 40

On the evening of June 17, 1961, Alan Freeman was the guest presenter of ITV's big pop show *Thank Your Lucky Stars*. He introduced Tommy Cooper, along with Helen Shapiro, The Mudlarks and Petula Clark. Tommy proceeded to perform 'Don't Jump Off The Roof Dad' and stole the show. The track was released as a single and a couple of weeks later it had entered the UK top 40.

Honor Blackman – wearing those kinky boots – and Patrick MacNee as Cathy Gale and Steed in TV's The Avengers

35. KINKY BOOTS Honor Blackman & Patrick MacNee (1964)

The single was first released in 1964 to cash in on the boots worn by Honor Blackman in her role as Cathy Gale in the popular TV series *The Avengers*, in which she starred with Patrick MacNee, who played John Steed. Surprisingly, at the time of release the duo's record failed to chart. But some 26 years later when it was reissued in time for Christmas in 1990, it climbed to number five on the UK charts.

36. BO DUDLEY Peter Cook & Dudley Moore (1966)

Cook and Moore were always acknowledged as quite non-PC (even outside of their legendarily potty-mouthed Derek & Clive guise) this song certainly falls into that category – a send-up of blind blues singers. Jazz musician 'Bo Dudley' here gives an explanation of the Harlem song he's singing to the presenter. The track was actually released as the B-side to their equally non-PC song, 'Isn't She A Sweetie'.

37. ALL I WANT FOR CHRISTMAS IS A BEATLE Dora Bryan (1963) *UK No 20*

Johnny Gregory was the musical director on this Dora Bryan Christmas hit, with words and music credited to Gladys Benton. Early pressings came in a picture sleeve depicting Dora holding a guitar and wearing a Beatles wig. It was during a run of the play *Six Of One* at the Adelphi Theatre, in which she appeared, that Dora was asked to record the song.

But she insisted in rewriting some of the words. The record received considerable airplay, despite being voted the 'best bad record' of 1963. The Beatles embraced the record and even sang part of the song on one of their giveaway fan-club Christmas records.

38. THE GONK SONG The Gonks (1964)

The Gonks were named after a stuffed doll that came in various shapes and sizes but which were basically heads with arms and feet minus a body and usually without legs. They were not very intelligent; they bounced, whistled and spoke rubbish and were popular in the mid-Sixties. The B-side of the single was their version of Arthur 'Big Boy' Crudup's 'That's Alright Mama' popularised in the Fifties by Elvis Presley. The obscure British band who named themselves after these creatures once worked as the backing group for the singer Twinkle when she supported The Rolling Stones on their 1965 tour of the UK and Ireland and whose biggest hit was 'Terry'.

39. I PASS Godfrey Winn (1967)

Born in Edgbaston in Birmingham, Godfrey Winn began his career as a boy actor in John Galsworthy's play *Old English* at London's Haymarket Theatre. In 1928 he wrote his first of many novels, *Dreams Fade*. In 1936 Winn became a columnist for *The Daily Mirror* and two years later was writing for The Sunday Express by which time he was claiming to be the highest-paid journalist in Fleet Street. He made several appearances in Sixties movies, including *Billy Liar* and *The Great St Trinian's Train Robbery* and in 1967 recorded this oddity for Decca, 'I Pass'.

40. THE TIMES THEY ARE A-CHANGIN' Sebastian Cabot (1967)

Throughout the Fifties and Sixties, the actor Sebastian Cabot was one of America's top choices to play posh Englishmen. Despite being an actor who specialised in upper-class roles, he wasn't posh at all. He was Cockney-born, within the sound of Bow Bells, and worked both as a chef and a wrestler before turning his hand to acting. As the Sixties progressed, he was the narrator for Disney cartoons, including the *Winnie The Pooh* stories and *The Sword And The Stone*. In 1967, he found himself involved in an extraordinary project, 'acting out' the lyrics to Bob Dylan songs for an album with the catchy title of *Sebastian Cabot Actor, Bob Dylan Poet: A Dramatic Reading With Music*, from which this track is taken.

POP ON THE SCREEN

This chapter will deal with songs that were written specifically for, or which featured on, the soundtrack of popular movies during the Sixties.

1. PRIVILEGE Paul Jones (1967)

This song was written by Mike Leander and Paul Jones for the film of the same name, in which Paul starred with Jean Shrimpton, Max Bacon and Jeremy Child. It was a speculative account of how England would become in the Seventies – with the over-powerful welfare state manipulating the masses through the media, especially via pop stars!

2. THEME FROM THE VALLEY OF THE DOLLS
Dionne Warwick (1968) *US No 2*

The movie *Valley of the Dolls* starred Sharon Tate, Patty Duke and Susan Hayward (with a brief cameo appearance by Richard Dreyfuss), and was based on the Jacqueline Susann novel about three young women making their way in show business. The song was written by André and Dory Previn and had originally been intended for Judy Garland to perform before she was fired from the cast. At the suggestion of Barbara Parkins, one of the film's stars, Dionne Warwick was invited to sing the song, with a John Williams arrangement. But it had to be re-recorded for this release as a single under the direction of Burt Bacharach, because Warwick was signed to Scepter and the soundtrack was released on 20th Century Records.

3. LIVE NOW, PAY LATER Doug Sheldon (1962)

The title song from a British comedy movie that starred Ian Hendry, June Ritchie, John Gregson and Liz Fraser and which was nominated for a BAFTA. The story tells of Albert, an electrical goods salesman who has to collect payments from his customers every week. He befriends a young single mother who has been left to bring up a baby on her own. Doug Sheldon was a London lad from Stepney who moved with his parents to Skegness, where he worked in his father's fairground as a barker and bingo caller. After completing his Army National Service, he landed a small part in the movie *The Guns Of Navarone* and it has been said that he once shared a flat with Michael Caine and Terence Stamp. He also secured some television work as an actor, where he was spotted by Craig Douglas's manager, Bunny Lewis, who secured him a recording contract with Decca.

4. STROLL ON **The Yardbirds (1967)**

The story goes that legendary movie director Antonioni commissioned a song called 'Blow Up' for the movie of the same name from a group called The In Crowd, featuring guitarist Steve Howe, who apparently refused to smash up his guitar for the film. So the song was rejected and The Yardbirds were brought in to write this song, 'Stroll On'. Jeff Beck *did* smash up a guitar which, ironically, was a cardboard copy of Steve Howe's.

5. WHAT'S NEW PUSSYCAT **Tom Jones (1965)** *UK No 11*

The title song to the movie starring Peter Sellers, Peter O' Toole, Woody Allen and Ursula Andress, about a crazed fashion editor who goes to a psychiatrist for help over his problems with his love life. The song was written by Burt Bacharach and Hal David.

6. ACCIDENTS WILL HAPPEN **Patsy Ann Noble (1963)**

From the movie *Live It Up*, which was also known as 'Sing And Swing'. The title song was performed by ex-Tornado and Joe Meek protegé Heinz, who also starred in the movie alongside David Hemmings and a very young Stevie Marriott. Other musical guests included Patsy Ann Noble herself, Gene Vincent and Kenny Ball. The movie itself had some strong songs but a fairly weak storyline about a struggling pop group trying to make the big time. A sequel movie was released two years later in 1965 called *Be My Guest*.

Aussie singer Patsy Ann Noble, appearing in the movie Live It Up

7. BORN TO BE WILD Steppenwolf (1968) *US No 2/UK No 30*

The band took its name from the 1927 novel by cult author Herman Hesse. Most of the original band had previously been part of the Canadian group, Sparrow. 'Born To Be Wild' was featured in the opening sequence of the 1969 movie *Easy Rider*, elevating the song to its 'classic rock' status.

8. MIX ME A PERSON Adam Faith (1962)

This Adam Faith movie also starred Anne Baxter and Donald Sinden. Adam, in his first dramatic role, played a young rock'n'roll singer named Harry Jukes who gets a flat tyre when driving down a country road and then finds himself holding a smoking gun over the body of a dead policeman.

9. THE SYSTEM The Searchers (1966)

This song by The Searchers was from a movie directed by Michael Winner which was also known as 'The Girl Getters'. Starring Oliver Reed, Julia Foster, and David Hemmings, it told the story of hoodlum teenagers on the rampage and their romances at a British seaside resort.

10. BROKEN PIECES Elaine & Derek (1965)

From the bizarre movie *Gonks Go Beat*, which is set on the planet earth sometime in the future. The world is divided into two separate factions: Beatland, populated by mainly pop musicians and singers; and Balladisle devoted to those in favour of the slower ballads. The atmosphere is tense between the two continents and each year, the annual 'Golden Guitar' contest between both sides is always declared a draw, to try and keep the peace. That is until Wilco Rogers, an ambassador from the Congress of the Universe, arrives on the scene, charged with the task of settling the feud between the two groups of inhabitants. The movie stars Kenneth Connor, Terry Scott and Frank Thornton with music supplied by, amongst others, The Nashville Teens, Lulu & The Luvvers, The Graham Bond Organisation and Elaine & Derek. Derek was in fact Derek Thompson who later became better known for playing Charlie Fairhead in the TV series *Casualty*.

11. SECOND HAND ROSE Barbra Streisand (1965)
US No 32/UK No 14

This was Barbra's UK chart debut and also her introduction to the movie world. When she was first asked to play the less than attractive Fanny

Brice in *Funny Girl*, she was reluctant to take on the part because she felt self-conscious about her facial appearance and was worried it would be exaggerated on the screen. Omar Sharif, who played her Jewish husband, was condemned by the Arab press and considered a traitor as the film was released at the time of the Arab-Israeli Six Day War. There was even talk of revoking his citizenship. The story tells of the ambitious singer Fanny who is discovered by Nick Arnstein, a heavy gambler, who introduces her to producer Florenz Ziegfeld who gives her a job in his new revue. She soon becomes the show's biggest attraction and goes on to become a national celebrity – but not before marrying Arnstein, bringing with it the cause of much of her unhappiness in her life.

12. SWINGIN' SCHOOL **Bobby Rydell (1960)**
The 1960 movie from which this song is taken is *Because They're Young*, starring Dick Clark and Tuesday Weld. The plot tells of a gang of kids who force a nice, well-behaved student to help them commit a robbery. Inevitably, the robbery goes wrong. Other music featured included James Darren singing the title song and Duane Eddy playing 'Shazam'.

13. FERRY ACROSS THE MERSEY
Gerry & The Pacemakers (1964) *US No 6/UK No 8*
Written by Gerry Marsden, this was the title song from the movie that starred Gerry & The Pacemakers with guest appearances by Cilla Black, The Fourmost and Jimmy Savile. Directed by Jeremy Summers, it was the first movie to be shot on location in Liverpool after the city became famous world over for its music. Over the years, there have been a number of covers of the song including versions by Frankie Goes To Hollywood and Pat Metheny.

14. IN THE HEAT OF THE NIGHT **Ray Charles (1967)** *US No 33*
The title song to the movie of the same name starring Sidney Poitier, Rod Steiger and Warren Oates, about a redneck southern sheriff who is forced to accept help from a black detective in solving an unusual murder case. The movie won five Oscars including Best Movie and screenplay.

15. TO SIR WITH LOVE **Lulu (1967)** *US No 1*
Another Sidney Poitier movie – but a very different one. This song was the B-side of 'Let's Pretend', in the UK, and was the title song to the gritty movie, set in a tough school in the east end of London.

16. IF A MAN ANSWERS Bobby Darin (1962) *US No 32/UK No 24*

The title song from *If a Man Answers* was sung by Bobby Darin, who also starred in the film with his then wife, Sandra Dee, alongside Cesar Romero and Stephanie Powers. The light-hearted storyline pitted Darin as a feckless spouse to Dee, who attempts to mould him into the perfect husband using a variety of tricks. Both attempt to make each other jealous with their antics.

17. THE WINDMILLS OF YOUR MIND Noel Harrison (1969) *UK No 8*

The son of British actor, Rex Harrison, Noel sang this theme from the movie *The Thomas Crown Affair*, starring Steve McQueen and Faye Dunaway. The movie was re-made in 1999 with Pierce Brosnan playing the lead, with the same song was performed by Sting.

18. ON THE BEACH Cliff Richard & The Shadows (1964) *UK No 7*

This song derives from the movie *Wonderful Life*, which starred Cliff and The Shadows alongside Melvyn Hayes, Una Stubbs, Susan Hampshire and Richard O' Sullivan, who entertain diners aboard a luxury liner. After dark, the boys bring out their guitars, overloading the ship's power supply, bringing it to a grinding halt. The captain kicks them off the boat and they head for the coastline in a life raft (using their guitars as paddles, of course) only to find they've arrived on a film set. Making the most of the situation, they decide to make their own movie, using the leading lady without her knowledge. Confused? You will be.

19. COME OUT DANCING Rick Nelson (1965)

Rick's father, Ozzie bought the film rights to a short-lived Broadway show, *Love And Kisses*, which had no songs in it. He wrote, produced and directed a movie version and brought in songwriters to add music. Sonny Curtis wrote the title song and Clint Ballard Jnr wrote this track, 'Come Out Dancing'. The film starred Rick and his wife Kris with Jack Kelly and Kristin Nelson.

20. BECAUSE THEY'RE YOUNG Duane Eddy (1960) *US No 4/UK No 2*

The theme tune to the movie of the same name, starring Dick Clark and Tuesday Weld, this single from Duane Eddy would have been number one in the UK had it not been for The Shadows' first hit, 'Apache', hogging the top spot for the three weeks Duane remained at number two. Somewhat further down the charts at the time, there lurked a vocal version of 'Because They're Young', performed by another star of the movie, James Darren.

21. WHERE THE BOYS ARE Connie Francis (1961)
US No 4/UK No 5

Written by Neil Sedaka and Howard Greenfield, this was the title song from the movie *Where the Boys Are*, starring Connie and George Hamilton. The film's plot is about four young girls who have a holiday together, away from school and family for the first time.

22. THE HAPPENING The Supremes (1967) *US No 1/UK No 6*

Taken from a movie starring Anthony Quinn, Milton Berle and Faye Dunaway (in her debut screen role), in which a former gangster is kidnapped after he decides to become respectable. The Supremes' title song carried quite a pedigree: it was the last of 10 American number one hits for the girls written by the team of Holland-Dozier and Holland and the first song to carry a fourth name on the team's credits, that being Frank DeVol who wrote the score to the movie. It was also the last American number one to feature Florence Ballard in the line-up and it was also their last single to be billed as just The Supremes. Their follow up, 'Reflections', was billed as Diana Ross & The Supremes.

23. MAYBE TOMORROW Evie Sands (1969)

This haunting song was written by Quincy Jones with Alan and Marilyn Bergman for a little known movie from 1969, *John And Mary*, starring Dustin Hoffman and Mia Farrow. The song was probably the best feature of the film, which was generally panned by the critics and labelled innocuous and trite. It tells the story of the couple who meet up, have a quick fling, then can't decide if the relationship should be brought to an end.

24. TRUE GRIT Glen Campbell (1969) *US No 35*

The title song from the movie starring John Wayne and Glen Campbell, which tells of a young girl who hires the aging and drunken U.S Marshall, Rooster J Cogburn, to track down her father's killer. To do so, he must head into Indian Territory, where the killer is thought to be hiding. Wayne received an Oscar as best actor for his part as Cogburn and the song was also nominated in that year's awards. Wayne reprised his role in 1975 in a sequel, *Rooster Cogburn*, in which he starred opposite Katherine Hepburn.

25. WORK IS A FOUR LETTER WORD Cilla Black (1968)

The movie was directed by Peter Hall and starred David Warner as a worker in a big company that manufactures plastic daffodils, who would much prefer to spend time with his plant collection. Cilla Black plays his fiancée, Betty, who wants him to knuckle down to his job. But nothing gets in the way of the precious mushrooms that he cultivates in the boiler

Cilla and George Martin working on the song 'Work is a Four Letter Word' in 1968

room of the main building of his works. His activities turn him into an enemy of manager Mr Price, played by David Waller.

26. LET'S TALK ABOUT LOVE Helen Shapiro (1962) *UK No 23*

One of the many songs featured in the very first movie directed by Richard Lester. *It's Trad, Dad!* was re-titled *Ring-A-Ding Rhythm*, for the American market as they were unfamiliar with the term 'trad'. The story is based around two characters, Craig and Helen, played by Craig Douglas and Helen Shapiro who, along with a group of friends, take on a the local mayor who objects to the youngsters' love of traditional jazz and attempt to have the jukebox removed from the local coffee shop. Our two heroes gain support from disc jockeys Alan Freeman, David Jacobs and Pete Murray and, with many pop stars and trad jazz bands helping, decide to stage a big show in support of their music. The mayor, on learning about the performance, decides to stop the show by any means necessary. Naturally the movie ends with all the town's kids enjoying the music, to the displeasure of the adults. The movie also featured Kenny Ball & His Jazzmen, Acker Bilk & His Paramount Jazz Band, The Temperance Seven, Chubby Checker, Gene Vincent, Del Shannon and many, many more.

27. KEEP ON DANCING Brian Poole & The Tremeloes (1963)

Just For Fun was another teenage story of politics in which two main parties in the UK try to capture the votes of the young folk to no avail. The young decide to put forward their own candidates on the 'Just For Fun' party line and, of course, they win. The movie features Alan Freeman, David Jacobs and Jimmy Savile playing themselves, with support from Dick Emery, Irene Handl and Richard Vernon as Prime Minister. There's a huge line-up of musical guests, including a rare appearance on film by Dusty Springfield who, with The Springfields, sing the title song. There are also songs from Jet Harris & Tony Meehan, Freddy Cannon, Bobby Vee, The Crickets, Ketty Lester, Johnny Tillotson, Louise Cordet and others.

28. TWO LEFT FEET Bob Wallis & His Storyville Jazzmen (1963)

Many of the trad jazz bands created identifiable images for themselves by way of a sartorial gimmick. Acker Bilk and His Paramount Jazz Band became associated with bowler hats and striped waistcoats whilst Kenny Ball and Chris Barber's bands simply played in suits. Bob Wallis and His Storyville Jazzmen dressed as riverboat gamblers. 'Two Left Feet' is the title song from the movie of the same name and featured the band as well as starring Michael Crawford, Julia Foster, David Hemmings and Nyree Dawn Porter. It is an amusing insight into teen life in Britain before The Beatles.

29. LONELY Mr Acker Bilk (1962) *UK No 14*

Almost a year later after the phenomenal success of 'Stranger On The Shore', Mr Acker Bilk once again decided to cut another single with the Leon Young String Chorale. Having been asked to come up with a melody for the movie *Band Of Thieves*, a low budget comedy in which Bilk played himself, he composed 'Lonely' with Norrie Paramor. The film's title is self-explanatory as the story: the band in question is a jazz band comprised of ex-convicts, released from prison and attempting to go straight.

30. HERE WE GO ROUND THE MULBERRY BUSH Traffic (1967)

This is the title song to a movie that starred Barry Evans, Judy Geeson and Sheila White and was based on the novel by Hunter Davies. Stevie Winwood's previous band, The Spencer Davis Group, also contributed to the soundtrack and made a brief appearance in the film. This was their third single and its release had more to do with the fact that it had been used as the movie's title track than the band's actual wishes. It was also to be their last single: the group were liberated by the creative freedom which was offered when recording albums.

31. PISTOLERO Roy Orbison (1967)

Directed by Michael Moore, the movie *Pistolero* featured Roy Orbison in his only starring role as an actor, with Maggie Pierce and Sammy Jackson. It was a musical Western set towards the end of the American Civil War, in which Roy played Johnny Banner, a man with a bullet-firing guitar, hired as part of gang. Their daring mission was to rob gold from the United States Mint in San Francisco for the purpose of financing the beleaguered Confederacy to win the war.

32. THE BALLAD OF CAT BALLOU
Nat King Cole & Stubby Kaye (1965)

The film starred Jane Fonda (as Cat Ballou) and Lee Marvin, who won an Oscar for his dual role as Kid Shelleen and Tim Strawn. Nat King Cole was The Sunrise Kid and Stubby Kaye was Professor Sam The Shade – the pair of them cropped up from time to time to describe scenes in song.

33. MORGAN – A SUITABLE CASE FOR TREATMENT
Mike Vickers (1967)

Mike Vickers was one of the founder members of Manfred Mann and in the beginning played baritone and alto sax before the Manfreds decided to dispense with brass in their arrangements; Vickers then took up the guitar. The group went from success to success but Mike wanted to concentrate more on his composing and solo work. In 1967, he recorded his own album, *I Wish I Were A Group Again*, which included instrumental versions of several hits of the time including, 'Waterloo Sunset, 'Matthew And Son', 'Pretty Flamingo' and Johnny Dankworth's theme tune to the comedy movie, *Morgan – A Suitable Case For Treatment*, starring Vanessa Redgrave and David Warner.

34. AFTER THE FOX The Hollies, featuring Peter Sellers (1966)

The Hollies performed the Burt Bacharach and Hal David title song to the 1966 movie in which Sellers starred, *After The Fox*. According to Neil Simon, who wrote the screenplay, Sellers insisted that his new wife at the time, Britt Ekland, be cast as the Fox's sister. And although the director, Vittorio De Sica, didn't think her look or accent was right for the part, he gave into Sellers.

35. DON'T BRING LULU Dorothy Provine (1961) *UK No 17*

Dorothy Provine was born in Deadwood, South Dakota, but was raised in Seattle, Washington and discovered by Warner Brothers' talent executive Scotty Baiano, when he saw her in a college production of 'Charley's Aunt' at the University of Washington. 'Don't Bring Lulu', became a hit after it was featured in the Sixties TV series, 'The Roaring Twenties' in which she played the beautiful singer, Pinky Pinkham. Provine married director Robert Day in 1968 and retired from show business becoming something of a recluse in her retirement indulging in her love of reading and watching movies. On 25 April, 2010, she died of emphysema.

36. CATCH US IF YOU CAN The Dave Clark Five (1965)
US No 4/UK No 5

Written by Dave Clark and the group's guitarist, Lenny Davidson, this was the title song to a movie of theirs, which was renamed *Having A Wild Weekend* for the American market. In the Seventies, the song was played before the start of Shrewsbury Town Football Club's matches as the players ran onto the pitch: even now it is occasionally revived for big games.

37. JEAN Oliver (1969) *US No 2*

William Oliver Swofford was born in North Carolina. He began singing in the early Sixties with groups The Virginians and later The Good Earth when he was known as Bill Swofford. In 1969 he achieved a massive hit with 'Good Morning Starshine' from the musical *Hair*, following it with Rod McKuen's theme from the Oscar winning movie *The Prime Of Miss Jean Brodie*, starring Maggie Smith and called 'Jean'. Although not a hit in the UK, the record became Oliver's most successful release in the US.

38. LET'S SLIP AWAY Cleo Laine (1960)

This song, written by Johnny Dankworth and David Dearlove, was featured in the movie *Saturday Night And Sunday Morning*, starring Albert Finney, Rachel Roberts and Shirley Anne Field. The soundtrack featured a wide variety of music, with Dankworth providing all the jazz flavoured interludes that cropped up in the movie.

39. WE HAVE ALL THE TIME IN THE WORLD
Louis Armstrong (1969)

The record was first released in 1969 to tie in with the opening of the James Bond movie, *On Her Majesty's Secret Service*, in which the song was featured. Written by John Barry and Hal David, the title was taken from the final words uttered by Bond at the end of the film. Unfortunately Armstrong was too unwell to play his trumpet on the track, but Barry chose him to perform the song as he felt he would sing it with the right amount of irony. The record was reissued 25 years later in 1994, as part of a TV ad for a famous beer commercial, this time reaching number three in the UK.

40. MOON RIVER Audrey Hepburn (1961)

Over the years there have been many versions of the Henry Mancini and Johnny Mercer song, 'Moon River', which they wrote for the Blake Edwards movie *Breakfast At Tiffany's*, winning two Oscars for both 'Best Film Song Of The Year' and 'Best Original Score'. This was the original version, sung by Holly Golightly (as played by Audrey Hepburn) in the film itself.

41. SOME PEOPLE Valerie Mountain & The Eagles (1962)

Born in Bristol and raised in Weston-Super-Mare, Valerie joined the Cliff Adams Singers in 1960 whilst still retaining her day job with the Port Of Bristol Authority. In 1961, she was invited to appear in a play called *A Man Dies*, performing 16 songs in the retelling of the story of Jesus using a rock'n'roll score. Working alongside local group Rickey Ford and The Stranglers, they released a single from the show on EMI, 'Go It Alone Gentle Christ', followed by a cast album that was almost a decade before *Jesus Christ Superstar*. In 1962, Bristol was the chosen location for a movie, *Some People*, starring Kenneth More and David Hemmings for which Valerie was selected to perform the title song, backed by another local group, The Eagles. It was released as a single by Pye but neither the movie or the song proved strong enough to secure her with a regular recording contract and after her marriage in 1964, she gave up the business.

42. THE DREAM MAKER Tommy Steele (1963)

Written by Norman Newell and Philip Green, the song was arranged by John Barry and featured in the movie *It's All Happening*, released in

Valerie Mountain, of Valerie Mountain and The Eagles, with bandmate Richard Smith

America as *The Dream Maker*, and also starring Angela Douglas, Bernard Bresslaw and Michael Medwin, with further music items from Russ Conway, Danny Williams, Shane Fenton and The Fentones and The Clyde Valley Stompers.

43. DR GOLDFOOT AND THE BIKINI MACHINE The Supremes (1965)

The bizarrely titled movie *Dr Goldfoot and the Bikini Machine* was a direct spin-off from the *Beach Party* series of films starring Annette Funicello and Frankie Avalon, who both appeared in reprising roles alongside Vincent Price as the mad doctor of the title. The theme song to the movie was sung by The Supremes over a backing track which was later recycled for a single release by an obscure girl group, The Beas. The Supremes' version was issued as a one-sided promotional disc distributed to cinemas to play before screenings, so only a few copies were pressed, making it the group's rarest 45. The rest of the movie score was by Les Baxter, with more songs written – as it was intended to be a musical – but those scenes wound up on the cutting-room floor.

44. A HARD DAYS NIGHT The Beatles (1964)

The title song to the Fab Four's first full-length movie became their fifth number one both here and in America. The biggest problem with the filming of *A Hard Day's Night* was finding locations because, wherever they chose, the area would be swamped by fans within a few minutes as word got out.

45. STRANGERS IN THE NIGHT Frank Sinatra (1966)

This topped the US charts for one week but was number one in the UK for three. The song came from the movie, *A Man Could Get Killed*, an adventure comedy filmed around the Mediterranean which starred James Gardner and Sandra Dee.

46. LIVING DOLL Cliff Richard (1959)

Giving Cliff Richard his first number one hit and the biggest-selling single of 1959, this song was a UK number one for six weeks and remained in the best sellers at the beginning of the Sixties. Written by Lionel Bart, it was featured in Cliff's debut movie, *Serious Charge*, in which he played a layabout delinquent, Curley Thompson. One of the teenage gang members was played by an uncredited Jess Conrad in an early acting role.

47. THAT DARN CAT Buddy Greco (1965)

Written by leading movie composers, brothers Robert and Richard Sherman, this was the title song to the 1965 Walt Disney film *That Darn Cat*, starring Hayley Mills, Dorothy Provine and Roddy McDowall. Initially Buddy's voice was considered ideal for the song but in the final cut, a version by Bobby Darin was used over the credits. To confuse matters further, the soundtrack LP featured both Bobby Troup and Louis Prima performing alternative versions.

48. PAYROLL Reg Owen & His Orchestra (1961)

Payroll was a 1961 British crime thriller movie starring Michael Craig and Billie Whitelaw about a gang of villains who stage a wages robbery that goes disastrously wrong. The music was composed by Reg Owen who, with his orchestra, released a single of the theme in 1961.

THE PSYCHEDELIC ERA

It's hard to describe what puts a record into the category of psychedelic pop, as it covers a range of musical styles and influences – from folk to blues rock and Indian traditional music. But it is also associated with the state of consciousness sometimes brought about by the taking of mind-altering substances.

1. JOURNEY TO THE CENTRE OF YOUR MIND The Amboy Dukes (1968) *US No 16*

Ted Nugent first took up the guitar at the age of nine and formed his first band three years later. In 1965, with his family, he relocated to Chicago and formed another band, The Amboy Dukes. This was their only US hit, dominated by Nugent's sharp wrenchings of guitar. After many personnel changes, and with Ted being the only surviving original member of the group, they decided to call it a day in 1975.

2. SWEET YOUNG THING The Chocolate Watch Band (1967)

The single features a somewhat deranged vocal performance by lead singer Dave Aguilar who, when questioned about a certain line in the song, insisted he was singing 'If you're gonna bug around, I'm gonna split'. Many have suggested he was probably singing something different – the word 'bug' in particular. The group formed in San Francisco in 1965 as a Rolling Stones soundalike act, playing in local clubs before being signed to Capitol's Tower label in 1966.

3. GROUND HOG Spirit (1969)

Spirit consisted of vocalist Jay Ferguson (who wrote this song and later went on to form Jo Jo Gunne), Randy California on guitar, John Locke on keyboards, Mark Andes on bass (who joined the group Heart in 1983) and drummer Ed Cassidy. Just prior to recording this album, the group were invited by movie director Jacques Demy to provide the music to the belated follow up to his successful 1964 movie *The Umbrellas Of Cherbourg*, entitled *The Model Shop*. Unfortunately he spoke little English and was unable to communicate his ideas to the actors or the group, resulting in a good idea turning out half-baked. To add to their troubles, the film company insisted on having Gary Lockwood, star of *2001 – A Space Odyssey*, play the lead rather than the director's choice, the then unknown Harrison Ford.

4. DIAMOND HARD BLUE APPLE OF THE MOON The Nice (1968)

This first came to most listeners' notice as a bonus track from the reissue of The Nice's debut album, *The Thoughts Of Emerlist Davjack*, which was produced by The Rolling Stones' producer Glyn Johns (although the group had wanted Mick Jagger himself at the controls). The song was selected as the B-side to their only UK singles hit, 'America', and featured Keith Emerson playing the latest studio gizmo of the time, the Mellotron.

5. CAN'T BE SO BAD Moby Grape (1968)

Two former associates of Jefferson Airplane – Skip Spence, who had been their drummer, and Matthew Katz, the band's one-time manager – formed the group in San Francisco in 1966. The group took their name from the punchline to an old joke: 'What's big and purple and lives at the bottom of the sea?' In 1967 they were signed to Columbia records and released their self-titled debut album. In a marketing stunt, their label released five singles at once, but it backfired as they were accused of being over-hyped. Their second LP, *Wow! Grape Jam* was a double album sold for the price of one and was released the following year. It contained the track that introduced the band to a wider group of British fans, 'Can't be So Bad'.

6. EARLY MORNING Barclay James Harvest (1968)

Formed in Manchester in the summer of 1967, the group spent over a year working on their own material in the solitude of an old English farmhouse. Their first batch of demos led to the release of their debut single, 'Early Morning', on EMI's Parlophone label. The following year they were transferred to the company's newly created progressive label, Harvest, where they worked with The Beatles' sound engineer, Norman Smith, who also produced their first two albums.

7. WESTERN UNION The Five Americans (1967) *US No 5*

Under the leadership of guitarist Mike Rabon, this group originally began life as The Mutineers, playing local clubs and dance halls in Oklahoma. The group moved to Dallas, Texas and changed their name to The Five Americans, where they were discovered playing at a dive called Pirate's Nook by John Abdnor, the president of Abnak, a local record label. In the summer of 1965 they released their first single, 'I See The Light', reaching number 26 and winning them their first of six American Hot 100 hits. But this, 'Western Union', was the only one to make the top 10.

The Chocolate Watch Band started off as a Rolling Stones-inspired garage group, then scored a hit with 'Sweet Young Thing'

8. ME AND MY WOMAN The Keef Hartley Band (1969)

Hartley was once a member of The Artwoods, before joining John Mayall's Bluesbreakers in 1967. He left the following year to form his own band. His first album *Halfbreed*, for Decca's Deram label, was regarded as a masterpiece of the fusion of rock, jazz and blues. 'Me and my Woman' is taken from their second album, *The Battle Of The North West Six*, this track featured the new addition of Miller Anderson on vocals and lead guitar. Their first album had featured vocalist Sam Holland but Keef was unhappy with the results and decided to ring the changes, also bringing in contributions from Rolling Stone, Mick Taylor.

9. SHE COMES IN COLOURS Love (1967)

Taken from their second album, *Da Capo*, the group agreed that this was the most difficult song to record because of all the unusual chords. Drummer Michael Stuart-Ware was amused by the reference to Arthur Lee's visit to London in the lyrics, as he knew that Lee had never set foot on British soil at this point in his career. There's also another widely held belief that The Rolling Stones borrowed the title for inclusion in the lyrics of their 1967 track, 'She's A Rainbow'.

10. SOMEBODY TO LOVE Jefferson Airplane (1967) *US No 5*

San Francisco based Jefferson Airplane signed to RCA Records in 1966, with two albums and three singles already to their name, before the release of 'Somebody to Love' on their new label. Their original singer, Signe Anderson, was replaced by Grace Slick, who had previously been with The Great Society, and who had recorded an earlier version of the song as 'Someone To Love' for a small independent label. The song was recorded for the album *Surrealistic Pillow* at the RCA studios in Hollywood where The Rolling Stones had cut '(I Can't Get No) Satisfaction' and 'Get Off Of My Cloud', with the same engineer.

11. I'LL BE LATE FOR TEA Blossom Toes (1967)

Originally named The Ingoes, Blossom Toes released their debut album, *We Are Ever So Clean*, at the height of the Flower Power boom of 1967. It was produced by Giorgio Gomelsky who discovered both The Rolling Stones and The Yardbirds. Blossom Toes never really hit the big time but had played on the same bill as such acts as The Move, The Crazy World Of Arthur Brown and Pink Floyd during the days of Syd Barrett.

This was the first of just two albums they recorded in their short career between 1967 and 1969, the second was titled *If Only For A Moment*.

12. THE THIRD DEGREE Marc Bolan (1966)

The north London teenager made his recording debut for Decca in 1965 with 'The Wizard', which is now considered a psychedelic classic – long before the term actually existed within the music world. This, the follow -up, had a much harder feel, as did his third and final release for the label, 'Hippy Gumbo'. After he left Decca, he joined the group John's Children just prior to finding fame and fortune with Tyrannosaurus Rex, later better known as glam rock titans T. Rex.

13. BACK IN L.A. The Peanut Butter Conspiracy (1969)

This Californian group made it onto the music scene in the mid-Sixties when West Coast psychedelic groups were all the rage. Initially gaining experience at live dates in local clubs, they were first heard on record in 1966 with their debut single, 'Time Is After You'. The following year, they were signed to American Columbia and achieved limited recognition with their single 'It's A Happening Thing', following it with their first album *The Peanut Butter Conspiracy Is Spreading*. In 1968, their second

The Peanut Butter Conspiracy, a West Coast psychedlia group who were presumably deeply distrustful of Sun Pat

album *The Great Conspiracy* was released, but the prospect of any further success seemed unlikely. In 1969, a third album appeared on the market, *For Children Of All Ages*, made up of earlier tracks they'd recorded for a previous label – and from which this track is taken.

14. LOVE REALLY CHANGED ME Spooky Tooth (1968)

Spooky Tooth were one of the first acts to be signed to the Island label, and this was released as a single in 1968, taken from their album *It's All About*. The band promoted the album with a number of radio broadcasts, most of which were for Radio 1, where John Peel became a great supporter of their music. They were touring non-stop for over two years, clocking up 45,000 miles in a single year. As well as visiting Europe, they toured America four times, supporting The Rolling Stones, Janis Joplin and The Eagles.

15. TICKET TO RIDE Vanilla Fudge (1967)

This was the opening track from the self-titled debut – and most successful – album from the band Vanilla Fudge. It also contained the full seven-and-a-half minute version of their hit cover of The Supremes' 'You Keep Me Hanging On'. The group were originally named The Pigeons but changed their name in 1967. They were great admirers of The Beatles and it has been said that The Beatles themselves would play Vanilla Fudge's recorded versions of their songs to anyone who would listen.

16. HOLE IN MY SHOE Traffic (1967) *UK No 2*

Held off the number one spot by 'Massachusetts' by The Bee Gees, this was the group's second top-10 hit. It's widely believed that Steve Winwood didn't like the Dave Mason composition; he felt that it failed to represent the band's true musical style. Mason quit the band soon afterwards and Traffic began to develop a less commercial sound, which may well have contributed to the end of their run of hit singles in the UK. However their new material proved popular on American Rock stations and it gave the band a second wind across the Atlantic. The brief spoken passage in the middle of the song was performed by a girl named Francine Heimann. In July 1984, actor Nigel Planer, who played the role of Neil in the TV series, *The Young Ones*, released a cover version of the song, which reached the same number-two peak as the original.

17. EIGHT MILES HIGH **The Byrds (1966)** *US No 14/UK No 24*

The Byrds' first hit to be written by group members Gene Clark, Roger McGuinn and David Crosby, this was included on their album *Fifth Dimension*, and is considered to be one of the first songs to be labelled psychedelic rock. Although all three are credited, each one claims to have written it themselves. The song is about the group's flight from America to the UK. Although, most commercial aircraft fly at an altitude of six to seven miles, it was decided that 'eight miles high' scanned better. Regrettably the song was widely misinterpreted as being about recreational drug use and was banned by a number of radio stations.

18. A QUESTION OF TEMPERATURE **The Balloon Farm (1967)**

A garage punk quartet from New Jersey, The Balloon Farm fitted like a glove into the Sixties psychedelic music scene: this was the first of two singles by the group. They had previously been called Adam, with each group member adopting that name. After being dropped by their record company after their second single, 'Hurry Up Sundown', the band then evolved into Huck Finn for one further release, 'Two Of A Kind', before calling it a day. The group's Mike Appel went on to write songs for The Partridge Family and later became the first manager of Bruce Springsteen.

19. MAGICIAN IN THE MOUNTAIN **Sunforest (1969)**

In 1969, Sunforest were offered the chance to record for Decca's recently formed Nova label, which itself was an offshoot of Deram. The group had little live experience so had only a very limited following, but they sufficiently impressed the record label's bosses with their folk, ethnic and medieval musical influences to secure a recording contract. They cut just one album, *The Sound Of Sunforest* under the supervision of producer Vic Smith but, unsurprisingly, failed to sell in any significant quantities.

20. I'LL BE YOUR MIRROR **The Velvet Underground (1966)**

The Velvets, while only modestly successful at the time, have become one of the most influential groups in the history of rock. The band already had a lead singer, Lou Reed, but German model Nico joined the group at Andy Warhol's suggestion, and she first performed with the group on their debut album, *The Velvet Underground And Nico*. Although her voice was often criticized for being cool to the point of monotony, she added a slightly chilling decadence to the songs she sang.

21. THE JOLLY GREEN GIANT The Kingsmen (1965) *US No 4*

The group that brought us the classic 'Louie Louie' achieved their second-biggest American hit with a song based on an American TV jingle used to sell tins of Green Giant vegetables. The company didn't know what to make of this unauthorised breach of their copyright: the West Coast office sent the group boxes of their products to give away at their concerts, while the East Coast office tried to sue the group for defamation. The song was actually recorded at the end of one of their sessions as a joke and was never intended for release but a record company executive heard it and was convinced it was a hit.

22. WHITE BIRD It's A Beautiful Day (1969)

The single version was edited from their eponymous album and written by group members David LaFlamme and his wife Linda, who was inspired by looking out of the couple's attic window in Seattle. The pair felt like caged birds in that little space: their band was barely working in the bad weather, they had no means of transport and very little money. The song was later used in three episodes of the 1980s television series *Knight Rider* and in 1991 was included in the soundtrack of the movie, *A Walk On The Moon* set against the backdrop of the Woodstock festival of 1969 and the moon landing of that year.

23. 96 TEARS Question Mark & The Mysterians (1966)
US No 1/UK No 37

The biggest mystery about this single at the time was the identity of the lead singer. Although it was a mystery in 1966, it's no secret today. Behind the sunglasses, which he never removed in public, Question Mark was Mexican-born Rudy Martinez. He was raised in Michigan, as were his fellow group members. The song '96 Tears' was written by Rudy some four years before the group came together and started out as a poem called 'Too Many Teardrops'.

24. TIME The New Tweedy Brothers (1968)

By the time the New Tweedy Brothers put out their only album in 1968, the group had been on the San Francisco music scene for several years, opening for such acts as The Grateful Dead, Them and The 13th Floor Elevators. Their name was a tribute to an old- time folk band of several decades earlier (named The Tweedy Brothers).

Originally hailing from Portland, The New Tweedy Brothers could have easily risen to the top of the local rock scene, but disappointingly the Brothers simply sank into obscurity. This track wasn't included on their sole album and had been gathering dust in the archives until finally being released on CD in 2009.

25. SHAKE The Shadows Of Knight (1968)

Formed in Chicago in 1965 as The Shadows, they built up a local following and impressed bosses of the American Dunwich label when they performed their version of Them's 'Gloria' at a showcase held in The Cellar Club. They were signed to the label and after changing their name to The Shadows Of Knight (so as not to be confused with Cliff Richard's backing group), they released the song as their first single. It sold over 10,000 copies in the first 10 days and soon reached number 10 on the Billboard charts. They followed it with Bo Diddley's 'Oh Yeah', which also cracked the American top 40 but, by the Spring of 1967, internal strife led to the breaking-up the group.

26. DO UNTO OTHERS The Elastic Band (1968)

The Elastic Band was the starting point for Sweet guitarist Andy Scott, emerging from the ashes of Welsh mid-Sixties group The Silverstone Set. They recorded a couple of highly regarded blue-eyed soul singles for Decca in the Sixties including 'Do Unto Others'. After a year on the underground gig circuit supporting the likes of Jimi Hendrix and Pink Floyd, these new acts made a significant impact on the band's musical direction; when they returned to the studio in the summer of 1969 to record their album *Expansions On Life* their style had changed radically to a psychedelic/early progressive rock sound, which suggested that the new-look Elastic Band could be a major act. Inexplicably, though, Decca delayed the album's release until March 1970, by which time the band had fallen apart, lead singer Ted Yeadon having left in December

1969 to replace Steve Ellis in the group The Love Affair. As a result, Decca barely promoted the album, which duly sank without trace.

27. LAUGH LAUGH **The Beau Brummels (1965)** *US No 15*

Although this is probably their best-known single, their follow-up, 'Just A Little' was the bigger American hit, reaching number eight. The band took their name from Beau Brummell, a foppish nineteenth-century English gentleman: it was a way of identifying with the British pop boom in America. Additionally, they figured that since everyone bought, or browsed, Beatles records in shops, having a name that naturally followed The Beatles alphabetically would be a shrewd move. They also took to wearing British-influenced mod clothes. 'Laugh, Laugh' is listed in the rock'n'roll Hall of Fame as one of the 500 most influential songs that shaped rock'n'roll.

28. I CAN TAKE YOU TO THE SUN **The Misunderstood (1966)**

The late John Peel claimed on his *Top Gear* radio show 'that this is to my mind the best popular record that's ever been recorded'. It was Peel who persuaded members of this Californian-based group to relocate to the UK, where they recruited several British musicians to record this track. It's often hailed as one of the all-time psychedelic singles. Unfortunately, their dreams of success were shattered when the American members of the group were deported back to America, having been unable to obtain long-term work permits, and were drafted into the Vietnam War.

29. JUST DROPPED IN (TO SEE WHAT CONDITION MY CONDITION WAS IN) **Kenny Rogers & The First Edition (1968)** *US No 5*

The first American hit for the group with lead singer Kenny Rogers, who later made a name for himself as a major country performer, this single is now a collectable amongst the psychedelic music fans. Written by Mickey Newbury, who was responsible for Elvis Presley's 'American Trilogy' and Tom Jones's 'Funny Familiar Forgotten Feelings', the song was intended as a stark warning against the use of hard drugs. It was first recorded in 1967 by Jerry Lee Lewis, for his album *Soul My Way*, but he decided not to release it as a single.

30. ABBA ZABBA **Captain Beefheart (1966)**

Captain Beefheart was born Don Van Vliet and began playing the saxophone and harmonica at the age of 13. By 1959, he had joined a local blues band in California called The Blackouts, during which time he became friends with Frank Zappa. In 1963, they formed The Soots. Turned down by several record labels, Zappa went off to form The Mothers Of Invention leaving the Captain to form his first Magic Band. They were given the opportunity of recording five tracks for A&M records in 1965, two of which were released as singles. A subsequent album was shelved after the company decided the material was unsuitable. They then signed to Buddah and recorded the album *Safe As Milk*, from which this track has been taken.

31. FLY ME TO THE EARTH **The Wallace Collection**
Released as their second single and taken from their debut album, *Laughing Cavalier*, one of the last albums released in both mono and stereo format by EMI. The band hailed from Belgium and were formed from the ashes of a group called Sylvester's Team. They based themselves in the UK, taking their name from the famous museum based close to EMI's headquarters at the time. Their debut single, 'Daydream', featured on the album and became a hit in 21 countries, going to number one in Belgium – which resulted in the group being invited to tour Europe, America and Mexico. Future singles, although reasonably successful in parts of Europe, couldn't hit the levels of their debut and the group split in 1971. They reunited in 2005 with a somewhat different line-up.

32. I AM JUST A MOPS **The Mops (1968)**
Originally released in Japan on RCA in April, 1968, The Mops' debut album, *Psychedelic Sounds In Japan*, was the country's first self-proclaimed psychedelic release. Although they wore the uniformed kaftans, beads and *Sgt. Pepper* jackets, the group were considered by many to be too rough and tough in their musical taste to be true flower power people but more garage punkers.

33. THIS WHEEL'S ON FIRE
Julie Driscoll, Brian Auger & The Trinity (1968) *UK No 5*
Written by Bob Dylan and Rick Danko, a member of his backing group, The Band, this track has often been covered. The Band's own version appeared on their 1968 album, *Music From Big Pink*, the same year that Julie Driscoll with Brian Auger and The Trinity covered it for a single release in the UK.

Driscoll and Auger's treatment of the song strongly reflected the psychedelic era of British music, complementing the group's flamboyant dress and performances, In 1992, Driscoll recorded the song again with Adrian Edmondson for the theme music to the BBC comedy series *Absolutely Fabulous*, whose main characters were throwbacks from that era.

34. IN-A GADA-DA-VIDA Iron Butterfly (1968) *US No 30*

This is the single edit of the track from the group's album of the same name. The original version runs for over 17 minutes and occupies the entire second side of an LP. The song was originally called 'In The Garden of Eden' but the lyric was misinterpreted by the group's drummer, Ron Bushy who wrote the title down incorrectly. When he later told composer and singer Doug Ingle that he loved 'In-A-Gada-Da-Vida' it stuck. The track was played by the group in the studio as a try-out whilst they were waiting for their producer, Jim Hilton. The engineer had the tape machine running and captured a performance that they were never able to better: that version was released.

35. MAGIC POTION The Open Mind (1969)

Formed in the early Sixties as The Apaches, playing covers of hits of the day, the group renamed themselves The Drag Set in 1965, building up a solid reputation playing more self-composed blues-style numbers. In 1967, they secured a deal with the Go label, a subsidiary of the independent Strike records, and released a track called 'Day And Night'. For the next couple of years they continued to play live and searched for their next record contract, which they found in 1969 and they recorded an album for Philips that was eventually released as *The Open Mind*, with original copies now fetching around £800. The album received poor reviews and failed to sell. But they were still invited back into the recording studios to cut this single, 'Magic Potion', which has been widely regarded as the group's finest moment.

36. PSYCHOTIC REACTION Count Five (1966) *US No 5*

Although their American label was called Double Shot, Count Five had just one shot at fame – this release being their only hit of their career before they headed back to oblivion. For all that, this single was an important release for fans of the psychedelic music scene, and even though they

Paul Revere & the Raiders were named after a legendary American political rebel, and dressed in historical garb at their shows

were accused of ripping off The Yardbirds' sound, the group made a record that remains as exciting today as when it was first recorded.

37. THE GREAT AIRPLANE STRIKE Paul Revere & The Raiders ft Mark (1966) *US No 20*

The group achieved over a dozen top-40 hits in America but never managed to touch the charts in the UK. Many considered their sound too American but on this track, lead singer Mark Lindsay owes a lot to Mick Jagger; he relates the tale of a frustrating journey where almost everything goes wrong. The production was by Terry Melcher, the son of Doris Day.

38. JENSKADAJKA The Orange Bicycle (1968)

The Orange Bicycle had been in existence since the early Sixties and were originally called Rob Storm and The Whispers. But as fashions changed they became The Rob Storm Group and for a while worked as Paul and Barry Ryan's backing band, morphing into The Orange Bicycle in 1967 after the psychedelic revolution arrived. By this time they had become largely studio-based, releasing five singles for EMI's Columbia label before switching to Parlophone for their one self-titled album, featuring a number of songs written by Elton John and Bernie Taupin. This was their fourth Columbia single.

39. LIKE A TEAR The World Of Oz (1969)

The track comes from The World of Oz's eponymous album: it featured a sleeve that caused deep confusion, as it featured sketches of the group's previous line-up yet most of them barely featured on the record. The design utilised characters from L. Frank Baum's *Wonderful Wizard Of Oz* universe, while the back cover had images of their producer, Wayne Bickerton and musical director, Mike Vickers. The track 'The Muffin Man' became a hit in several European countries outside of the UK.

40. A QUESTION OF TEMPERATURE The Balloon Farm (1967)

A track that epitomises the spirit of the Sixties garage punk scene, it was the first of two Balloon Farm singles by New Jersey quintet, The Balloon Farm, released on the Laurie label in America and on London in the UK. The group had previously recorded as Adam, with each of them adopting the first-name Adam – inspired by a leading New York night-club. After being dropped by their label after the release of their second single, they evolved into Huck Finn for one further release on Kapp. The group's Mike Appel went on to write songs for The Partridge Family and for a while managed Bruce Springsteen.

41. RIDE Caravan (1968)

Although never achieving the commercial success many had expected, Caravan had a long-lasting appeal with their very British style of performing and writing music, much of which was down to their guitarist, Pye Hastings. In May, 1968, the group performed at the legendary London underground club, Middle Earth, which led to a recording contract with Verve, making them one of the first signings to their new London based operation. Entering the recording studios in the summer of that year, they set about recording their self-titled first album consisting mainly of material they'd performed at their live gigs, with 'Ride' being one of the few exceptions.

42. HEY MR FLOWERMAN The Floor (1967)

The chances are that you've never heard of The Floor – unless you live or have spent time in Denmark where this English psychedelic pop group found fame in 1967. Prior to that, most of the band were The Hitmakers then the summer of love arrived and they decided that a change was required and the group needed reconfiguring. A guitarist was added and they settled on their new name before setting about recording an album under the direction of song writer, Johnny Reimar together with the cream of Copenhagen's session musicians. Unfortunately, after its release and a single (the aptly titled 'You Ain't Going Nowhere') in 1968, they decided to call it a day.

43. HOT SMOKE AND SASSAFRAS The Mooche (1969)

This was a cover of an American hit by The Bubble Puppy. This UK band created quite a following in the East Anglia area and this single, their only release, was produced by John Schroeder. The group's sax player, Dave Winthrop went on to become a member of Supertramp in the early Seventies and was later involved with Babe Ruth and Secret Affair.

44. CAN'T SEEM TO MAKE YOU MINE The Seeds (1966)

This was the first song to be recorded by The Seeds and, as well as being the first track on their eponymous first album, it was also their first single release. It was written by the lead vocalist, Sky Saxon and first released in 1965 but re-issued two years later, reaching number 41 on the American charts. After writing the song, Sky hawked it round the record labels and received little response until he finally made a deal with the Crescendo label that allowed the group studio time to complete the recording.

45. LITTLE GIRL The Syndicate Of Sound (1966) US No 8

At the time of release, the group from Northern California were young and inexperienced – thrust into the American spotlight with only this one hit under their belt. After winning a talent competition in 1964, they made their first record for a small local label, Scarlet, before coming to the attention of Garrie Thompson, a Lockheed Aviation employee who ran his own record label, Hush, as a sideline with his parents (who both had experience in music publishing and had helped launch the career of Joe Simon). A fellow worker at Lockheed, whose son was a member of The Syndicate Of Sound, approached Thompson about the group and a few weeks later they were in the studio recording 'Little Girl'.

46. SOMEONE MUST HAVE LIED The Fun & Games Commission (1967)

The Fun & Games Commission evolved out of a Texas-based group, The Sixpenz, and released two singles. They then learned that there was another group already in existence called Sixpence and were forced to change their name to The Fun & Games Commission, releasing this their first single under their new name. After which they shortened it to simply The Fun & Games.

47. GROOVIN' IS EASY The Electric Flag (1968)

When guitarist Mike Bloomfield decided to leave The Butterfield Blues Band, he formed The Electric Flag in 1967 with drummer Buddy Miles and keyboard player Barry Goldberg, and featuring various other leading musicians from time to time. Their first recording was the soundtrack album to the movie *The Trip*, starring Peter Fonda. They then began work on their first proper album, *A Long Time Comin*, from which this track is taken. But soon after its release, Bloomfield quit the group – although many reports suggested that the group left him due to his affiliation with drugs.

48. CHERRY BLOSSOM CLINIC The Move (1968)

Taken from their eponymous debut album, the only one which was recorded by the group's initial line-up – prior to the departure of bassist Ace Kefford. The last track, 'Cherry Blossom Clinic', was intended as a single at the end of 1967. However, the release was cancelled, as the lyrics were about the inmate of a mental home, and in the wake of the controversy which had dogged the previous single 'Flowers In The Rain', with its promotional postcard featuring an allegedly libellous drawing of Harold Wilson, it was felt that to risk further allegations of bad taste and scandal would harm their career irreparably.

49. APPLES AND ORANGES Pink Floyd (1967)

After the success of the singles, 'Arnold Layne' and 'See Emily Play', the group decided on another Syd Barrett composition for the follow-up. The group were booked to perform the song on *Top Of The Pops* but Syd refused to move his mouth along with the rest of the band to the lip-synched track on the grounds that John Lennon had also refused on an earlier edition of the show with The Beatles. To compromise, Roger Waters appeared to be singing lead, despite the fact that he didn't do any vocal work on the record.

50. OVER UNDER SIDEWAYS DOWN The Yardbirds (1966)
US No 13/UK No 10

The single was taken from their album *Roger The Engineer*, their only LP to contain all original material written by the group. The record was first officially titled simply *The Yardbirds*, but has since been named *Roger the Engineer*, a title stemming from the drawing on its front cover, a cartoon of the studio engineer Roger Cameron by band member Chris Dreja.

THE COLLECTABLES

A long-term favourite section of the programme, here are 50 of the most sought-after 45s on the planet – and not all them always carrying a high price.

1. A ROAD TO NOWHERE Carole King (1966)

After the success of 'It Might As Well Rain Until September', Carole released two further singles that failed to make any impact. It wasn't until nearly four years later that she released another single, 'A Road To Nowhere', a song about the break-up of her marriage to Gerry Goffin, but by then the interest in the artist had long gone and the record disappeared into a black hole despite having her original version of Dusty's 'Some Of Your Loving' on the B-side. However, she then made a spectacular comeback in 1971 with her Grammy Award-winning album, *Tapestry*.

2. THE MADMAN RUNNING THROUGH THE FIELDS
Dantalian's Chariot (1967)

This single was released in August 1967, and the B-side was called 'Sun Came Bursting Through My Cloud'. The group were a psychedelic reincarnation of Zoot Money's Big Roll Band whose stage show boasted one of the finest light shows on stage in the UK, surpassing even that of Pink Floyd. This, however, was the only single they ever released and, should you be lucky enough to find an original copy on the Columbia label, then expect to pay or sell it for at least £150.

3. BO STREET RUNNER The Bo Street Runners (1964)

The Bo Street Runners gained a huge following at their weekly residency at The Railway Hotel in Harrow. Their fans constantly asked if they'd released any records, so, as a response to their requests, they went into the studios in 1964 and recorded tracks for their fans who wanted a memento of the gig. The record was sold on Sunday nights at the gig for five shillings. A mint copy of the EP can fetch as much as £1,500: not a bad investment!

4. SHAKE, SHAKE, SENORA
The Ram Jam Band with Geno Washington (1965)

Geno Washington was in the UK whilst on leave from the American Services and met up with The Ram Jam Band, who were looking for a replacement front man. Up and coming record producer John Schroeder had discovered the band and signed them to a recording contract with Pye Records' new offshoot label, Piccadilly. However, The Ram Jam Band had already recorded a single for EMI after Geno had replaced former front men, Ram John Holder and Errol Dixon. The single, now a rare collectors' item, was an adaptation of Gary U.S. Bonds' 1962 American top-10 hit, 'Twist, Twist, Senora', which itself was inspired by the calypso, 'Shake, Shake, Senora'.

5. MY CLOWN July (1968)

The track originally appeared on their self-titled album *July*, an original vinyl copy of which exchanged hands on eBay for a surprising £788. Now the album has been given a long overdue re-issue on the Rev-Ola label and features the original single mix of the song. They started out as a skiffle act from Ealing called The Playboys, and then became an R&B combo, The Tomcats. John (Speedy) Keen, who later was successful as part of Thunderclap Newman, was part of the group for a while. In 1966, The Tomcats went to Spain as Los Tomcats with a new line-up that would later develop into July. There they achieved chart success with four EPs, one of which was all in Spanish! They returned to the UK in 1968, basing themselves in Ealing and recording as July.

6. SHEILA'S BACK IN TOWN Tinkerbell's Fairydust (1969)

The group went through several name and personnel changes before arriving at Tinkerbell's Fairydust. Formed in 1960 by brothers Gerald and Chaz Wade as The Moonrakers, they then became the short-lived Ramrods – short-lived because an American group of that name already existed. Then they were The Ricochets, releasing one single, 'I Should Have Known'. In early 1967, they evolved into The Rush and released two further singles on Decca, 'Happy' and 'Make Mine Music', before finally settling on Tinkerbell's Fairydust, whose debut release was a cover of Spanky And Our Gang's 'Lazy Day'. Six months later, a Bach-inspired single, 'Twenty Ten' was released, and despite heavy promotion from both John Peel and Kenny Everett, the single failed to chart. In January 1969, their third and final single, 'Sheila's Back In Town', appeared but again without success, apart from in Japan where it reached number two – only held off number one by The Beatles' 'Hey Jude'. Towards the end of 1969, Decca records were about to release their debut album but, just days before it was due to hit the shops, they decided to cancel the project. Although copies were pressed and ready to be mailed out to the media for review, most pressings were destroyed. It is now estimated that a mint copy of the vinyl album is worth in excess of £2,000. Only staff working at Decca at the time would have had access to the handful of copies that weren't destroyed.

7. LIGHTEN UP BABY Ty Karim (1966)

Ty was a stunning-looking, tall and elegant LA soul singer with a raw emotive vocal delivery who recorded from the mid-Sixties to early Eighties. Her recordings were mainly original dance-inspired numbers – always very dynamic and great vehicles for her husky voice. The Sixties' tracks are Northern soul at its best and their rarity and excellence has put three of them into the £1000+ bracket, with 'Lighten Up Baby' being one of the most collectable. Sadly, Ty died in 1983. Her daughter Karime, inspired by her mother, moved to the UK eventually, leading to her singing her parents' wonderful music to very appreciative crowds on today's Northern soul circuit – a repertoire that includes a great blues version of 'Lighten Up Baby'.

Ty Karim: a favourite of Northern Soul collectors

8. GIRLS Mark Raymond & The Crowd (1964)

In the late Fifties, Ken Hoban, an employee at one of Cadbury's chocolate factories, formed The Wildcats. Then, by the beginning of the Sixties, he became lead vocalist with The Rayvons. Changing his name to Mark Raymond, the group became a big attraction in the Birmingham area. A chance meeting with agent Bob Wooler, who had gone to see the Rayvons perform at The Majestic Ballroom in Birmingham, resulted in the group being booked to appear at Liverpool's famous Cavern Club where they were well received.

In 1963, Mark was invited to take over as lead vocalist with another local group, The Cyclones, and the following year auditioned for EMI Records' producer Bob Barrett, who offered them a contract. Travelling to London, they recorded several tracks at the famous Abbey Road studios, and one of the group's own songs, 'Girls', was selected as a single. Just prior to the release of the record, it was discovered that there was already an American recording group called The Cyclones, so – a quick name change – and Mark Raymond and The Crowd were born. Despite the commercial appeal of the disc, it somehow missed out on a chart placing and unfortunately would turn out to be their only record release.

9. NOTHING'S TOO GOOD FOR MY BABY The Springers (1966)

This Northern soul classic, 'Nothing's Too Good For My Baby', is so sought-after that in the spring of 2001, a vinyl copy of the single sold for over $5,000 on eBay. The group from Philadelphia recorded a number of tracks with producer Thaddeus Wales, who also named the group and worked with studio musicians who evolved into MFSB who helped create the Philly sound.

10. WHEN A BOY FALLS IN LOVE Mel Carter (1963)

This is a truly hard-to-get single. It's also hard to even hear the thing: there have been several Mel Carter compilations released over the years, but they all managed to leave this track out. Many other artists have recorded the song but this version has been considered the best among soul fans.

It was written by Sam Cooke and was the title track to an extremely rare 1963 Mel Carter album released on Sam's Derby label. It exchanges hands today at around £300.

11. THERE ARE EIGHT MILLION COSSACK MELODIES AND THIS IS ONE OF THEM Group X (1963)

The single was originally released in a picture sleeve in 1963 and is now quite a valuable and collectable piece of vinyl. They issued one further single later in the same year, 'Roti Calliope', that also fetches good money at actions. For a time it was believed that Group X were, in fact, The Tornados in search of another hit but further investigation suggests they were more likely to have been a lesser-known group, The Mark Leeman Five. Mark himself was tragically killed in a car crash in 1965 just after the group had released their first single under their own name.

12. ELEPHANT RIDER The Hush (1968)

This is a monstrously rare and sought-after slab of psychedelia/ freakbeat from 1968. Great guitar work and vocals from this five-piece who hailed from Manchester. The record was produced by songwriters Albert Hammond and Mike Hazelwood and, as far as we can tell, this was their only single release. The only known line-up of the group are five guys named Peter, Geoff, Chris, John and Mac.

13. 'TIL YOU SAY YOU'LL BE MINE Olivia Newton-John (1966)

Valued by *Record Collector* magazine at around £150 for an original copy of this single, this is far more thrashy and distorted than the tracks Olivia went on to successfully record throughout the Seventies and Eighties. Written by Jackie De Shannon, this became her first venture into the world of recording and was released the year she arrived in London after belatedly claiming a prize of a trip to England for winning an Australian talent contest. Although she was unconvinced she should leave Oz, it was her mother that finally persuaded her to make the move that resulted in her being booked with her friend and then singing partner Pat Carroll on a bill with The Shadows. As a result she met Bruce Welsh, with whom she became involved romantically, and it was this connection that led to an introduction to Cliff Richard and her being booked to appear on his TV shows and future stardom.

14. I HAPPEN TO LOVE YOU The Myddle Class (1966)

This is among the most collectable items by the writers Carole King and Gerry Goffin, as it was one of the few singles issued on the short-lived Tomorrow label, formed by the couple in 1965. The group were championed by a journalist friend and neighbour of the Goffins, Al Aronowitz, who convinced the talented couple to write and produce tracks for his protégées. After spending around $15,000 on the act, Carole is believed to have asked him, 'What are you going to sell us next, The Brooklyn Bridge?' As things turned out, soon after Carole relocated to Los Angeles after her split from Gerry, she married the group's bass player, Charles Larkey, in 1968.

15. BREAK MY MIND Duane Eddy (1969)

The song was written by John D Loudermilk and became something of a country classic. Although Eddy's version, released in 1969, was recorded for the Reprise label in The States, it came out on CBS in the UK. Since then it has become something of a rarity and quite a collector's item, although surprisingly doesn't come with a price value of much more than £10, should you be lucky enough to find a copy.

16. SAVE MY SOUL Wimple Winch (1966)

Should you be fortunate enough to find an original copy of this single on the Fontana label in your collection, then you'll be pleased to know that in mint condition it's worth over £400. Formed in 1961 as The Silhouettes but, with any number of groups with that name, later changed it to The Four Just Men, playing their first gig at Liverpool's Cavern Club on 22 August, 1962 with Gerry & The Pacemakers and The Beatles. In 1964 they recorded their first single, 'That's My Baby', for Parlophone. After a few

It wasn't until they renamed themselves Wimple Winch that they could be sure they had a band name that hadn't already been taken

more unsuccessful releases, changes in personnel and a new manager, they became Wimple Winch, signing to the Fontana label. Their first single, 'What's Been Done', followed by 'Save My Soul' – both recorded at their initial session – brought them a huge following.

17. WE'RE GONNA LOVE Wilfred Jackie Edwards (1960)

This single was issued in the UK in 1960 on the Starlite label and was this artist's first British release. It is believed to have been one of the earliest Jamaican singles to be issued here as a 45, and the original single has become a rare collectors' item. Jackie was often described as the Nat King Cole of Jamaica and was a huge star of the island. In 1962, after being spotted by Chris Blackwell, owner of the Island Records' label, he was persuaded to relocate to the UK, where he became more successful as a songwriter than as a performer, composing three top-20 hits for The Spencer Davis Group and 'Come On Home' for Wayne Fontana. He suffered a fatal heart attack on August 15, 1992, aged just 54.

18. HE DOESN'T GO ABOUT IT RIGHT We The People (1966)

Should you be fortunate to own a mint copy of 'He Doesn't Go About It Right' issued in the UK on the London American Label in 1966, you could expect to sell it at an auction for well over £100. The group released three other singles in 1966: 'My Brother The Man' for the small Hotline label, before signing to Challenge where they released 'Mirror Of Your Mind', followed by this collectable, 'He Doesn't Go About It Right'.

19. BLACK SHEEP R.I.P The Australian Playboys (1967)

In their homeland down under, they were known simply as The Playboys but renamed The Australian Playboys for other territories to avoid confusion with Gary Lewis & The Playboys. Working as a backing group for fellow Australian Normie Rowe, the group came to England in 1966 without a recording contract or any promise of work. They thought their luck had changed when Andrew Oldham signed them to his Immediate label and issued their only UK release, a deranged reworking of the nursery rhyme 'Ba Ba Blacksheep', which now exchanges hands for over £1000 – but watch out for bootleg copies. The group broke up in 1967 and most of them returned home, although guitarist and singer Mick Rogers later went on to join Manfred Mann's Earthband.

20. THE FOX HAS GONE TO GROUND Bamboo Shoot (1968)

No one has yet managed to discover the true identity of the group Bamboo Shoot. This was their one and only single release, which they recorded for EMI's Columbia imprint, now exchanges hands for around £250. Many have compared the lead vocalist to Steve Marriott in this song that takes a rather unexpected turn when it goes semi-religious half way through the track with gongs and chants.

21. HIDE AND SEEK The Thyrds (1964)

An original copy of this hard-to-track-down single, first issued on the tiny Oak label in 1964, can fetch as much as £250 in mint condition. A somewhat less valuable re-issue by Decca, later that same year, is still worth around £50. As far as we can tell, this was the group's only release, but both issues had different B-sides. The Oak single had the band's interpretation of the classic R&B song, 'Got My Mojo Working', as the flip, whilst the Decca release had a song called 'No Time Like The Present' as the other track.

22. APPLES AND ORANGES Pink Floyd (1967)

The follow-up to 'See Emily Play', today a mint copy of this single in its original picture sleeve on EMI's Columbia label would exchange hands for around £150. This was the last Floyd single to be written by Syd Barrett, who soon after its release was replaced by David Gilmour. The band filmed a promotional clip in a Belgian fruit market for this track – one of the few songs recorded by Pink Floyd with a 'love' theme.

23. WALK ON GUILDED SPLINTERS Marsha Hunt (1969)

Former model and one-time girlfriend of Mick Jagger, Marsha Hunt grew up in Philadelphia but moved to Britain in the mid-Sixties, living for a time in Edinburgh. In 1967 she met Mike Ratledge of Soft Machine. At the time she was having trouble acquiring a visa and she persuaded him to marry her just before the band headed to France on an extensive tour. Their relationship was short but they remained married and good friends for many years. In 1968 she found fame when she starred as Dionne in the first rock musical, *Hair*. The following year she appeared at The Isle Of Wight Music Festival with her own band, White Trash, and released her first single, a cover of Dr John's 'Walk On Guilded Splinters' (sic) that is now a most collectable 45.

24. I'M A LOVER NOT A FIGHTER **The Brand (1964)**

The Brand were another Birmingham-based group whose wild and raw sound stretched to just this one single for the Piccadilly label. However, their limited legacy made quite an impact on record collectors and this revival of Lazy Lester's song created plenty of excitement without the need for any extra session musicians. A mint copy of this single was valued at £100 by *Record Collector* magazine.

25. 10,000 WORDS IN A CARDBOARD BOX
The Aquarian Age (1968)

John Wood formed the group with John Alder, both of whom were still part of Keith West's group Tomorrow when they recorded this self-penned song that was produced and arranged by Mark Wirtz. Keith was enjoying success as a solo performer with his 'Excerpt From A Teenage Opera'. They released this one single that now fetches around £150 for a mint-condition copy. They also recorded a future track, 'Me', that was never released, as John suffered a drug-induced nervous breakdown and cirrhosis of the liver that nearly killed him. The situation made him rethink his way of life and he decided to quit the music business, thus Aquarian Age never really got off the ground and Tomorrow stopped playing together at the end of the Sixties.

26. I MUST BE DREAMING **Billy Fury (1964)**

'I Must Be Dreaming' has a special significance to Billy Fury fans. The song was announced in 1964 as Billy's next release, but 'I'm Lost Without You' appeared in the shops instead and subsequently all tapes of the song were deemed lost forever. A BBC radio recording of the song was discovered but a real breakthrough came in 2006, when an astounding version was found in the record company's archives but, to this day, hasn't been given an official release.

27. I'M READY **The Quakers (1965)**

The song was written by blues legend Willie Dixon and performed here by The Quakers, a highly-rated band who released this single on the small but successful independent Oriole label in 1965. After that, there is little more we can tell you about this disc but they did release a single on the little-known Studio 36 label in the same year called 'She's Alright', which is currently listed at a value of £450 plus – not surprising as there were only 50 copies pressed.

28. I FOUGHT THE LAW The Bobby Fuller Four (1966)
UK No 33/US No 9

Written by Sonny Curtis in 1961 and first recorded by The Crickets that year. In the States, an earlier Bobby Fuller version was originally released on the small Exeter label in 1964 and sold very few copies – but making that label's recording a very collectable item worth around £200. As the single entered the American top 10, Bobby was found dead in his mother's parked car near his home in California. It was put down to suicide due to asphyxiation but most who knew him believe to this day that he was murdered.

29. SECURITY Thane Russell (1967)

This was a cover of an Otis Redding classic and a huge hit across Australia, but sank without trace in the UK. The identity of Thane Russell was for a time something of a mystery, with reports coming from Oz that it might have been Mick Jagger. This proved to be untrue, although he is thought to have been the tea boy at one of The Stones' recording sessions. Thane's real name is Doug Gibbons. He secured a deal with CBS, and changed his name for the two singles he recorded for the company, which are both worth around £130 in the collector's market.

30. ALL FOR YOU Earl Van Dyke & The Soul Brothers (1965)

More Motown mysteries surround keyboard player Earl Van Dyke, who was the leader of the renowned label's house band known as both The Funk Brothers and The Soul Brothers. They were featured on most of the label's hit records and Van Dyke also recorded a few singles under his own name and toured the UK with the very first Motown review. Composed by William 'Mickey' Stevenson, Ivy Joe Hunter and Henry Cosby, this was originally titled 'Make No Mistake'. Lyrics were later added and Marvin Gaye recorded it as 'Lucky, Lucy Me', before Jimmy Ruffin got his hands on it when it became 'All For You'. Neither version was given a release at the time. Although this version shows up in *Rare Record Guide*, there's no evidence that any copies were ever pressed.

31. TO THE ENDS OF THE EARTH Tony Middleton (1966)

Tony Middleton was born in Richmond, Virginia, later moving to New York. There, he developed skills in various sports and began boxing as an amateur in his late twenties. He became the lead singer with a group called The Five Willows, later to be called just The Willows, before leaving them in 1957 and finding a strong cult following around Europe as a solo singer. This 1966 release on Polydor is his cover of a Nat King Cole hit that has become a much sought-after single, in mint condition fetching a price close to £500.

32. SOME THINGS ARE BETTER LEFT UNSAID
Ketty Lester (1964)

The daughter of a farmer, Ketty was born Revoyda Frierson in Arkansas. She was one of 15 children and began singing in clubs in the early Fifties under the name of Ketty Lester and later toured as a singer with Cab Calloway's Orchestra. In 1961, she signed to the American Era label, releasing a single, 'I'm A Fool To Want You'; but DJs preferred the B-side, a revival of 'Love Letters', and turned it into a hit. In 1962 she toured the UK supporting The Everly Brothers, but was unable to repeat her success on the recording front. In 1964, she recorded what is now a highly collectable Northern soul Classic, 'Some Things Are Better Left Unsaid', copies of which now exchange hands for over £100.

33. BOOGIE CHILDREN **The Playboys with John Fred (1964)**

You may remember 'Judy In Disguise With Glasses' by John Fred & His Playboy Band from 1968. Four years earlier, he had recorded 'Boogie Children', a lesser-known track that was first released in America on the Jewel label – to whom John Fred & The Playboys were under contract. However, a couple of months later, the same record appeared on N-Joy, for whom it is believed the track was originally recorded, but this time was released simply as John Fred. So whether you have a copy by The Playboys or by John Fred, it's still a much sought-after 45.

34. HEAD OVER HEELS **The Stylos (1964)**

Popular in their hometown of Manchester, The Stylos were recognised as a great R&B combo. Although they only managed to achieve one record release through the Liberty label, the single has now become a collectors' item that would fetch around £120 in mint condition. Their self-penned 'Head Over Heels' is still considered one of the best examples of Manchester rhythm and blues from the Sixties.

35. WHATCHA GONNA DO
The Lloyd Alexander Real Estate (1967)

The wonderfully-named Lloyd Alexander Real Estate were a local group from Hackney in the East End of London who later evolved into the progressive rock band, Audience. This collectable 45 from 1967 that was released on the President label would cost you a cool £100 in mint condition, if you were fortunate enough to turn up a copy. The main vocalist was Howard Werth, whose middle name was Alexander. Although he wasn't present on this track, his name probably was the inspiration behind the collective group's billing.

36. TOFFEE APPLE SUNDAY **Toby Twirl (1968)**

The track was produced by Wayne Bickerton and written by the Newcastle-based group's drummer, John Reed, and guitarist, Nick Thorburn. The song was inspired by the Spanish City funfair in Whitley Bay, North East England. A mint copy of this single on the Decca label is currently valued at just over £200.

37. TWO LOVERS MAKE ONE FOOL **The Serenaders (1963)**

The Cleethorpes Northern Soul Weekender was a big event in the town where a selection of favourite tracks were performed live by artists at the famous and longest-running weekender venue in the country. This track by The Serenaders with Sidney Barnes was a favourite amongst the crowd, and a copy of the original single has sold for over £100.

38. INDIVIDUALITY **Hoyt Hudson (1962)**

It's fairly certain that this single by American singer Hoyt Hudson – who worked mainly in the clubs around the Houston area in Texas – wasn't ever released in the UK. There is very little information about the artist, but this is a well sought-after record by collectors and a copy in reasonable condition was on sale via the internet for just over £90.

39. RED SILK STOCKINGS **Freddy Finkhouse Four (1964)**

This ultra-rare single features legendary Memphis rock 'n'roll guitarist Travis Wammack, who wrote and recorded his first song at the age of 11. By the time he was 17, he'd hit the American charts with the instrumental 'Scratchy'. He worked as a session musician at the renowned Fame Studios in Muscle Shoals from the early Sixties until

1975, and in 1984 became Little Richard's bandleader for 11 years. The rare-to-find 'Red Silk Stockings' features American session musicians and, as far as we can tell, failed to get released in the UK.

40. EVERYBODY'S TALKING 'BOUT MY BABY
The Beatstalkers (1965)

The group were formed in Glasgow in 1962 and by 1964 had become one of the city's leading music attractions specialising in covering rare and obscure R&B songs. Dubbed as Scotland's answer to The Beatles, a 1965 open-air concert in Glasgow had to be abandoned when fans rushed the stage. That same year they were signed to Decca and released their first single, 'Everybody's Talking 'Bout My Baby', with two follow-ups in quick succession, none of which managed to capture the record-buying public's attention. Moving to London in 1967, they secured a residency at the famous Marquee Club and switched labels to CBS, but still that hit record eluded them. They then released 'Silver Tree Top School For Boys', written by David Bowie, again to little interest, and the group called it a day in 1969 after their equipment was stolen. Today, however, all their singles are highly collectable and fetch around £100 each.

41. MINE EXCLUSIVELY The Olympics (1966)

The song was written by Shirley Mae Matthews, who gained quite a reputation in America for singing backing vocals for many leading names, including Barbra Streisand, Neil Diamond, Paul McCartney

The Beatstalkers: initially praised as Scotland's answer to The Beatles, they released a David Bowie song, but split up, hitless, in 1969

and Elton John. This high-energy track was recorded by The Olympics in 1966 and made the American top 40 R&B charts, but didn't find a release in the UK until 1969 when it was licensed to the soul label, Action. It was also one of the first records to cause a demand for 'old soul' – what we now call Northern Soul Classics – and this one would fetch around £80.

42. BAJA John Paul Jones (1964)

This is indeed a very rare record, released on the Pye label in 1964 by John Paul Jones, and is a highly collectable 45 for those seeking Led Zeppelin-related material. Jones, of course, became the bass player with Zeppelin after he ended his association with the Tony Meehan Group. 'Baja', copies of which now fetch around £150, was composed by Lee Hazlewood and produced by The Rolling Stones' manager, Andrew Loog Oldham

43. REFLECTIONS OF CHARLES BROWN Rupert's People (1967)

The complex story of Rupert's People began when Howard Conder, manager of a group named Sweet Feeling, asked his band to record 'Charles Brown', a song he'd written with the group's Rob Lynton. They released it on the B-side of their 1967 single 'All So Long Ago'; but, weeks later, with a new arrangement based on Bach's 'Air On A G String', Conder recorded the song again with a group called The Fleur De Lys, whom he'd heard perform at a London club. For the purposes of the record, the band were renamed Rupert's People and the title changed to 'Reflections Of Charles Brown'. Soon after the release of the record, The Fleur De Lys decided they didn't want any further involvement with the project and pulled out, leaving Conder with the problem of putting together a new group. Original copies of this single now exchange hands for around £60.

44. OPEN THE DOOR TO YOUR HEART Darrell Banks (1966)
US No 27

Darrell Eubanks was born in Mansfield, Ohio. Later, the Eubanks' family moved to Buffalo, New York, where Darrell began singing in a local church choir. His debut single was also the first release for the small Revilot label. Although Banks claimed to have written the song, the fact was heavily disputed by Donnie Elbert some years later, who claimed that he originally named it 'Walk Right In'. A court battle pursued and Elbert finally won out. There were further complications with the UK release as promo copies were distributed, at the same time, by both Decca's London label and EMI's imprint, Stateside. After more legal wrangles, it came to light that EMI had gained the official rights, with the upshot that the rare London 45s are now worth over £1000.

45. LUCY LEE Lloyd George (1962)

In the Sixties, the London label licensed 'obscurities' from many American labels, and this is the reason why numerous collectables today are on this particular label. And they really don't come much more obscure than this 1962 country-blues single, 'Lucy Lee' by Lloyd George that was released in The States on Imperial. Lee was almost 64 when he recorded this track, although he had first recorded in the early forties as part of the comedy duo Lonzo and Oscar, and again in the following decade as Ken Marvin.

46. I THINK I LOVE YOU Helen Troy (1962)

This thundering Northern Soul favourite by New Yorker Helen Troy presently holds a price tag of around £200 (and growing) for a mint American pressing on the Kapp label. The song was written, and believed to have been originally recorded, by vocal group The Sierras.

47. KING OF SIAM
East Of Eden (1968)

In 1971, radio sets across the UK were being turned up to the sound of the top-10 hit 'Jig-A-Jig' by East Of Eden that featured the lively violin playing of Dave Arbus, a founder member of the group who were formed in 1968. It was in that year that they recorded a one-off single called 'King Of Siam' for the Atlantic label, before they signed to Deram in 1971. This has become a most collectable item, as it has, as far as we are aware, never yet appeared on any album or compilation.

48. OLE MAN RIVER The Righteous Brothers (1965)

The song was written by Jerome Kern and Oscar Hammerstein II for their 1927 Broadway musical *Showboat*, in which it was performed by Jules Bledsoe. It also gave Paul Whitman and His Orchestra an American number one in 1928, with vocals by Bing Crosby. However, the most well-known rendition was sung by Paul Robeson in the 1936 movie version of the show. The Righteous Brothers recorded their version for their now long-deleted 1965 album *You've Lost That Lovin' Feelin'*.

49. THE DAY BEFORE YESTERDAY Gordon Lightfoot (1963)

This very rare single was released in the UK on the Fontana label and credited to 'Gordie Lightfoot'. Although it's one of 11 songs he recorded as a soloist back in 1962, at a time when he was part of a duo called The Two Tones with Terry Whelan, 'The Day Before Yesterday' wasn't released until the following year. It was the only song that wasn't included on an album of those tracks called *Early Lightfoot* that was eventually released in 1971.

50. WINKIE DOLL Billy Dolton (1961)

Co-Written by Jerry Fuller, 'Winkie Doll', about a short-lived Japanese dance craze, was released in the UK in 1961 on the Parlophone label, and went virtually unnoticed as no one had any idea who Billy Dolton was or where he came from. Years later, it emerged that he was none other than successful country star Glen Campbell using a pseudonym. The single has since become a collector's item, although copies have been found for around £15.

THEY SANG IT FIRST

This section of the book looks at a collection of hit songs that had been recorded prior to the version or versions that finally made it into the charts.

1. SOME OF YOUR LOVIN' **The Honey Bees (1965)**

Written by Carole King and Gerry Goffin, who produced this original American version of 'Some Of Your Lovin'' with a female group called The Honey Bees (who were The Cookies under another name, with a different lead singer). The line-up was believed to have included Barbara Alston, a former member of The Crystals. Carole King also released her own version of the song a few months later.

2. BEND ME, SHAPE ME **The Outsiders (1967)**

The group were so named because they considered themselves to have been physically mismatched as they came in all shapes and sizes, ranging from founder member Tom King, who stood six foot five inches, to lead vocalist Sonny Geraci, who was an entire foot shorter. In 1966, they changed their name from The Starfires to The Outsiders and achieved four American top-40 hits in that year before being offered 'Bend Me Shape Me' by songwriters Scott English and Larry Weiss. The group duly buried this track in the middle of their debut album. The composers were still convinced the song had the potential to be a hit, and a few months later The American Breed took it into the top five, a feat repeated in the UK by Amen Corner.

3. THE WRITING ON THE WALL **Adam Wade (1965)** *US No 5*

Released in America as a double A-side with a song called 'Point Of No Return', this release quickly ran out of steam mainly due to an alternative version by Gene McDaniels that reached number 21. That was of little concern to Adam Wade as 'The Writing On The Wall' continued to sell thousands of copies, but lost out yet again in the UK when it was covered by Tommy Steele, whose version reached number 30.

4. KEEP ON DANCIN' **The Gentrys (1965) US No 4**

This garage rock band from Memphis, Tennessee, had vocals by Bruce Bowles, Larry Raspberry and Jimmy Hart, who later took up managing professional wrestlers and was known as 'The Mouth From The South'.

Hulk Hogan was one of his biggest clients. The song 'Keep On Dancing' later became the 1971 debut hit for The Bay City Rollers.

5. A WALKING MIRACLE **The Essex (1963)** *US No 12*

The Essex were originally formed by a group of marines who were still in active service when they had their biggest hit, 'Easier Said Than Done', which gave them an American number-one hit in 1963. The single also became a minor hit in the UK where it was becoming increasingly difficult for American acts to break through owing to the outbreak of Beatlemania, which hadn't yet crossed the Atlantic. The follow-up single, 'A Walking Miracle', just failed to make the American top 10 but missed the UK charts completely. However, this song eventually made the UK top 10 in the Seventies via a cover by Limmie And Family Cooking.

6. BYE BYE BABY **The Four Seasons (1965)** *US No 12*

Written by Bob Crewe and Bob Gaudio, this became their seventeenth American top-40 hit but failed to register in the UK. However, the song was successfully revived in 1975 by The Bay City Rollers, who took the song to the top of the UK charts, selling in excess of a million copies in the first six weeks of its release.

7. DON'T MAKE ME OVER **Dionne Warwick (1962)** *US No 21*

Her debut hit in the US had a successful cover version in the UK in 1966 by The Swinging Blue Jeans, which reached number 31 in the charts. Dionne's superior version was written by Burt Bacharach and Hal David and arranged and produced by Burt. Dionne wanted to record the writers' song 'Make it Easy On Yourself', but was told that it had already been given to Jerry Butler. Furious, Dionne stormed out of Burt's office shouting 'Don't make me over, man!', inspiring him to write the song exclusively for her – after which, all was forgiven.

8. WALKING IN THE RAIN **The Ronettes (1964)** *US No 23*

The record amazingly failed to make the British charts, although the song was successfully covered three years later by The Walker Brothers. Written by Barry Mann and Cynthia Weil with producer Phil Spector, and arranged by the legendary Jack Nitzsche, the record earned sound engineer Larry Levine a Grammy nomination for his work on the production.

9. SKI-ING IN THE SNOW **The Invitations (1966)**

One of their previous releases, 'What's Wrong With Me Baby', had been a popular Northern Soul hit. One year later came 'Ski-ing In The Snow', which became a much sought-after single in the Sixties and was later covered in the UK by Wigan's Ovation, reaching number 12 in the charts in 1975. The Invitations' lead singer, William Morris, died in November 2004, aged 66.

10. PAPER ROSES **Anita Bryant (1960)** *US No 5/UK No 24*

The song was covered in the UK by The Kaye Sisters, who had the bigger hit here, reaching number seven in the charts. Anita Bryant first sang in public in 1942 at the age of two when she performed 'Jesus Loves Me' to a congregation at an Oklahoma Baptist church. Anita was, on all accounts, still-born, but the quick-thinking doctor ordered a pan of iced water, stuck her head in it and whacked her extremely hard, forcing her to draw breath. She signed her first recording contract in 1958 with New York label Carlton, where she achieved her first top-40 hit with 'Til There was You', from the musical *The Music Man*. Several more releases followed, but it was in the spring of 1960 she achieved her biggest hit with 'Paper Roses', selling over a million copies in America alone. The song was later successfully revived in 1973 when Marie Osmond's version reached number two.

11. (THERE'S) ALWAYS SOMETHING THERE TO REMIND ME **Lou Johnson (1964)** *US No 49*

This original version of the number-one hit for Sandie Shaw was written and produced by Burt Bacharach for Lou Johnson, a former gospel singer from Brooklyn, New York, who established himself as one of the finest interpreters of the complex Bacharach and David compositions, a view even expressed by Dionne Warwick and the composers themselves; yet many of his recordings would become more successful in the hands of other artists. Other songs he'd been the first to record include, 'Message To Martha', a UK hit for Adam Faith, and 'Reach Out For Me', a hit for Dionne Warwick.

12. PAINTER MAN **The Creation (1966)** *UK No 36*

This was their only single to make the top 40 and features an instrumental break by guitarist Eddie Phillips, whose trademark was playing with a violin bow. He was reputedly the first musician to develop this technique although Jimmy Page would do the same, gaining much greater acclaim. When they played 'Painter Man' on stage, singer Kenny Patrick would create images by spraying paint onto a canvas, and then a member of the road crew would set light to the artwork. 'Painter Man' was successfully revived in 1979 by Boney M when they took the song into the UK top 10.

13. BREAKAWAY Jackie De Shannon (1963)
This is Jackie's original 1963 demo recording featuring Leon Russell on piano. It was recorded at the time when Al Bennett was the head of her record label, Liberty, and was trying to build a catalogue of copyrights for their publishing arm. They spent just under an hour recording the track, after which the song was sent to Irma Thomas who eventually released a version as a single that went virtually unnoticed. However, a good song will always come through, and two decades later Tracy Ullman achieved her first chart success with her 1983 top-10 hit version of the song.

14. I'M INTO SOMETHING GOOD Earl-Jean (1964) *US No 38*
The Cookies were a female vocal group who recorded the original version of 'Chains', which was made popular by The Beatles on their first LP. The Cookies were Darlene McRea, Margaret Ross and Dorothy Jones, and the three girls also provided backing vocals for many top American recording stars, including Neil Sedaka, Little Eva and Ray Charles. In fact, Darlene left The Cookies to join Ray's own backing group The Raeletts, and her sister, Earl-Jean, replaced her, releasing her solo single that was covered in the UK by Herman's Hermits and reached number one.

15. YOUNG, GIFTED AND BLACK Nina Simone (1969)
The original version of the song that became a top-five hit in 1970 for reggae duo Bob and Marcia, this song was the final uncompromising political statement Nina recorded for the RCA label. The title was taken from a play of the same name written by her friend Lorraine Hansberry, who had died at the age of 34 from cancer. Later it became something of an anthem of the Civil Rights movement after one of its members declared it to be the national song of black people in America.

16. STAY Maurice Williams & The Zodiacs (1961) *US No 1/UK No 14*
The Hollies covered the song in 1963, reaching number eight in the charts and giving them their first breakthrough into the top 10. Maurice Williams

and The Zodiacs originally recorded as The Gladiators and had a minor hit in 1957 with his own composition and original version of 'Little Darling', which was made famous the same year by The Diamonds. Maurice also wrote 'Stay' but was told by his record label to change a line in it that said, 'Let's have another smoke', believing that radio stations wouldn't play anything that encouraged young people to take up cigarettes.

17. SAILOR (YOUR HOME IS THE SEA) Lolita (1960) *US No 5*

This was the original recording of a song 'Seaman' that was covered successfully in the UK by both Anne Shelton, whose version reached number 10, and Petula Clark, who achieved a number one; these releases, both in 1960, kept Lolita's versions at bay. Lolita was the show business name of Austrian-born Ditta Zuza Einzinger, whose singing in a local church choir led to her winning a regular spot on a radio show in Linz. She was signed to Polydor records and made a name for herself in German-speaking Europe, giving her an unlikely American top-five single.

18. SILENCE IS GOLDEN The Four Seasons (1964)

The Four seasons did in fact record the original version of 'Silence Is Golden' for the B-side of their big hit single, 'Rag Doll'. However, The Tremeloes, being a big fan of the group's tight harmonies, decided to make the song their own, giving them their first and only UK number one after the departure of Brian Poole.

19. A LOVE LIKE YOURS (DON'T COME KNOCKING EVERY DAY) Martha & The Vandellas (1966)

Back in 1963, the song, originally recorded by Martha & The Vandellas, was the B-side to their US hit 'Heatwave'. Three years later, the song was once again relegated to the B-side of Kim Weston's 1966 single 'Helpless'. Writers Holland-Dozier and Holland needn't have worried because later the same year Phil Spector got hold of the song and recorded it with Ike and Tina Turner, achieving a UK top-20 hit with it.

20. I JUST DON'T KNOW WHAT TO DO WITH MYSELF Tommy Hunt (1962)

No one has ever been able to explain the failure of the breath-taking original version of the Burt Bacharach and Hal David song 'I Just Don't Know What To Do With Myself', by Pittsburgh-born Tommy Hunt.

Produced by Jerry Leiber and Mike Stoller with Bacharach's own arrangement, it had everything going for it. Nevertheless, the former Flamingos' lead singer could do no better with his fourth release of 1962 than with his previous three. A copy of his record found its way into the hands of Dusty Springfield via Mr Bacharach, who was scheduled to produce some tracks with her in 1964; but, due to prior commitments on his part, this never happened. This was one of the songs they were hoping to record; but she still took the song to producer Johnny Franz and Ivor Raymonde who came up with a great arrangement. This became Dusty's third solo single, and it reached number three in the charts.

21. I LIVE FOR THE SUN The Sunrays (1965)

The song was successfully covered in the UK in 1968 when it became the debut hit for Vanity Fare. The Sunrays' record was produced by Murry Wilson, the sour-grapes father of Beach Boy members Brian, Carl and Dennis, who was determined to out-do his famous sons after being fired as their manager. The vengeful Murry was hoping to create a bigger success than his children's group. It's interesting to note that the Tower label, a subsidiary of Capitol, was started just for The Sunrays.

22. MR CUSTER Larry Verne (1960) *US No 1*

Eighty-four years, three months and 15 days after the climactic battle fought at Little Big Horn between the troops led by General George

The Sunrays were a Beach Boys-style Californian group. They were actually produced by Murry Wilson, father of three of the Beach Boys

Custer and 3000 Sioux Indians, which left Custer and all his men dead, Larry Verne's comical plea to the General, telling him he didn't want to fight, was at the top of the American charts. Turned down by every label in the country, the copy of the disc the writers were taking round had worn out, so they went into the studio to cut a new one. Herb Newman, the owner of Era Records, happened to be in the hallway and overheard the track and offered to release it. Ten months after the original session, a shortened version made it into the stores. In the UK, the song was covered by Charlie Drake and reached number 12 in the charts. The original American version topped the charts in the second week in October, for just one week, before being replaced by 'Save The Last Dance For Me' by The Drifters.

23. SHORTNIN' BREAD The Bell Notes (1960)

The original American recording of a song that was based on a traditional folk song from 1905, successfully covered at the same time in the UK by the Viscounts. The Bell Notes were from Long Island in New York and were regular performers at a bar in The Bronx. In 1959 they achieved an American top-10 hit with 'I've Had It' for the small Time label. Then, in 1960, they signed to Autograph Records and issued 'Little Girl in Blue', followed by two singles for Madison Records, the latter being 'Shortnin' Bread', which hit just number 96 in the U.S. and was to be their last hit before they broke up by 1962.

24. TIME Jerry Jackson (1961)

Craig Douglas was always one for covering American originals. After the success of 'A Hundred Pounds Of Clay', he heard a record by little-known singer Jerry Jackson called 'Time'. With his cover of this track he had yet another smash. Jackson's original came about when the former automobile body-shop worker walked through the doors of New York's Brill building and met Buddy Kaye and Phil Springer – Springer being one of the first songwriters to produce their own material. They liked what they heard from Jackson and recorded their song 'Time' on his first session.

25. EVERLASTING LOVE Robert Knight (1967) UK No 19

Knight made his recording debut with a group called The Paramounts who were signed to Dot records in 1960, releasing 'Free Me' the following year. After a number of failed singles, they broke up but, still under contract to the label, they were all prevented from recording for over four years. Knight went to Tennessee State University to study chemistry and whilst there formed The Fairlanes, with whom he was spotted performing by Buzz Cason and Mac Gayden, owners of the small Rising Sons label who signed him in 1967. They had just written 'Everlasting Love' and agreed he had the right voice for the song. The record reached number 13 on the Hot 100 and was covered in the UK by The Love Affair, who took it to number one. In 1968, Knight released the single 'The Power Of Love', with 'Love On A Mountain Top' on the B-side. Over five years later in 1973, with the growing popularity of Northern Soul music, the DJs discovered the hidden B-side and created a huge demand, resulting in its UK reissue and eventual top-10 chart placing.

26. THE PIED PIPER The Changin' Times (1965)

The 'Pied Piper,' a UK hit for both Crispian St Peters and Bob and Marcia, was written by Artie Kornfeld and Steve Duboff, who were founder members of a band named The Changin' Times that went on tour as the opening act to Sonny & Cher in 1965. The pair also wrote the Sixties American hits 'The Rain, The Park And Other Things' and 'We Can Fly' for The Cowsills. Steve went on to become a record company executive and wrote songs for, amongst others, The Turtles, Ringo Starr and The Monkees, whilst Artie, who by the time he was 24 also held a senior position in a music company, had written over 60 American hits for the likes of Freddy Cannon, Gene Pitney, The Shirelles and Connie Francis, as well as being one of the founders of the famous 1969 Woodstock festival.

27. YESTERDAY HAS GONE Little Anthony & The Imperials (1967)

A UK hit for Cupid's Inspiration that was originally recorded by Little Anthony And The Imperials and taken from the album *Reflections*, with 11 of the 12 tracks written by one of the great unsung heroes of soul music, Teddy Randazzo.

28. IF YOU GOTTA MAKE A FOOL OF SOMEBODY
James Ray (1961) *US No 22*

Successfully covered later in Britain, giving Freddy and The Dreamers their first hit with their version that reached number three in the UK charts. James Ray was once homeless, living rough on a roof in Washington, D.C. He had released a single in 1959 as Little Jimmy Ray but when the record flopped, he fell on hard times. A couple of years later, Gerry Granahan, the boss of Caprice records, heard him singing in the street and took him into the studio to record 'If You Gotta Make A Fool Of Somebody'. Ray was in his early twenties when he died in 1964, reportedly of a drug overdose.

29. MUSTANG SALLY Sir Mack Rice (1965)

The original version of the song by composer Sir Mac Rice. Rice was a member of vocal group The Falcons from 1957 to 1963. After that he was signed to the Blue Rock label, a soul music subsidiary of Mercury, after being introduced to Andre Williams, who ran the Chicago operation. The introduction came through Ted White, who at that time was married to Aretha Franklin. One day, Ted invited Mac round to their home to play a couple of songs to his wife. Whilst playing 'Mustang Sally' that he originally called 'Mustang Mama', it was Aretha who suggested changing it to Sally because of the part of the song where he sang, 'Ride, Sally, ride'.

30. WILD THING The Wild Ones (1965)

Many believe that 'Wild Thing' was a Troggs original song. Well, it's not. In 1965, one-time recording artist Gerry Granahan was having huge success as a producer for United Artists records and signed New York rock band The Wild Ones – a competent group that lacked their own material, who needed to be launched with a hit single. Gerry contacted songwriter Chip Taylor and asked him to come up with a song, resulting in him sending 'Wild Thing' along in time for their recording session. No one took much notice of the song and the band vanished without trace apart from drummer Jordan Christopher, who became an actor, appearing in films including 'The Return Of The Magnificent Seven'.

31. SOMETHING STUPID Carson & Gaile (1967)

C. Carson Parks, the older brother of Van Dyke Parks, got into folk music in the late Fifties, forming a duo named The Steeletown Two in Los Angeles where he'd taken a job with a company that made TV commercials. Parks later formed a new group with his brother, calling themselves The Steeletown Three. Barely scraping together a living, Carson joined various other groups before he met Gaile Foot, whom he married in the mid-Sixties. Together they recorded an album as Carson and Gaile and from it came their first single, 'Something Stupid'. Later, the song was to catch the attention of Frank Sinatra, who decided to record it with his daughter Nancy. Their version went on to sell millions of copies around the world.

32. BABY SITTIN' BOOGIE **Ralf Bendix & Little Elizabeth (1961)**

Bendix, who was also known by his birth name Karl Heinz Schwab, recorded 'Baby Sittin' Boogie', a hit for Buzz Clifford in 1961. The Bendix version was first released in German as 'Baby Sitter Boogie' and featured Little Elizabeth, who, as far as we can tell, was his baby daughter.

33. ALONE AGAIN OR **Love (1968)**

Although now considered a rock classic – and The Damned made the top 40 in 1987 with their version – the record was never a major hit. Love's recording was first released in 1968 but failed to make the charts either here or in America. It was re-issued in the US in 1970 and this time just managed to creep into the Hot 100 at number 99. The group's lead singer, Arthur Lee, was sentenced to 12 years in jail in 1995 for the illegal possession of a gun but served only five and a half years after an appeal court found the prosecutor at his original trial guilty of misconduct and the charge was reversed. The following year, Lee put together a new incarnation of Love.

Freddy Cannon: his records were as explosive as his surname

34. BUZZ BUZZ A DIDDLE IT
Freddy Cannon (1961)

A minor American hit that was successfully revived in the UK by British group Matchbox, reaching number 22 in

The Valentinos: Bobby Womack's band released 'It's All Over Now' a mere month or so before The Stones' version

1980. Written by Frank C. Slay and the Four Seasons' producer, Bob Crewe, it has often been described as the best Bo Diddley record never recorded by Bo Diddley himself. Cannon's nickname was 'Boom Boom' because of his big-sounding records that leapt out of tinny car radios and portable record players, back when rock 'n'roll was first taking over the music industry's consciousness.

35. IT'S ALL OVER NOW The Valentinos (1964)

Written by Shirley and Bobby Womack, and originally recorded by The Valentinos, who were Bobby, Cecil and Harry Womack. They were signed to Sam Cooke's Sar label and wanted to record the song with a full orchestral backing, but Cooke overruled them saying it would spoil the sound. It was released in the spring of 1964, the same time The Rolling Stones were on their first tour of North America. The Stones got to hear the disc and recorded it nine days later at the Chess Studios in Chicago. Bobby Womack was furious. Six months later, when he received the royalty cheque for the song, he informed Mick Jagger that he could have any song he wanted.

36. MOUNTAIN OF LOVE Harold Dorman (1960) *US No 21*

Mississippi-born Harold Dorman was an American one-hit wonder, whose only hit was probably better known to many Stateside music fans from the 1964 remake by Johnny Rivers that became a bigger hit. British fans may well remember the Kenny Lynch cover; but Dorman's is not only the original version, he also wrote the song. As a composer, he also enjoyed another major US success in 1974 when his song 'Mississippi Cotton Picking Delta Town' became a top-five Country hit for Charley Pride.

37. BOSSA NOVA BABY Tippie & The Clovers (1962)

The group were a re-formed version of The Clovers that had broken up in 1961. This was not only the first single for over a year, but also the final one, to be released on the American Tiger label. Despite being Billboard magazine's 'Pick Of The Week', it promptly disappeared from sight a few days later. The record was released in the UK on EMI's Stateside label and was dusted off a year later by Elvis Presley for his movie *Fun In Acapulco*, and reached number 13 on the UK charts.

38. THE NIGHT THEY DROVE OLE DIXIE DOWN
The Band (1969)

Written by Robbie Robertson and first recorded by The Band on their 1969 self-titled debut album. In 1971, Joan Baez covered the song, releasing it as a single and achieving her last UK top-10 hit to date with it. The lyrics tell of the last days of the American Civil War and its aftermath. Robertson claimed that when he came up with the melody, he had no idea what the subject would be about; but, after extensive research into the war, the foundations were laid.

39. YOUR MA SAID YOU CRIED IN YOUR SLEEP LAST NIGHT
Kenny Dino (1961) *US No 24*

Doug Sheldon's British cover was the hit in this country, but this is the original American recording by Kenny Dino from Queens in New York. Whilst he was signed to the Dot label, he was given this song that he absolutely hated and said they should pass it onto Lonnie Donegan as a follow up to 'Does Your Chewing Gum Lose It's Flavour On The Bedpost Overnight'. However, he was talked into recording it. When played to the boss of the label, he threw it against a wall in disgust. Kenny, with composers Steve Schlaks and Irv Glazer, walked out of his office in shame. The tape remained on a shelf for over six months until Kenny was signed to Musicor in The States, who had a different view about the track.

40. UNDER THE MOON OF LOVE Curtis Lee (1961) *US No 46*

Curtis Lee only managed two American Hot 100 hits, 'Pretty Little

Angel Eyes' and this, 'Under The Moon Of Love'. Both songs were co-written by Tommy Boyce and both were successfully covered in the UK in the Seventies by Showaddywaddy, the latter reaching number one for them in 1976. Lee made his first record for Warner Brothers in 1959 but nothing came of it. Some months later, he was spotted singing in a club by Ray Peterson, who was about to form his own label. Offering him a contract, Lee spoke of his songwriting friend, Tommy Boyce; an introduction was made and he too was signed to Dunes as a writer.

41. RUBY DON'T TAKE YOUR LOVE TO TOWN
Johnny Darrell (1967)

Johnny Darrell must be one of the unluckiest performers ever to put his voice on record for he cut the original versions of both 'The Green Green Grass Of Home', a hit for Tom Jones, and 'The Son Of Hickory Holler's Tramp', a major success for O. C. Smith. To make matters worse, he hit more bad luck with his original version of 'Ruby Don't Take Your Love To Town', released in 1967, with music programmers virtually ignoring his version along with all his other releases. Two years later, Kenny Rodgers and The First Edition covered the song and had a worldwide hit with it.

42. DENISE Randy & The Rainbows (1963) *US No 10*

Formed in New York in 1961 as The Dialtones, the following year this band began working with songwriter Neil Levenson. Neil introduced them to Bright Tunes Productions, a company run by The Tokens of 'The Lion Sleeps Tonight' fame. Changing their name to Randy & The Rainbows, the group recorded Levinson's song, 'Denise' in the style of The Four Seasons. Released through the American Laurie label, this record earned them their one and only US hit. The song was later revived as the 1978 UK debut hit for Blondie under the slightly altered title of 'Denis'.

43. TWIST AND SHOUT The Top Notes (1961)

The song was composed by up and coming producer and songwriter Bert Berns under the pseudonym of Bert Russell, along with Phil Medley. Before this version was recorded by The Top Notes, the original title of the song was 'Shake It Up Baby'. When the finished track was delivered to Atlantic records boss Jerry Wexler, he hated the arrangement and the tempo –but still decided to release it, despite knowing it would fail.

Berns then took the song to The Isley Brothers and convinced them to record it the way he felt it should be sung. The result was a number-one R&B hit and a top-20 success in the summer of 1962.

44. YOU'RE NO GOOD Betty Everett (1963)

Written by Clint Ballard Jnr and first recorded by Dee Dee Warwick in 1963; in the same year Betty Everett achieved her first entry into the Billboard Hot 100 with the song, peaking at number 51. Her label boss, Calvin Carter, had planned to record it with Dee Clark, another of his artists. He decided it was too much of a negative song for a guy to sing about a girl but no problem the other way round, so he passed the song onto Betty. During the playback of what was to have been the final take, vocal group The Dells, who were hanging around the studio had begun stomping their feet to the beat of the song. Producer Carter heard the effect it made to the track and decided to record it once more to include the foot stomping, giving it its heavy beat. The song gave The Swinging Blue Jeans their third and final UK top-20 hit in 1964.

45. SOME OTHER GUY Richie Barrett (1962)

Written by Jerry Leiber and Mike Stoller together with its performer, Richie Barrett, whose original version of the song was first released as a single back in 1962. The song later became a firm favourite amongst the Merseybeat groups, with The Beatles often performing it in their live sets at The Cavern Club. A 1963 recording by The Big Three even made the UK top 40, and John Lennon paid homage to the song by using the two-chord intro for the beginning of his 'Instant Karma'. A copy of the valuable Barrett single was found in John Peel's treasured record box after his death.

46. HANDBAGS AND GLADRAGS Double Feature (1967)

Written by Mike D'Abo, who played the song to record producer Mike Hurst. Hurst was looking for material for a new group called Double feature. Believing it to be the ideal song, he went ahead and recorded it. In the meantime, Andrew Oldham also got hold of the song and recorded it with Chris Farlowe. Oldham then contacted Hurst and persuaded him to withhold the release of his version in order to give Farlowe a head start. Reluctantly, Hurst agreed. The upshot was that Chris's version made the top 40, leaving Double Feature's copies to be melted down in order to recycle the plastic.

47. I CAN'T LET GO **Evie Sands (1965)**

Born in Brooklyn, New York, Evelyn Lourette Sands had released her first single when she was in her teens, and in 1965 signed to the Blue Cat label – a subsidiary of the famed Red Bird Records. She toured with label mates The Shangri-Las, and began a long collaboration with composers and producers Al Gorgoni and Chip Taylor with the recording of the single 'Take Me For A Little While'. A pre-release white label of her disc was stolen by a Chicago-based producer who handed it to Chess Records' artist Jackie Ross. Ross, who had just had a hit with 'Selfish One', rushed into the studio and covered the song, unaware of the bad practise that had taken place. Because of Ross's name, his version gained the majority of the airplay and the subsequent legal battle set back Evie's career before it had a chance to get started. Her follow up, 'I Can't Let Go', was released during the chaos surrounding her previous single, leaving the coast clear for The Hollies to cover 'I Can't Let Go', with which they had an American top-50 hit and reached number two in the UK.

48. I'VE GOT MY MIND SET ON YOU **James Ray (1963)**

Written by Rudy Clark, who is best remembered for his song 'It's In His Kiss', this is the original version of the song by James Ray (who was also the first to record 'If You Gotta Make A Fool Of Somebody', a hit for Freddy and The Dreamers in 1963). Ray had a very short recording career, with only one completed album to his name; it is believed he died of a drug overdose in 1964. 'I've Got My Mind Set On You' became a UK top-five hit and a number one in America in 1987.

49. I'VE LOST YOU **Matthews' Southern Comfort (1969)**

Elvis Presley's hit version of 'I've Lost You' (1970) was written by Ken Howard and Alan Blaikley (best known for writing hits for acts such as Dave Dee, Dozy Beaky, Mick and Tich, The Herd and The Honeycombs) and first recorded the previous year by Matthews' Southern Comfort. The composers became involved with the management of Ian Matthews and wrote 'I've Lost You' (under the pseudonym of Steve Barlby) for inclusion on his 1969 debut album *Matthews Southern Comfort* that would soon become the name of his band.

50. HIS LATEST FLAME **Del Shannon (1961)**

After exploding onto the international pop scene in 1961 with his debut release, the multi-million selling single 'Runaway', Shannon's record company pressured him to get an album completed in time to cash in on the success. The tracks for the project included six of his own compositions, a Bacharach and David song and three by the prolific writing team of Doc Pomus and Mort Shuman. The latter's contribution included '(Marie's The Name Of) His Latest Flame'. This was a song that Elvis also chose to record, making it a million seller. Although Del probably recorded the song after Presley, his album was released first, making it more of a separate attempt at the song rather than a cover and, as far as the public is concerned, Del sang it first.

51. A ROCKIN' GOOD WAY
Brook Benton & Dinah Washington (1960) *US No 7*

'A Rockin' Good Way (To Mess Around And Fall In Love)' was written by Brook Benton and Clyde Otis with Luchi De Jesus. Although popular belief was that Brook's version with Dinah Washington was the original, the song had been recorded two years earlier by Priscilla Bowman and The Spaniels, but with little success. When Benton's record company suggested he recorded a few duets with Dinah, they agreed to give the song a try – and just as well, as it gave them their second top-10 hit together. The song later became a top-10 hit in the UK in 1984 when it was revived by Shakin' Stevens and Bonnie Tyler.

52. THE PIED PIPER **The Changing Times (1965)**

This is the original version of the 1966 top-five UK hit for Crispian St Peters. It was released a year earlier in The States by composers Artie Kornfeld and Steve Duboff under the group name of The Changing Times. Although their version made the American Hot 100, reaching no higher than number 87, St Peters' cover was a top-five hit on both sides of the Atlantic the following year. The song was yet again revived in 1971 by Bob and Marcia, whose version reached number 11 in the UK.

53. HIGHER AND HIGHER **The Dells (1967)**

Chicago-based group The Dells cut the pulsating 'Higher And Higher' for Chess during the early part of 1967 and were planning to release it as a single. The song was written by staff writers Billy Davis and Raynard Miner, the company's premier composers who had created the most chart success for the label in the Sixties. Less satisfied with their lot were Gary Jackson and Carl Smith who decided to quit the company and took with them a copy of the arrangement for 'Higher and Higher'. Keeping the basic melody but re-writing part of the lyric, they presented the song as their own work to Carl Davis, the boss of Brunswick Records, who immediately gave it to Jackie Wilson. Wilson jumped at the opportunity to record it and ended up having a smash hit. Davis and Miner immediately sued when they realised that they weren't even credited as co-writers, resulting in them being awarded 80% of all royalties on the song.

54. THEY LONG TO BE CLOSE TO YOU Adrienne Posta (1966)
Written by Burt Bacharach and Hal David, and popularised by The Carpenters in 1970, this song was originally recorded by actor Richard Chamberlain on his 1963 album *Twilight Of Honour* and was also the B-side of his single 'Blue Guitar'. Dionne Warwick also cut a version in 1964 on her album *Make Way For Dionne Warwick* and also issued it as the B-side of the single 'Here I Am'. Actress and singer Adrienne Posta had more faith in the song and, in 1966, released it as an A-side; but, despite substantial airplay, the song had to wait until The Carpenters' version came along four years later for its greater success.

55. IT'S RAINING Irma Thomas (1962)
In 1981, Shakin' Stevens reached number 10 in the UK charts with a song called 'It's Raining' that many believed was his own composition. In fact the song was written by Allen Toussaint under his pseudonym of Naomi Neville and originally recorded in 1962 by Irma Thomas. Irma had gained her first real break whilst working as a waitress in a local New Orleans night club where Wednesday nights were new talent nights. One such evening, Irma decided to get on stage, claiming she could out-sing resident band Tommy Ridgley's vocalist, Miss LaVell. This she did and after rapturous applause she was promptly sacked – but the silver lining was that Tommy agreed to guide her musical potential in the right direction.

56. SHE WEARS MY RING Roy Orbison (1962)
Written by Nashville husband-and-wife team Boudleaux and Felice Bryant, the song became a major hit in the UK when revived in 1968 by Solomon King. The melody is based on a Mexican song, 'La Golondrina',

composed by Narciso Serradel Sevilla. Roy's early 1962 version first appeared on his album *Crying*, and was later covered by Elvis Presley on his 1974 album release *Good Times*.

57. THE SHOOP SHOOP SONG Merry Clayton (1963)

Also going under the title of 'It's In His Kiss', Merry's recording was arranged by Jack Nitzsche for Bobby Darin's TM Production company and released on Capitol. The song had first been offered to, but rejected by, The Shirelles. There have been conflicting debates as to who recorded the original version of this Rudy Clark song as there was another version by Ramona King. Ramona's version was released around the same time as Betty Everett's hit recording in 1964. The backing vocals on Merry's 1963 disc were provided by The Blossoms.

58. SOMEDAY WE'LL BE TOGETHER Johnny & Jackey (1961)

There's an interesting story attached to this song that was written by Harvey Fuqua, along with Johnny Bristol and Jackey Beavers who originally recorded it in 1961 as Johnny & Jackey. It was released in America on the Tri-Phi label that was later bought out, along with the rights for the publishing on the back catalogue, by Tamla Motown. 'Someday We'll Be Together' was then chosen by Diana Ross for her first solo single; but, instead, it was decided to release it as her final outing with The Supremes in 1969 – even though the other two members of the group, Mary Wilson and Cindy Birdsong, weren't featured. Nevertheless, credited to The Supremes, it gave them their twelfth American number one.

59. I CAN HEAR MUSIC The Ronettes (1966)

After a number of big hit records, The Ronettes hit a bad patch with their releases, so much so that in 1966 promotional copies of their single 'I Can Hear Music' had been pressed up and sent out to DJs and reviewers. But at the last minute it was withdrawn from sale – thus making the value of such a copy today worth in excess of £100.

Three years later, in 1969, the girls were signed to A&M Records and released just one single, 'You Came, You Saw, You Conquered,' and guess what was on the B-side? Seeing that The Ronettes' record didn't get a proper initial release, The Beach Boys saw an opportunity for a hit and brought out their own version, also in 1969, scoring a UK number 10.

60. NO REGRETS
Tom Rush (1968)

According to Tom Rush, 'No Regrets' was one of the first real songs he wrote and was inspired by his girlfriend of many years, Jill, whose photograph – taken by Linda Eastman in New York's Central Park – graces the cover of the album *The Circle Game*, on which the song first appeared. Jill lived in

The Ronettes' 'I Can Hear Music' was withdrawn shortly after it's release, making it very rare

Boston and on one occasion after she had come to visit Tom and he had to see her off on a plane home, he wrote the song about saying goodbye to the woman he loved. The situation proved prophetic, as a few years later she left him for someone else. The song became a huge hit for The Walker Brothers in 1976 and also for Midge Ure in 1982.

61. HI-HO SILVER LINING The Attack (1967)

Written by Scott English and Larry Weiss, it is widely believed that the original version of the song was recorded by Jeff Beck; but in fact mod group The Attack released their version on 3rd March, 1967, three weeks ahead of Beck's recording. Larry Weiss had played the song to record producer Mickey Most, who decided to cut it with Beck. At the same time, Scott English had sent it to manager Don Arden, who decided to give it to The Attack.

62. LOVE OF THE COMMON PEOPLE The Four Preps (1967)

Clean-cut college boys Glen Larson, Bruce Belland, Ed Cobb and Marvin Inabnett decided to form a group whilst at Hollywood High School where they made their stage debut at a talent competition in 1956. A year later, they were signed to the Capitol label where they released a number of unsuccessful records before hitting the big time with 'Big Man' in 1958. Over the next few years, they made the charts with a couple of other releases but, as the Sixties wore on, The Four Preps popularity wore out. In 1966, Ed Cobb left the group and was replaced by David Somerville, former lead vocalist with The Diamonds. His first release with his new group was singing lead on 'Love Of The Common People', which songwriters John Hurley and Ronnie Wilkins had personally played to the group. Although not a hit at the time, the song gave Nicky Thomas a top-10 hit in 1970 and did the same for Paul Young in 1983.

63. SHA-LA-LA The Shirelles (1964)
The Shirelles released their original version of 'Sha-La-La' at the beginning of 1964 in America but their recording only managed to climb to number 69 on the Hot 100. Some months later, Manfred Mann decided to cover it as the follow-up to their equally daftly titled 'Do Wah Diddy Diddy' that had topped the charts. In the UK, the Manfred's version reached number three and, to the surprise of many, number 12 in the US.

64. DON'T MAKE MY BABY BLUE Frankie Laine (1963)
In 1965, The Shadows made the charts for the second time with a vocal hit, a song written by Barry Mann and Cynthia Weil, 'Don't Make My Baby Blue'. Fans of the group believed it to be a brand new composition, most unaware that it had been released two years earlier by Frankie Laine, who in the same year had issued the original version of 'I'm Gonna Be Strong' (also written by Mann and Weil and later to become a massive hit for Gene Pitney).

65. A GROOVY KIND OF LOVE Diane & Annita (1965)
The general perception was that this Toni Wine and Carole Bayer Sager song had originally been recorded on a B-side by Patti Labelle & The Bluebells and then discovered by The Mindbenders after Wayne Fontana left them. That was the way the music history books had been written until a bunch of dedicated record collectors unearthed this apparently earlier version by an obscure duo named Diane and Annita, who both sang with Ray Anthony's Orchestra before trying at solo careers. Together they released a couple of records on the American Wand label in 1965, the year an EP of their material was issued in France and contained a version of 'A Groovy Kind

Of Love,' sounding remarkably like a demo and did not appear to be the voices of the two girls but an entirely different singer (who is now believed to be Carole Bayer Sager). To confuse matters further, the publishers claim that the original song demo had been recorded by the other composer, Toni Wine, leaving us still wondering who is actually singing on this track.

66. HELLO HOORAY Judy Collins (1968)

The song is best known to music fans as the top-10 hit by Alice Cooper from 1973 that was slightly re-titled as 'Hello Hurray'. Written by Canadian singer-songwriter Rolf Kempf, this very different version by Judy Collins was released some five years earlier on her album, *Who Knows Where The Time Goes* that featured many leading musicians, including James Burton, Van Dyke Parks and Stephen Stills.

67. HE'S A REBEL Vikki Carr (1962)

Written by Gene Pitney, the offer of this song was turned down by The Shirelles. Subsequently, Vikki Carr, who had just signed to Liberty, decided to record it as her debut single; but producer Phil Spector also got to hear the song and, learning that Vikki's disc was soon to be in stores, decided to rush out his own version. The Crystals were on tour at the time so he arranged with Darlene Love to sing lead, backed by The Blossoms. The Crystals were shocked to learn they apparently had a new record out. They still received the credit on the label for the version that ended up being the hit.

68. ANY WAY THAT YOU WANT ME Tina Mason (1966)

Tina released her first single on Capitol in 1965 as Tina & The Mustangs after being discovered by record producer David Axelrod when the band held a residency at Disneyland in Hollywood. The following year, in 1966, she released her first solo record, a song written by Toni Wine and Carole Bayer, 'Finders Keepers', and tucked away on the B-side was the Chip Taylor composition, 'Any Way That You Want Me' – that later that year would become a massive hit for The Troggs. Tina went on to record one album for Capitol, *Something Wonderful*, before becoming a session singer and finally becoming a massage therapist in Los Angeles for more than 20 years.

69. ONE WAY LOVE The Drifters (1964)

Written by Bert Russell and Jerry Ragovoy, the song first appeared on The Drifters' album *Under The Boardwalk* and featured the voice of Johnny Moore on lead vocals. This was released as a single just prior to the album's title track that re-established The Drifters into the American top 10 after the relative failure of 'One Way Love' that peaked at number 56 – although Cliff Bennett's UK cover did somewhat better, reaching number nine in the UK charts.

70. WHEREVER I LAY MY HAT (THAT'S MY HOME) Marvin Gaye (1963)

This track had first appeared on Marvin's 1963 album *That Stubborn Kinda Fellow* and was one of Norman Whitfield's earliest productions. In contrast with the A-side, it also demonstrated how Motown had moved on in six years. In 1983, Paul Young covered the song that he'd first heard on his mother's Dansette record player, and ended up with a number-one hit.

71. A MESSAGE TO MARTHA Jerry Butler (1963)

Although Lou Johnson's version of this Bacharach and David composition that he titled 'Kentucky Bluebird' is often mistaken for the original recording, the song was first recorded two years earlier in 1962 by Jerry Butler, but not released until the following year on his album *Need To Belong*. Jerry's recording career was on the decline in America so his record label dispatched him to New York to work with Burt Bacharach and Hal David who wrote and produced his 'Make It Easy On Yourself', which re-established him in the top 20; but, inexplicably, 'Message To Martha' – recorded at the same sessions – was left in the can until two years later, leaving the way clear for Lou Johnson and Adam Faith, whose UK cover gave him his final top-20 hit.

THE ALBUMS

My personal selection of albums: from each of the albums here, I've selected a track that I feel to be an outstanding song.

1. JUST A LITTLE LOVIN' **Dusty Springfield (1969)**

Taken from her last album of the Sixties, *Dusty In Memphis*, this song was written by Barry Mann and Cynthia Weil. When Dusty went to Memphis to record the tracks, she was quite taken aback by their methods of recording. She had been used to turning up at the studio to find all the arrangements written; the musicians would record the track in two or three takes. Not so for this album. The musicians would spend several hours working out an arrangement in their heads, record it, discuss it and continually make changes until everyone was happy with the result.

2. I'LL COME RUNNING OVER **Lulu (1965)**

Taken from Lulu's debut album, *Something To Shout About*. As there were no songwriters in her backing group, The Luvvers, or anyone within her management or production team with composing skills, the songs were made up mainly of American cover versions of a wide range of material, from Motown to Spector. However, Lulu has subsequently been recognised a successful songwriter having written songs for other artists including Tina Turner. The complex vocal harmonies were difficult to replicate live, so this album's songs were rarely heard onstage.

3. EVERYTHING UNDER THE SUN **The Walker Brothers (1967)**

The opening track to their third top-10 album *Images*, released in 1967, which became their last of the Sixties. Their previous two LPs had both made the top 10 and in 1966, they were the third most successful album act in the UK, just behind The Beatles and The Beach Boys. This album appeared in August, 1967, when Scott had already embarked on a solo career. Although it contains some of their most ambitious performances and arrangements, the album was somewhat overlooked due to the pending split.

4. THE PICTURE **Cupid's Inspiration (1969)**

'Cupid's Inspiration' was taken from their only album, *Yesterday Has Gone*, which was also the title of the first and biggest of their two hit singles. This four-piece band came from Lincolnshire and was originally called The Ends. They secured a recording deal on the strength of the amazing voice of lead singer, Terry Rice-Milton. The follow up single, 'My World', made the top 40 but no further hits followed and after recording their album, they disbanded at the end of the year.

5. MEAN OLD WORLD Chicken Shack (1968)

Taken from their second album, *OK Ken*, this was written by the legendary blues artist, Aaron 'T-Bone' Walker. After the success of their debut album, *Forty Blue Fingers*, producer Mike Vernon found it increasingly difficult to get the band to agree on material and return to the studio to record the follow-up, as the record label were demanding new product. Finally work began in June 1968 and continued in dribs and drabs until *OK Ken* was finally completed in October of that year. The album title came about through singer Christine Perfect going through a period when she decided to call everyone Ken.

6. DEAR JILL Blodwyn Pig (1969)

Recorded at Morgan studios in Willesden and produced by Andy Johns (brother of Glyn Johns, who'd worked on most of The Rolling Stones' tracks). The song was released as a single and comes from their1969 debut album, *Ahead Rings Out* and was one of just two LPs released by the band, formed by Jethro Tull's ex guitarist, Mick Abrahams in 1968. Their second album, released the following year, was called *Getting To This*.

7. ALL YOUR LOVE John Mayall's Blues Breakers (1966)

This is the opening track to The Bluesbreakers' album with Eric Clapton, and is often referred to as the *Beano* album, because the front cover depicts Clapton sitting with the rest of the group reading a copy of *The Beano*. Clapton joined the band in 1965 after he left The Yardbirds in favour of playing in a more bluesy style. But he and Jack Bruce left the following year to form Cream.

8. RIDE MY SEE-SAW The Moody Blues (1968)

Released as a single, it just failed to make the top 40, peaking at number 42 in the UK. It was also their last single to get anywhere near the charts in the Sixties. Written by John Lodge, it was taken from their album, *In Search Of The Lost Chord*. The song became a long standing encore favourite of the band. 'Ride My See-Saw' made a piece of pop history by becoming the first rock song ever to be recorded on an eight-track multi-track recording machine.

9. MAKE THE NIGHT A LITTLE LONGER The Shirelles (1962)

The Shirelles

A track from The Shirelles' third album, *Baby It's You*, it was written by Carole King and Gerry Goffin. As with their two previous albums, *Tonight's The Night* and *The Shirelles Sing To Trumpets And Strings*', the repertoire was a mix of already-issued singles and old and new songs they'd recorded as possible future hits. It also became their first LP to make the American album charts and the first to feature a picture of the girls on the front cover. Whilst it was climbing the charts, the group were heading for New York to record material for their next project, 'Twist Party', with sax player King Curtis.

10. COME ALL YE Fairport Convention (1969)

This is the opening track from their album, *Liege And Lief*, which Fairport began recording in the summer of 1969. The group were actually on the brink of splitting up following a traumatic road accident that had resulted in the deaths of their drummer Martin Lamble and Richard Thompson's girlfriend, Jeannie Taylor. As they came round to the idea of continuing, they decided they had to take a new musical direction, with completely new material, so they would never have to revisit the music they'd played with Martin. Sandy Denny began playing the band traditional ballads and bass player Ashley Hutchings began researching different arrangements of the songs. Ironically, the two prime catalysts for their new direction would be the first musicians to leave, soon after the release of the album.

11. LONG TIME GONE Crosby, Stills & Nash (1969)

Taken from the multi-million-selling self-titled debut album, released by Crosby, Stills & Nash in 1969, this song was written by David Crosby. The picture on the album cover shows (from left to right), Nash, Stills and Crosby, in a different order than their band name. The photo was taken before they'd settled on what to call themselves and they found a house across from a Santa Monica car wash that they thought would be a perfect fit for their image. For no particular reason, they posed for the photo in the order of Nash, Stills, and Crosby, then a few days later after they decided on the name and to prevent confusion, they went back to the house to re-shoot the cover in the correct order. But when they got there, they found the house was reduced to a pile of rubble.

12. SUNSHINE OF YOUR LOVE The Fifth Dimension (1969)

This song was taken from The Fifth Dimension's fourth album, released in the spring of 1969, named *The Age of Aquarius* after their biggest hit single. It became the best-selling LP of the group's career. It held down the number-two position on the US Hot 100 for two weeks and remained on the charts for just under a year and a half. Included on the album were songs by Laura Nyro, Jimmy Webb and this unusual choice for a cover of Cream's self-penned 1968 hit, 'Sunshine Of Your Love.

13. YOU CAN'T DO THAT Nilsson (1967)

'You Can't Do That' was taken from Harry Nilsson's second album for RCA, *Pandemonium Shadow Show*, which established him as one of both John Lennon and Paul McCartney's favourite artists. Lennon listened to the album for 36 hours after being given a copy and then called Nilsson to congratulate him; this began a friendship that would last for the rest of Lennon's life. Paul McCartney was once asked to name his favourite American group. He replied, 'Nilsson'. This is a cover of a Beatles track in which Harry cleverly referenced 20 of their other songs into the reworked lyrics. The Beatles' own version was first released as the B-side to 'Can't Buy Me Love'.

14. OL' MAN RIVER Cilla Black (1966)

Cilla with a swing: this one is taken from her debut album, called just *Cilla*, with a big-band arrangement by the legendary Johnny Spence. Jerome Kern and Oscar Hammerstein II wrote the song for the 1927 musical, *Showboat*, first performed in the original stage production on December 27 of that year by Jules Bledsoe who also sang it in the part-talkie 1929 film version. Still the most famous rendition was by Paul Robeson in the classic 1936 movie. I'm sure the composers never envisaged it to be performed quite the way Cilla and Johnny did.

15. SHINE ON BRIGHTLY Procol Harum (1968)
With 'A Whiter Shade Of Pale' being the most talked-about record of the summer of 1967 and their first album climbing the album charts, fans were wondering if they would be able to keep up the standard with their second LP, *Shine On Brightly*. They need not have worried, with Tony Visconti in the producer's chair and the superb guitar playing of Robin Trower, Gary Brooker's voice was pushed to its limits.

16. SIDEWALK SURFIN' Jan & Dean (1964) *US No 25*
Taken from their album, *Ride The Wild Surf*, which was their fourth, album release of 1964 – yes, four albums in one year – and also the soundtrack to the movie of the same name, starring Fabian and Shelley Fabares. They also wrote the humorous sleeve notes. 'Sidewalk Surfin'' started life as a Beach Boys song, 'Catch A Wave', but ended up with its title after new lyrics were added by Jan Berry relating to skateboarding.

17. PRISCILLA MILLIONAIRA Zalman Yanovsky (1968)
1967 was a momentous year in the life of Zalman Yanovsky. He went from the height of fame as lead guitarist with The Lovin' Spoonful to relative obscurity as a solo performer. Departing from the group in June, 1967, over the following 18 months he recorded a single that flopped, fathered a daughter, co-founded a production company and released his only solo album, *Alive And Well And Living In Argentina*, which was released on the Buddah label in 1968.

18. FIND ME A GOLDEN STREET The Shadows (1961)
Following the success of their single, 'Apache', The Shadows recorded and released their debut self-titled album, which became the first instrumental LP to reach number one in the UK charts. With sleeve notes written by Cliff Richard, this was the only Shadows album to feature all of the original line-up, which included Jet Harris and Tony Meehan. Each track was completed twice without overdubs – once

for the mono version and then again for the stereo release. 'Find Me A Golden Street' was the second track on side two and was written by Norman Petty, who originally recorded it with his trio. A later version appeared on the B-side of The Fireballs' single 'Carioca'.

19. ABOUT THE CHILDREN Tom Paxton (1969)

Tom Paxton was born in Chicago and at the age of 11 moved with his family to Oklahoma with the dream of becoming an actor. He began learning the trumpet before an aunt gave him his first guitar but it didn't replace his desire to act which led him to pursue a course in drama during which time he was introduced to folk music and began writing his own material that he performed for friends at which point he decided he'd rather become a folk singer. After a brief stint in the US army, he travelled to New York and visited Greenwich Village, where he became part of the growing folk scene and mingled with the likes of Joan Baez and Bob Dylan – as well as performing at some of the small clubs, including The Gaslight where he recorded his first album. His songs were being covered by many big names and despite the decline in the popularity of folk music towards the end of the Sixties, Paxton's output remained constant. In 1969 he released his fifth album, *The Things I Notice Now*, from which this song was taken.

20. GOODBYE JOE Laura Nyro (1966)

Laura Nyro is probably best known as a songwriter, whose work includes 'Wedding Bell Blues' and 'Stoned Soul Picnic' for The Fifth Dimension, 'Stoney End' for Barbra Streisand and 'Eli's Coming' for Three Dog Night. However, she released a constant flow of her own albums from 1967, when her debut was released, titled *More Than A New Discovery*. This song, 'Goodbye Joe', was the opening track. Sadly Nyro died of ovarian cancer in Danbury, Connecticut, in April 1997, at the age of 49, the same age at which the disease had claimed the life of her mother.

21. THE THOUGHTS OF MARY JANE Nick Drake (1969)

'The Thoughts Of Mary Jane comes from the first of Nick Drake's three albums released in his lifetime, *Five Leaves Left*. It came out in 1969 and featured accompaniment from members of the British folk-rock groups Fairport Convention and The Pentangle. Drake's primary instrument was the guitar, though he was being proficient at piano, clarinet, and saxophone. Despite his great talent, he sadly failed to find a wide audience during his life. But Drake's work has grown steadily in stature, to the extent that he now ranks among the most influential English singer-songwriters of the last 50 years. In November, 1974, Drake died from an overdose of prescribed antidepressants; he was 26 years old. Whether his death was an accident or suicide has never been resolved.

22. NEVER TELL YOUR MOTHER SHE'S OUT OF TUNE
Jack Bruce (1969)

Jack Bruce, who is probably best known for his work with Cream, dedicated his first solo hit album, *Songs For A Tailor* to the group's clothes designer Jeannie Franklyn who had recently passed away. Although considered to be his debut LP, he had previously recorded *Things We Like*, but the album was shelved by his record label until 1970. *Songs For A Tailor* reached number six on the UK album charts and the opening track on side one is 'Never Tell Your Mother She's Out Of Tune'. It's a song that he wrote – along with the rest of the repertoire – with poet and lyricist Pete Brown, and it features George Harrison on guitar.

23. KATHY'S SONG Paul Simon (1965)

In 1964, a young Paul Simon jumped on a plane in New York and headed to England, having been discouraged by the cool reception given to the first Simon & Garfunkel album, *Wednesday Morning 6AM*. Very soon he found himself immersed in London's underground folk scene, performing in local clubs and writing new material inspired by his new found life. Several of the songs he recorded during his stay would later be re-recorded for future Simon & Garfunkel releases.

24. BABY YOU'VE BEEN ON MY MIND Linda Ronstadt (1969)

Produced by Chip Douglas of The Turtles, *Hand Sown ... Home Grown* was Linda Ronstadt's debut solo album after her departure from the group The Stone Poneys. Her choice of material saw her move away from folk-rock into country-rock, with material by writers including John D Loudermilk, Randy Newman, fellow Stone Poney Kenny Edwards and Bob Dylan, whose 'Baby You've Been On My Mind' was the opening track on side one of this collection.

THE BIG BALLADS

A selection of 30 great dramatic ballads with big orchestral arrangements mixing hits with lesser-known recordings.

1. PLAY THE DRAMA TO THE END Clodagh Rodgers

Written by Richard Kerr and Joan Maitland, who had been responsible for Don Partridge's second hit, 'Blue Eyes', this was Clodagh Rodgers' first release for the RCA label. Although she had been releasing records since 1962 for both the Decca and EMI Columbia labels, she had met with little success. 'Play The Drama To The End' received an impressive number of plays on the radio, helping to establish her name. The following year she finally achieved her first hit with 'Come Back And Shake Me'.

2. YOU DON'T HAVE TO SAY YOU LOVE ME Dusty Springfield (1966) *UK No 8*

Although Dusty achieved 15 top-40 hits in the Sixties, this was her only number one. Dusty heard the song at the Italian San Remo song contest as 'Io Vhe No Vivo Senza Ta', performed by its composer, Pino Donaggio. She brought a copy home and asked her good friend Vicki Wickham, producer of *Ready Steady Go*, to write an English lyric, which she did with the help of The Yardbirds manager, Simon Napier-Bell. The song later returned to the top 10 on two occasions in the Seventies.

3. WITHOUT LOVE (THERE'S NOTHING) Tom Jones (1969)
US No 5/UK No 10

This became Tom's sixteenth UK top-40 hit and eleventh in The States. It was also his final hit of the Sixties, by which time he'd become a huge success with his live act in Las Vegas – where women would throw not only their underwear onto the stage but also their hotel-room keys. 'Without Love (There Is Nothing)' was written by Danny Small and originally recorded by Clyde McPhatter in 1957 whose version reached number 19 in America 14 places lower than this later cover.

4. HUNG ON YOU The Righteous Brothers (1965)

After The Righteous Brothers' success with 'You've Lost That Lovin' Feelin'' the search was on for a suitable follow-up. Having written their big hit, Barry Mann and Cynthia Weil were expected to provide the next song. But to everyone's surprise, Mann and Weil lost out to Carole King and Gerry Goffin's 'Just Once In My Life'. The record company then changed their minds and swerved in favour of a different Goffin-King composition. 'Hung On You' was issued in its place. But that was then usurped in turn, completely overshadowed by the B-side, the Righteous Brothers' revival of 'Unchained Melody'.

5. HURT Timi Yuro (1961) *US No 4*

Timi Yuro's father discouraged her singing but her mother secretly paid for her to have private operatic voice training. By the late Fifties she was singing in her parents' Italian restaurant in Chicago. 'Hurt' was previous an R&B hit in 1955 for Roy Hamilton.

6. MY HEART BELONGS TO YOU Eddie Fontaine (1961)

Fontaine began his singing career at the age of five by singing in intermissions at neighbourhood theatres in his home town of Queens in New York. He became a busker in his teens and after a three-year spell in the US Navy, he graduated to being a successful night-club performer. In 1954 he was signed to RCA records and made an appearance on the very first Alan Freed TV Show on Easter Sunday 1955. He appeared in one of the great rock'n'roll movies, *The Girl Can't Help It* in 1957, and the following year he released a single of his own composition which he wrote in 15 minutes, 'Nothin' Shakin' (But The Leaves On A Tree)', which was covered in the UK by several artists, including Billy Fury. In 1961, he moved to Hollywood and obtained a residency at Puccini's night club, owned by Frank Sinatra. It was there that a Warner Brothers executive heard him and hired him for an acting role in a new TV series called '*The Gallant Men*; it was in this series he performed 'My Heart Belongs to You'. After that he made guest appearances in many top TV shows including *Ironside*, *The Rockford Files*, *The Six Million Dollar Man*, *Quincy* and *Starsky And Hutch*. He died on April 13, 1992.

7. STAY WITH ME Lorraine Ellison (1966)

Lorraine Ellison sang with two gospel groups, The Ellison Singers and The Golden Chords, before going solo. She made several other recordings after 'Stay With Me', but unfortunately everything was inevitably compared – unfavourably – with this classic. Nothing came close in power.

8. ANGELICA **Jordan Christopher (1966)**

Actor and singer Jordan Christopher managed to stretch out his 15 minutes of fame into 20 years of steady work. A former hairdresser, Christopher became an instant celebrity when, in the mid-Sixties, he married Sybil Burton, the former wife of film-star Richard Burton. The handsome Christopher caught the eye of several film and TV directors, appearing in *Return of the Seven* (1966), *Brainstorm* (1980) and *That's Life* (1986). He performed with his backing band, The Wild Ones, and in 1966 recorded this Barry Mann and Cynthia Weil song, 'Angelica'.

9. TURN AROUND LOOK AT ME **The Vogues (1968)** *US No 7*

They came together at high school in Pennsylvania as The Val-Aires in 1959 and made their recording debut the following year with a song called 'Laurie My Love'. In 1961, they changed their name to The Vogues but it wasn't until 1965 that they came to prominence, reaching the American top 10 with their cover of Petula Clark's 'You're The One'. In 1967, they signed to Frank Sinatra's Reprise label and with a change of vocal style, scored the following year with this revival of a song recorded several years earlier by Glen Campbell.

Kathy Kirby, who represented the UK at Eurovision in 1965

10. DON'T WALK AWAY **Kathy Kirby (1964)**

This was Kathy's sixth single for the Decca label and was originally called 'Walk Away', but the writers and record company decided to change the title as Matt Monro had a record in the charts at the time of release with a completely different song called 'Walk Away'.

11. THE WONDERFUL WORLD OF THE YOUNG
Danny Williams (1962) *UK No 8*

This Danny Williams record, *The Wonderful World Of The Young* had first been recorded by Andy Williams and gave Danny his biggest hit after his number one with 'Moon River'. This became his third and final UK top-20 hit and was written by Sid Tepper and Roy Bennett, whose dozens of successes include hits for both Cliff Richard and Elvis Presley.

12. IF I CAN DREAM **Elvis Presley (1968)** *US No 12/UK No 11*

After releasing a number of singles from his many movies, Presley returned unconditionally to proper albums and non-soundtrack recordings. Just prior to his return to live performances in Las Vegas, he made a TV special on which he premiered 'If I Can Dream', written in direct response to the assassinations of Martin Luther King and Bobby Kennedy, claiming that he'd never sing another song he didn't like – nor make another movie he didn't believe in.

13. LOVE ME WITH ALL OF YOUR HEART **Karl Denver (1964)**
UK No 37

This was the last of 11 consecutive top-40 hits for Karl Denver who was born Angus McKenzie in 1934. He reportedly jumped ship in America while en route back to Britain, after serving with the famous Scottish army regiment, The Argyll & Southerland Highlanders in Korea. He spent the next three years working in country & western clubs in America before being caught and deported. He made his UK TV debut in 1959 on Granada's *Bandstand* and soon after that was spotted performing in a Manchester pub by producer Jack Good, who convinced Decca to sign him up for a record deal. 'Love Me With All Of Your Heart' is an English-language version of the Mexican song, 'Cuando Caliente El Sol'.

14. I CAN'T MAKE IT ALONE **P.J. Proby (1966)** *UK No 37*

Yet another classic ballad from the pens of Carole King and Gerry Goffin. Although, at this time, P.J. Proby was still turning out great records, the media were far more interested in his tax problems and forthcoming bankruptcy than his music. So, sadly, this Proby single only just scraped into the top 40.

15. SOFTLY AS I LEAVE YOU **Matt Monro (1962)** *UK No 10*

Matt was discovered by pianist Winifred Atwell, who heard him singing and suggested to her record label, Decca, that they should sign him up. His real name was Terence Perkins and she helped change it to Matt Monro: Matt after a journalist friend of hers, Matt White, and Monro from Atwell's father's name. He had little success with the records he made for Decca but got a lucky break when George Martin asked him to make a demo of a song in the style of Frank Sinatra, for Peter Sellers to use on his forthcoming album *Songs For Swinging Sellers*. The recording was so good they knew they couldn't improve on it and included it on the LP under the name of Fred Flange. George immediately signed Matt to the Parlophone label, where they produced a string of hits together. 'Softly As I Leave You' was originally an Italian song called 'Piano', written by Antonio De Vita and Giorgio Calabrese and was sung by top star of the country, Mina at the San Remo Song Festival in 1960. British lyricist Hal Shaper heard the song and wrote English words to the melody, giving it its new title.

16. AT LAST **Etta James (1960)** *US No 47*

The song was written by Mack Gordon and Harry Warren and was first made famous in 1942 by The Glenn Miller Orchestra. Gordon and Warren composed other hits together, including 'Chattanooga Choo Choo', 'Serenade in Blue', and 'You'll Never Know'. Before teaming up, they were successful composers on their own and wrote numerous other songs with other partners. Gordon wrote the lyrics and Warren wrote the music. Etta has battled various drug addictions through the years, but it has rarely affected her music. She was in the midst of her addictions and other personal and professional problems when 'At Last' was recorded. It was one of her finest performances but was not typical of her work. Many of her songs have more of a blues feel and often contain darker lyrics that reflect the challenges she's faced.

17. MY LOVE FOR YOU **Johnny Mathis (1960)** *US No 47/UK No 9*

At high school, Johnny Mathis excelled in athletics and later entered San Francisco State college, with the intention of becoming an English teacher. However, his sports achievements led him to consider teaching physical education after he set the college record for the high jump. He was even invited to try out for the 1956 Olympic Games, but he turned down the offer in order to pursue a career in music. He had become interested in jazz and began singing in local nightclubs, and at one of them he was spotted by an executive for Columbia Records, who took him to New York to record some tracks. His first album was very jazz-influenced and failed to make much impression. But his label recognised his talent and steered him away from jazz towards the soft ballad approach as displayed on his first hit in 1957, 'Wonderful! Wonderful!

18. LET IT BE ME Peter & Gordon (1966)

Peter Asher and Gordon Waller were both sons of doctors. They became the first British act after The Beatles to hit the number-one spot on the American charts with 'A World Without Love', a song written by John Lennon and Paul McCartney. The lead track from their self-titled 1966 album, 'Let It Be Me' was originally a French song written by Gilert Béaud, Mann Curtis and Pierre Delanoe, with English lyrics added later by Jill Corey. Dozens of versions of the song have been recorded over the years including The Everly Brothers, Nancy Sinatra, Tom Jones, Bob Dylan Elvis Presley, and more recently, Paul Weller.

19. ROSECRANS BOULEVARD Gordon Waller (1968)

After four years as one half of the successful duo Peter And Gordon, and with Peter Asher's increasing success as a record producer, Londoner Gordon Waller decided to go it alone. This was his first solo single, a song written by Jim Webb. Unfortunately the single failed to capture the record-buying public's imagination. But he persisted with a further four singles and an album before abandoning the world of pop in favour of a career in agriculture. Subsequently, Peter and Gordon toured together again.

20. LOVE IS ALL Malcolm Roberts (1969) *UK No 12*

Considered by many to have been one of the most underrated singers of the Sixties, with only three hit singles to his name he became one of the few British singers to conquer Las Vegas. He was unable to build on his success there, yet remained a popular draw on the cabaret circuit. 'Love Is All' is the song with which Malcolm represented Britain at the Rio de Janeiro Song festival – and won.

21. THE WORST THAT COULD HAPPEN
Brooklyn Bridge (1968) *US No 3*

Written by Jim Webb, Brooklyn Bridge were made up of a vocal quartet and seven-piece band from Long Island in New York. They decided on their name when an employee at their manager's office commented that it would be easier to sell the Brooklyn Bridge than a band of this size. Lead singer Johnny Maestro had achieved an American top three hit some 10 years earlier with 'Sixteen Candles' as a member of The Crests.

22. HANDBAGS AND GLADRAGS Chris Farlowe (1967) *UK No 33*

Long before The Stereophonics had their 2001 top-10 hit with their cover of this song, Chris Farlowe recorded it. Mike D'Abo, who wrote it, claims that the moral of the song is telling impressionable teenagers that the way to happiness is not necessarily being trendy – there are far deeper values in life. The song has also been recorded by Rod Stewart and was used as the theme song to the TV series *The Office*.

23. PRINCESS IN RAGS Gene Pitney (1965) *US No 37/UK No 9*

As 1964 drew to a close, so did Gene Pitney's run of top-20 hits in America, ending with 'I'm Gonna Be Strong', but back in the UK, his popularity was stronger than ever. 'Princess In Rags' became his fourth in a run of seven consecutive top-10 chart entries. The song was written by Helen Miller, who also co-wrote 'It Hurts To Be In Love' for Pitney, and Roger Atkins, who co-wrote The Animals hit, 'It's My Life'.

24. MAKE IT EASY ON YOURSELF The Walker Brothers (1965)
US No 16/UK No 1

Their American record label, Smash, who bought the rights to the record in the US, were determined to make a hit out of this Walker Brothers release – despite Jerry Butler's original version having been a top-20 hit a mere three years earlier. They issued the promotional copies of the single in a folded picture sleeve, included an insert, and placed ads in all the leading music trade papers. Their efforts were rewarded when this Burt Bacharach and Hal David song was once more in the American top 20.

25. LIGHTS OF CINCINATTI Scott Walker (1969) *UK No 13*

Written by Tony Macaulay and Geoff Stephens, this became the last of three solo releases from Scott during the Sixties, all of which became top-20 hits. Between 1967 and 1969, he released three albums without The Walker Brothers and didn't release another single until 1971 when 'I Still See You' failed to chart. Scott still records today, although much

The Walker Brothers – none of whom were actually siblings

of his material is a million miles away from his commercial hits, having embraced a much more avant-garde musical direction.

26. WALK WITH ME MY ANGEL **Don Charles** (1962) *UK No 39*

Born Walter Scuffham in Hull, Don Charles broke into the entertainment business whilst in Hong Kong, where he combined his naval duties as a diver with his bookings ashore as a singer with a local band. Changing his name to Don Bennett, he decided to try his luck back home in Blighty where, in 1961, he met up with George Martin. He was signed to Parlophone and released the unsuccessful 'Paintbox Lover'. He was then introduced to Joe Meek, who suggested Don change his name to Don Charles – as Bennett was too close to Tony Bennett. Don then produced a single for Decca: a song he'd originally recorded as an album track with John Leyton, 'Walk With Me My Angel', which became his only top-40 hit. Meek often stated that he considered Don to have been the best voice he ever recorded.

27. I PUT A SPELL ON YOU **Nina Simone** (1965) *UK No 28 (in 1969)*

Nina's version of the Screaming Jay Hawkins song was first released in 1965 and became a minor hit, reaching just number 49 on the UK charts. Some three and a half years later in 1969, it was reissued and made the slightly more impressive number 28. Nina even called her 1991 autobiography *I Put A Spell On You*. The song is listed in *Rolling Stone* magazine's '500 Greatest Songs Of All Time', with dozens of other versions having appeared over the years, including recordings by Tom Waits, Alan Price, Ray Charles, Roxy Music and Katie Melua.

28. TOWER OF STRENGTH Frankie Vaughan (1961) *UK No 1*

Frankie always maintained that he never just looked for songs that would become hits, but for material he could really give a performance to in his stage act. When he heard the original Gene McDaniels' American version of this Burt Bacharach and Bob Hilliard song, he knew it fitted all his requirements. The record was also helped along its way by Frankie's appearance, close to the time of its release, on the 1961 Royal Variety Show at the Prince of Wales Theatre, London, which also included Shirley Bassey, Sammy Davis Jr and Jack Benny.

29. WHERE ARE YOU NOW (MY LOVE) Jackie Trent (1965) *UK No 1*

The first hit song to be written together by Jackie and her then husband, Tony Hatch, 'Where Are You Now (My Love)' held the number-one spot in the UK for just one week in May, 1965. The song was commissioned by Granada Television for their drama series *It's Dark Outside* starring Keith Barron and William Mervyn. When the song first hit the screen, viewers contacted the TV company trying to find out where they could buy the song, so Pye Records rush-released it in order to get it into the shops whilst the series was still being aired.

30. I WILL FOLLOW HIM Little Peggy March (1963) *US No 1*

Little Peggy March was a few days past her fifteenth birthday when 'I Will Follow Him' went to number one on the American charts in April 1963, making her the youngest female artist ever to achieve that accolade. Born in Pennsylvania, she began singing at the age of two and was heard at a cousin's wedding by a friend who introduced her to Hugo Peretti and Luigi Creatore at RCA who suggested she should record the French song, 'Chariot', once English lyrics had been added by Arthur Altman and Norman Gimble, turning her into an international star.

THE EPs

The EP was big news in the Sixties – often released after an artist had put out two or more singles. Their label would issue both sides on a four-track EP; alternatively, a successful album would be issued in sections of four or six tracks once sales had subsided. Very occasionally, an EP would be released of material that was not available in any other format. There was even a dedicated EP chart for a while. Here are 25 of these now collectable releases.

1. SHAKE, RATTLE AND ROLL The Swinging Blue Jeans (1964)

This one's taken from their only record to make the EP charts, 'Shake With The Swinging Blue Jeans', which contained four shaking tracks: 'Shaking Feeling' (the B-side of their 1964 top-20 hit revival of 'Good Golly Miss Molly'; 'Shakin' All Over', their biggest hit; 'The Hippy Hippy Shake'; and the classic 'Shake, Rattle And Roll'.

2. DANCE WITH ME Billy J Kramer & The Dakotas (1963)

Originally a 1960 top-20 hit for The Drifters, Billy and the boys' version appeared on no fewer than two of their EPs, both titled after hit singles. It first surfaced on the 1963 EP 'I'll Keep You Satisfied', on which they also included Ricky Nelson's 'It's Up To You', then the following year it cropped up again on the four-track, 'From A Window' EP, which also included their version of 'The Twelfth Of Never'.

3. THE SHRINE ON THE SECOND FLOOR Cliff Richard (1960)

UK No 14

This was one of the rare occasions that an EP sold enough copies to make the UK singles chart. Reaching number 14, this four-track disc contained Cliff's number-two hit, 'Voice In The Wilderness' along with 'Bongo Blues', 'Love' and this track, 'The Shrine On The Second Floor'. The movie it came from – *Expresso Bongo* – starred Laurence Harvey and Sylvia Syms with Cliff Richard as Bongo Herbert, working his way up the ladder as a pop singer.

4. DIMPLES The Animals (1965)

The Animals first made the EP charts at the beginning of 1965 with a four tracker called 'The Animals Is Here', consisting of their first three hit singles and reaching number three in the charts. Later that year, EMI released a self-titled EP that, although didn't chart, contained the first four tracks they ever recorded for the company on January 22, 1964. All the tracks were completed on that day but the recordings were shelved for the time. The songs were Chuck Berry's 'Around And Around', Fats Domino's 'I've Been Around' and two John Lee Hooker classics, 'Boom Boom' and 'Dimples'.

5. THREE WHEELS ON MY WAGON
The New Christie Minstrels (1966)
Although they made several well-known records such as 'Green Green' and 'Corn Whisky', this was the only time The New Christie Minstrels made the UK chart. This four-track release that reached number five on the EP charts contained the songs, 'Chim Chim Cheree', 'The Last Farewell', 'Kisses Sweeter Than Wine' and this, the title track with lead vocals by Barry McGuire.

6. ST LOUIS BLUES Helen Shapiro (1962)
Helen Shapiro released a total of seven EPs during the Sixties, three of which were made up of A-sides and B-sides of her hits, two which were tracks from her album *Tops With Me*, and her first and last gave her the chance to sing the blues. The first was called simply 'Helen'

Helen Shapiro: in the early Sixties, her hit-scoring abilities were as rock-solid as her hairstyle

and contained her version of 'The Birth Of The Blues' and the last, 'A Teenager Sings The Blues' had just three tracks – the title song, 'Blues In The Night' and this extended version of 'St Louis Blues'.

7. SHAKE SHERRY SHAKE Bern Elliott & The Fenmen (1964)

With the success of two hit singles, 'Money' and 'New Orleans', both covers of American hits, Bern Elliott & The Fenmen's record label, Decca, released their self-titled EP at the beginning of 1964 that reached number 10 on the format's top 20 chart and contained a further six covers that were, 'Please Mr Postman', 'Chills', 'I Can Tell', '(Do The) Mashed Potato', 'Shop Around' and a song originally recorded by The Contours, 'Shake Sherry Shake'.

8. LITTLE HONDA. The Beach Boys (1964)

'Little Honda' is taken from their disc 'Four By The Beach Boys', which reached number 11 on the EP charts, with three of the four songs written by group members Brian Wilson and Mike Love – 'Little Honda', 'Wendy' and 'Don't Back Down'. The fourth song was a Doc Pomus and Mort Shuman composition, 'Hushabye'. 'Little Honda' was covered by in America by The Hondells whose version reached number nine on the US Hot 100 in 1964.

9. MR PITIFUL Chris Farlowe (1966)

Soon after signing with Andrew Oldham's newly formed Immediate label, Chris released an EP called 'Farlowe In The Midnight Hour', which reached number six on the EP charts. Apart from the title track, he recorded versions of '(I Can't Get No) Satisfaction', the oddly chosen 'Who Can I Turn To' from the musical *The Roar Of The Greasepaint, The Smell Of The Crowd* and this interpretation of the Otis Redding classic, 'Mr Pitiful'.

10. YOU BETTER MOVE ON The Rolling Stones (1964)

Taken from The Rolling Stones' self-titled four-track debut, which topped the EP charts. It was released by Decca Records in 1964 not only to capitalise on the Stones' first top-20 single, 'I Wanna Be Your Man', but to test the group's commercial appeal before committing to letting them record a whole album. The four tracks were Chuck Berry's 'Bye Bye Johnny', Berry Gordy's 'Money', Leiber and Stoller's 'Poison Ivy' and Arthur Alexander's 'You Better Move On'.

11. SAN FRANCISCO BAY The Four Pennies (1964)

Philips, The Four Pennies' record label, made sure that the group were well represented on the EP front, with no fewer than four being issued during 1964 alone, the first being 'Spin With The Four Pennies'. It was the only one to make the EP charts, reaching number six. Their second, self-titled EP that contained the tracks 'I Found Out The Hard Way' (their top-20 hit single from that year), a cover of Roy Orbison's 'Running Scared', their own composition, 'Miss Bad Daddy' and 'San Francisco Bay'.

12. WILD IS THE WIND Unit 4 + 2 (1964)

Taken from their eponymous – and only – EP, 'Wild Is The Wind' was one of four tracks by the oddly named group Unit 4 +2 included. The other three songs were, 'Cotton Fields', 'Cross A Million Mountains' and a non-album track, 'To Be Redeemed'. The disc climbed to number 11 on the EP charts in 1965.

13. THERE'S NO LIVING WITHOUT YOUR LOVING
Manfred Mann (1965)

This is the title track to the Manfred's number-one EP, 'No Living Without Your Loving', which also contains their version of the classic, 'I Put A Spell On You', together with a cover of the Ray Charles hit, 'Let's Go Get Stoned' and the mouthful of a title, 'Tired Of Trying, Bored With Lying, Scared Of Dying'.

14. SORRY I'M GONNA HAVE TO PASS Lonnie Donegan (1960)

Although he released several EPs throughout the Sixties, this, 'Yankee Doodle Donegan' was the only one to make the EP charts, reaching number eight in 1960. The four songs included were 'Corrine, Corrina', 'Junko Partner', 'Nobody Understands Me' and this Jerry Leiber and Mike Stoller song, 'Sorry But I'm Gonna Have To Pass', originally recorded by The Coasters. The EP was released just a few weeks before Lonnie's next hit single, 'Lively', which was recorded at the same session in New York under the supervision of Leiber and Stoller.

15. CLOSE THE DOOR Georgie Fame (1967)

Georgie achieved four top-20 hit EPs during his stay with EMI Records and when he moved to CBS in 1967 he continued to make the charts, but his style of music changed. This self-titled four-tracker was his only hit EP for the label and this cover of the Joe Tex song was considered to have been the closest he ever came to recording a straight-down-the middle Sixties soul track for the company. The other three tracks included are, 'Knock On Wood', 'All I'm Asking' and 'Didn't I Want To Have To Do It'.

16. THE LOOS OF ENGLAND Dave Dee, Dozy, Beaky, Mick and Tich (1967)

This is the title track of the only EP record by the group to make the EP charts – hitting number eight in 1967. 'The Loos Of England' first appeared on their album, *If Music Be The Food Of Love, Prepare For Indigestion*. It was written by Ken Howard and Alan Blaikley, who also contributed two other compositions, 'Over And Over Again' and 'Nose For Trouble' plus a number by the group, 'All I Want To Do'.

17. A NEW KIND OF LOVE The Dave Clark Five (1965)

Their first of three 45s to make the EP charts for the group, from which this track is taken, the self-titled 'The Dave Clark Five', and it reached number three in 1964, followed by 'The Hits Of The Dave Clark Five' in 1965, which made it to number 20, then finally, in the same year, 'Wild Weekend', which got to number 10. The title of the latter was taken from the American name of the group's movie, *Catch Us If You Can* – in the US it was titled *Having A Wild Weekend*.

18. KEEP AWAY Billy Fury (1963)

Taken from his EP 'Billy Fury & The Tornados', this was one of two compositions on this four-tracker that was written by the singer, the other being 'What Did I Do?' The other two tracks included were 'Nobody's Child' and 'I Can't Help Loving You'. The record spent 16 weeks on the EP chart, reaching its highest position of number two.

19. TO THE CENTRE OF THE EARTH Pat Boone (1960)

Both the movie *Journey To The Centre of The Earth*, which starred Pat Boone and James Mason, and Boone's EP, were released towards the end of 1959 but neither found true success until early in 1960. The four songs featured on the disc – and on the movie soundtrack – were 'The Faithful Heart', 'My Love Is Like A Red, Red Rose', 'Twice As Tall' and the title song, 'To The Centre Of The Earth'.

20. TELL THE BOYS Sandie Shaw (1967)

This EP was released around the time that 'Puppet On A String' was selected to represent Great Britain in the 1967 Eurovision Song Contest. The EP contained the four other songs that she performed each Saturday night on the Rolf Harris Show on BBC TV, from which 'Puppet' was selected as the winner. Sandie has often claimed that it was her least favourite of the five choices. 'Tell The Boys' is the title track of the EP and was written by Mitch Murray and Peter Callander along with Roger Webb's 'I'll Cry Myself To Sleep', 'Had A Dream Last Night' by Chris Andrews and 'Ask Any Woman', written by Geoff Langley and John Stewart.

21. I REMEMBER Eddie Cochran (1960)

During the Sixties, it was a common practice of record companies that each time a popular artist had released two singles, they would then issue both A and B-sides on an EP. Such was the case with Eddie Cochran in 1960. Soon after his death the London label released the four-track 'Something Else', which also included 'Boll Weevil Song' together with 'Teenage Heaven' and 'I Remember'.

Sandie Shaw was another UK Eurovision representative, with 'Puppet on a String'

22. GOT MY MOJO WORKING The Mojos (1964)

The group's self-titled EP reached number 12 on the EP records chart and if you're fortunate enough to own a copy, then look after it: it has now become a real collector's item. The other three tracks on the disc are 'The One Who Really Loves You', 'Nobody But Me' and their biggest hit, 'Everything's Alright'. Originally called The Nomads, they were one of the few Merseyside groups to be signed to Decca. After their first single failed to chart the Mojos departed for Hamburg following the trail well worn by so many UK rock'n'roll bands of the period. While they were in Germany they cut their self- penned second single 'Everything's Alright' that became the group's only top-10 hit.

23. EARTHY The Tornados (1962)

With the group's 'Telstar' riding high in the charts, Decca were reluctant to release their follow-up single, 'Globetrotter', which they held back and instead released this EP, which spent a total of 27 weeks on the EP charts and the other three titles were 'Ridin' The Wind', 'Red Roses And A Sky Of Blue' and 'On A Cloud'. In 1963, they released a follow-up EP, 'More Sounds Of The Tornados', which also became hugely successful.

24. TON MEILLEUR AMI François Hardy (1964)

Taken from her disc, 'C'Est Fab', which reached number five on the EP charts largely on the strength of her hit single at the time, 'Tous Les Garçons Et Les Filles', which was included in the track listing along with the B-side, 'L'Amour S'En Va', alongside 'C'Est L'Amour Auquel Je Pense' and 'Ton Meilleur Ami'.

25. GET A BUZZ The Pretty Things (1965)

The Pretty Things had two top 20 EPs in the Sixties, the first being their eponymous four-tracker, which contained the A and B-sides of their hits 'Don't Bring Me Down' and 'Rosalyn'. The second EP was titled after one of its tracks, 'Rainin' In My Heart'. This was not the Buddy Holly song but one written by Jerry West and James Moore, better known as Slim Harpo. Members of The Pretty Things wrote the other three tracks, 'London Town', 'Sittin' Alone' and 'Get A Buzz'.

THE ONE BEFORE THE HIT

So what was that previous release before the major breakthrough? Here are some examples of the record before that first hit.

1. CHILLS AND FEVER Tom Jones (1964)

Tom's career really began in 1963, when he became the front man for local Welsh group Tommy Scott & The Senators. The following year they recorded several tracks under the supervision of Joe Meek but, despite being armed with the material, he was unable to secure a record deal. Running out of possibilities, Decca suddenly showed renewed interest after Gordon Mills spotted the group in a local working men's club. But he was more interested in the singer, who he renamed Tom Jones. His first release for the label was a cover of a minor American hit in 1961 for Ronnie Love, 'Chills And Fever', after which Tom didn't have to wait long to find himself at number one with 'It's Not Unusual'.

2. AS LONG AS YOU'RE HAPPY BABY Sandie Shaw (1964)

Dagenham girl Sandie Shaw was discovered by Adam Faith, who introduced her to his manager, Evie Taylor, who in turn acquired her a recording contract with Pye Records in 1964, releasing this, her debut single, which she successfully followed with the chart-topping Bacharach and David song, '(There's) Always Something There To Remind Me'.

3. NO, NO, NO Crispian St Peters (1965)

Born Robin Peter Smith in Swanley, Kent, after leaving school St Peters began working in a paper mill, playing local gigs at night, before his career was interrupted by National Service in the Army. Once discharged, he formed The Beat Formula Three and met up with David Nicolson, who became his manager. Nicolson gave him his new name and secured him a recording contract with Decca. The Beat Formula Three were dumped and replaced by The Puppets, who were deemed more suitable. St Peters' first single, 'At This Moment' was released at the beginning of 1965. It was a monumental failure, as was his next release, 'No, No, No'. But yes, yes, yes... the big hit, 'You Were On My Mind' eventually followed.

4. PRETTY GIRLS EVERYWHERE The Walker Brothers (1965)

On 17 February, 1965, three young men set off from California to the UK on the greatest adventure of their lives, leaving behind a series of lucrative club and television engagements. Calling themselves The Walker Brothers – although none of them were related – they signed to Philips, who had high hopes for them. But because John and Scott had both made records in the past, neither of them regarded this deal as particularly significant. John sang lead on their debut for the label, the uptempo 'Pretty Girls Everywhere', but it vanished without a trace. Then Scott took over for their first hit, 'Love Her'.

5. TURN AROUND AND TAKE A LOOK The Lemon Pipers (1968)

The Lemon Pipers were made up of the remnants of two Ohio-based groups, The Bandits and Ivan and The Sabres. Modelling themselves on a mix between The Byrds and The Who, they recorded their first self-written single, 'Quiet Please', in 1966 for the local Carol label. The following year they were signed by Buddah records, releasing their first record for them, 'Turn Around And Take A Look', written by guitarist Bill Bartlett. Little did they know they were one release away from an American number one with 'Green Tambourine'.

6. I DIDN'T MEAN TO HURT YOU The Rockin' Berries (1964)

Formed initially as The Bobcats in Birmingham in 1959, they backed Jimmy Powell and established a residency at Hamburg's famous Star club. Then, three years later, part of the group defected to form a new group, Jimmy Powell & The Dimensions. But instead of calling it a day, they recruited a couple of old mates from back home, leading to a contract with Decca. After a couple of failed singles, the label dropped them but, unfazed, they continued to work seven nights a week around the local clubs.

Over at Pye records, John Schroeder was looking for new talent to sign to their Piccadilly label and signed them to a deal, allowing them to release a version of a Shirelles' B-side, 'I Didn't Mean To Hurt You', which almost became a hit, but just missed the top 40. The very week the record made an appearance just outside the top 40, Pye decided to release 'He's In Town', killing off any chance of the other record climbing any higher. The reason was, however, that after hearing 'He's In Town' everyone became very excited. But word was out that the original version by The Tokens was about to be released, so Pye had no alternative but to rush out The Berries' own recording. The gamble paid off and they had their first top-10 hit.

7. ADIOS AMOUR (GOODBYE MY LOVE) The Casuals (1968)

The group, blessed with the unique voice of lead singer, John Tebb, based themselves in Italy for many years, working clubs around central Europe, before returning to England in the mid-Sixties where they took part in the TV talent show, *Opportunity Knocks*, winning it three weeks on the trot. This led to a recording deal with Fontana and the single, 'If You Walk Out', was released to little interest. They then returned to Italy where they recorded Italian versions of British hits for CBS. In 1968, they switched to Decca and released the single, 'Adios Amour (Goodbye My Love)' written by Tom Springfield and Norman Newell, little knowing they were one record away from a massive hit with 'Jesamine'.

8. ALMOST THERE BUT NOT QUITE The Traffic Jam (1967)

The original line-up of The Scorpions came together in 1962, a Peckham-based four-piece led by Mike Rossi, who was barely in his teens. Following a change in personnel, they became The Spectres and by 1966 – under the guidance of manager, Pat Barlow – they secured a deal with Pye Records. They had been recommended to John Schroeder, who was always on the lookout for new talent and had been put in charge of the subsidiary label, Piccadilly. Under his direction, they recorded a version of 'I Who Have Nothing'. The record failed, as did their next two releases. By January, 1967, they opted for another new name, Traffic, only to learn Stevie Winwood had already chosen that name for his new group and brought forward the release of their first single. So this Traffic became The Traffic Jam, capitalising on the publicity and releasing a single with the title 'Almost There But Not Quite'. Just how true that was they could not have guessed, as their next release, 'Pictures Of Matchstick Men' gave them that first taste of chart success under the name Status Quo.

9. SHE SMILED SWEETLY The Love Affair (1967)

Originally called The Soul Survivors, the band changed their name when they recorded their first single for the Decca label in 1967: a cover of the Mick Jagger and Keith Richards song, 'She Smiled Sweetly', taken from The Rolling Stones' fifth British studio album, *Between The Buttons*. Lead singer Steve Ellis has always claimed that he hated the song but was forced into recording it. After the record failed, they were released from their contract but were soon snatched up by CBS and topped the charts with 'Everlasting Love'.

The Love Affair: these lads charted with a Jagger/ Richards song

10. LOVE AND FURY **The Tornados (1962)**

Their first single, 'Swinging Beefeater', vanished without trace but then they secured the position as Billy Fury's live backing group, following the departure of The Blue Flames. Producer Joe Meek summoned the group into the studios to record 'Love And Fury', a tune he'd written as a dedication to Billy. The keyboard player on the record was Norman Hale, who soon fell out with Meek and by the time the record was released, had left the group and replaced by Roger LaVern.

For the follow up to 'Love And Fury' Meek had decided to record a new treatment of 'The Breeze And I', but just before its scheduled release, drummer Clem Cattini discovered that Shane Fenton's group, The Fentones, were about to release their version. The track was shelved and Meek was left with the problem of finding an alternative. The answer arrived a few days later when on July 11, 1962, the first live television pictures were beamed across the Atlantic via a new satellite called 'Telstar'. So inspired, Meek immediately set to work on writing a tune using that title and a multi-million selling record was created.

11. SHAKE YOUR MONEYMAKER **Fleetwood Mac (1967)**

Their first hit album was the bluesy, self-titled *Fleetwood Mac*, released on the Blue Horizon label in February 1968 and hugely successful in the UK. Before that, in 1967, they released Robert Johnson's 'Dust My Broom', which they recorded under its original title of 'I Believe My

Time Ain't Long', copies of which now fetch around £100. Their first top-40 hit was 'Black Magic Woman' but before that came their version of an Elmore James song, 'Shake Your Moneymaker', taken from their second album, *Mr Wonderful*.

12. GIVE PEACE A CHANCE Hot Chocolate (1969)

The eighteenth single to be released on The Beatles' Apple label and the first by Hot Chocolate, who went on to achieve a string of hits in the Seventies and Eighties, it was produced by former Shadows drummer, Tony Meehan. Lead singer, Errol Brown decided he wanted to make changes to John Lennon's original lyrics. Naïve with the workings of the music business, he didn't realise he needed the songwriters' permission to make any changes. A copy of the finished track was sent to Lennon who fortunately gave it his seal of approval. Shortly after, Hot Chocolate signed to Mickie Most's RAK label and scored a top 10 hit with 'Love Is Life'.

13. CAN I GET TO KNOW YOU BETTER The Turtles (1966)

The group were formed in California in 1965 by Howard Kaylan and Mark Volman as The Crossfires From The Planet Mars, signing to the newly formed White Whale label and changing their name to The Tyrtles (to keep in tradition of misspelling as inspired by The Beatles and The Byrds). But when their first single was released, the Bob Dylan song, 'It Ain't Me Babe', their name was spelt in the traditional way and the record reached number eight in America. They continued to achieve lesser-sized hits with 'Let Me Be', 'You Baby' and 'Grim Reaper Of Love' in the US but none of them charted in the UK. Then towards the end of 1966, much to the annoyance of the group, their label decided to release a song, 'Makin' My Mind Up', even before they'd had a chance to complete the recording. The response was so unfavourable that it was instantly withdrawn and replaced with this Steve Barri and PF Sloan song, 'Can I Get To Know You Better'. It only reached number 89 in America but they need not have worried as that elusive international hit was on its way – in the shape of 'Happy Together'.

14. WISE MAN Desmond Dekker & The Aces (1967)

Desmond first auditioned for companies in Jamaica in 1961 but failed to obtain a deal until he tried producer Leslie Kong's Beverley label. Although they signed a deal, he didn't record until 1963 because Kong

It took The Turtles several attempts, but they eventually struck lucky with 'Happy Together'

wanted to wait for the ideal song. That turned out to be 'Honour Your Mother And Father', which became a huge local hit. Several more successful records followed and his 'King Of Ska' turned him into one of the island's biggest stars. He then recruited four singers, Clive, Wilson, Patrick and Barrington, who became his backing band, The Four Aces and began recording with them.

In 1967 the group became a trio and became simply The Aces. With them, Desmond recorded 'Wise Man', which was well-received in the UK and Desmond's fan base was growing. It was when the follow up '007 (Shanty Town)' was released, he became a hit with pop and reggae fans alike. The disc received heavy support from the UK clubs and the pirate radio stations and eventually found a place in the top 20, the first Jamaica-produced record to achieve this level of success.

15. SO LONG BABE Nancy Sinatra (1965)

First signed to her father's Reprise label in 1961, Nancy Sinatra's early releases went virtually unnoticed and by 1965, still without a hit, she was on the verge of being dropped from the company's roster. Songwriter and producer Lee Hazlewood, who had been making records for over 10 years, notably with Duane Eddy, was drafted in to work with Nancy and crafted songs to suit her voice. Their first attempt produced the single 'So Long Babe', which reached the dizzy heights of number 86 on the American Hot 100, but little did they know that major success was just around the corner. Bolstered by a major change of image including bleached blonde hair, frosted lips and heavy eye make-up, Nancy made her mark on the American and British charts during the early part of 1966, reaching number one in her homeland for one week and in the UK for four weeks with her International hit, 'These Boots Are Made For Walkin''.

16. HOW MANY TEARDROPS Lou Christie (1963)

By 1966, Lou Christie had achieved two US top-40 hits 'The Gypsy Cried' and 'Two Faces Have I', but had failed to chart in the UK. The follow up to the latter only reached number 46 in The States in 1963 but he then had to wait until the beginning of 1966 for his only Stateside number one and first UK hit. The reason why there was such a long wait for Lou to achieve his first American chart-topper was the fact that he was drafted into the army in December 1964. On release, he recorded

'Lightning Strikes', which became his first release for the MGM label. True to form, two of his previous labels rushed out earlier recordings by Lou to try to cash in on his worldwide hit.

17. (DO I FIGURE) IN YOUR LIFE The Honeybus (1967)

Pete Dello and Ray Cane had worked separately in various groups before meeting up as part of Grant Tracy & The Sunsets, where the pair wrote much of the group's new material with little success. Both musicians turned down the opportunity to join Cliff Bennett's Rebel Rousers and instead concentrated on their writing. In 1965, they were back on stage backing soul singer, Steve Darbishire as part of the Yum Yum Band, recording five singles for Decca. Dello suffered a collapsed lung just before the start of a major tour and, after several months recuperating, decided it was time to form his own group to showcase his and Cane's material. And so The Honeybus was born.

In the spring of 1967, with the help of Russ Ballard and Bob Henrit from The Roulettes, they recorded and released their first single, 'Delighted To See You', which was released by Decca's recently formed Deram label. When the record flopped, the group completed their line-up by adding former Honeycombs member Colin Hare on guitar and drummer Pete Kircher, who had been with the band The Loving Kind, which also featured future Jimi Hendrix Experience bassist Noel Redding. The completed group went back into the studio to record their next single, '(Do I Figure) In Your Life', written by Dello under his real name of Peter Blumson. But despite heavy airplay and rave reviews,

The Honeybus: 'I Can't Let Maggie Go' became their one and only hit.

it failed to chart. They need not have worried, the big one was on the way. It was in March, 1968, that they released their third single, another Dello song, 'I Can't Let Maggie Go'. Within weeks, the record had climbed to number eight on the UK's national charts, resulting in TV appearances and a number of bookings for live gigs, all of which conflicted with Dello's vision for the future as he saw The Honeybus mainly as a studio project. With his record label screaming for more material, he found the pressure too much and quit his own group. Although it should have signalled the end of the band, the rest of the members decided to continue and recruited Jim Kelly to replace him. But despite a number of further releases, they were never able to repeat the success of their one and only hit.

18. YOU STILL WANT ME The Kinks (1964)

1964 was quite a year for The Kinks. In February they released their debut single, a cover of Little Richard's 'Long Tall Sally', which created a certain amount of media attention, then in April, with no chart action but in the middle of a major tour, their follow-up, 'You Still Want Me', an original Ray Davies song recorded on the same session as their debut single, was released as there was no time for them to go into the studios to record new material. This record also flopped, but little did they know how close they were to hitting the big time. A true case of third time lucky – but only after they'd recorded 'You Really Got Me' twice, despite the fact that their first effort satisfied producer Shel Talmy. The band persuaded their label, Pye to let them go back into the studio to remake it. Ray Davies picked the track apart in fine detail, making changes until he heard exactly what he wanted from the group. His judgement was confirmed when the record went to number one.

19. KEEP ON DANCING Brian Poole & The Tremeloes (1963)

The Tremeloes were signed to Decca in 1962 in direct preference to The Beatles. They were considered promising enough to be given a spot on *Saturday Club*, and in April that year released their first single, 'Twist Little Sister', followed by a couple of further unsuccessful releases. The year ended with the group appearing in the movie *Just For Fun* and performed the song 'Keep On Dancing', which would be their first release for 1963. But despite considerable publicity, the group just didn't fit in with what was happening musically in the UK and the record was a flop.

In April, 1963, the Beatles' debut album was the hottest selling record in Britain, EMI had started to promote The Dave Clark Five as London's big new stars, and so Decca became quick to market Brian and the boys in a similar way. What was required to complete that transformation was a red-hot powerful song. Producer, Mike Smith convinced them that a cover of 'Twist And Shout' was the answer. After some uncertainty, mainly because it was also the last track on The Beatles album, the decision was taken to record it, resulting in their first big hit.

20. LITTLE DARLING Wayne Fontana & The Mindbenders (1964)

Although popular belief has it that when Glynn Ellis changed his name to Wayne Fontana, he took his surname from that of his record label, it now transpires that was not the case at all – he named himself after the drummer, DJ Fontana. The Mindbenders made some impact with their first single, 'Hello Josephine', just missing making the top 40 when it stalled at number 46. There then followed two further singles that disappeared without trace, 'For You, For You' and the revival of The Diamonds' 1957 top-five hit, 'Little Darling'. After a promising start but with two failed records behind them, the group turned to American singer and songwriter, Jimmy Breedlove for their next release that happily gave them not one of their biggest hits but at least earned them their first top-40 placing with 'Stop, Look And Listen' before their next release that gave them the breakthrough they were looking for with 'Um, Um, Um, Um, Um, Um'.

21. GOOD DAY SUNSHINE The Tremeloes (1966)

With their lead vocalist, Brian Poole, The Tremeloes racked up eight top-40 hits between 1963 and 1965, but in that final year they released their last single together, 'Good Lovin'', which failed to chart. In May, 1966, Brian Poole issued his first solo single without the group, 'Hey Girl'. That too was a flop, as was The Tremeloes' debut without Brian, a cover of Paul Simon's 'Blessed'. The group then moved from Decca to CBS and their first single for the new label was a cover of the Lennon and McCartney song from the Revolver album, 'Good Day Sunshine' and although it received its fair share of airplay, sales were disappointing. It didn't chart but it showed the direction in which the group were heading. The group had discovered a Cat Stevens song, 'Here Comes My Baby', amongst some publishers' demos. They quickly gave it a makeover, turning it into an uptempo party track. The record entered the charts in February 1967 after which, until 1971, they were never far away from their next hit.

22. SAY THE WORD **The Brook Brothers (1960)**

Ricky and Geoff Brook really were brothers, and were originally called The Brooks Brothers. In 1958, they entered and won a talent contest in Southampton that was broadcast on Southern TV's *Home Grown*. The following year they were signed to the Top Rank label and placed under the supervision of up-and-coming writer and producer, Tony Hatch. After releasing a couple of the singles for the label, Hatch's talent was recognised by the bosses of Pye Records and they offered him a better deal, which he accepted. He took the brothers along with him, releasing their first single for the label, 'Say The Word' and dropping the 's' from their name. But after the record failed to chart, Hatch found the boys an obscure song written by Barry Mann and Howie Greenfield called 'Warpaint'. The record looked as though it was going to be another flop but, after almost four months, the record began picking up airplay and it entered the charts on March 30 1961, a few weeks later reaching number five.

23. THE SOUND OF SILENCE **Simon & Garfunkel (1965)** *US No 1*

Written by Paul Simon in 1964, following the assassination of President John F Kennedy, this song was originally recorded as an acoustic track for their first CBS album, *Wednesday Morning 3 AM*, but was later overdubbed with electric guitars at the instigation of their record company and released as a single the following year, reaching number one in the States on new Year's Day, 1966. It was that version that was included on their next album, *Sounds Of Silence*, the original title of the song. Both the singular and plural forms appear in the lyrics. The duo were robbed of UK chart success due to a cover version by the Irish group The Bachelors, who reached number three with their rendition.

So it was Simon & Garfunkel's follow-up, 'Homeward Bound', that was their debut into the UK charts. Written by Paul Simon at a time when he lived in the UK in Brentwood, Essex. He was travelling back from a gig and he got stuck at the railway station, so to pass the time he started work on this song with a double meaning: his desire for his train to arrive so he could get back to his girlfriend at the time, Kathy Chitty, but also his yearning to go to his home in the US.

THE ONE BEFORE THE HIT

24. GOODBYE **Barry Ryan (1968)**

Identical twin brothers, Paul and Barry Ryan achieved a handful of top 40 records as a duo on the Decca label between 1965 and 1967. Then the pair were signed to MGM, releasing further material, but none of the records made the charts. Towards the middle of 1968, Paul took the decision that he no longer wanted to perform but concentrate on his songwriting, leaving Barry to pursue a solo career. After the announcement, the fans were expecting Barry to record a new song composed by Paul, but that was not the case.

Still with MGM, his first solo outing was a song written by Clive Westlake and Mickey Most called 'Goodbye', but despite its fair share of airplay, the record was considered a flop. Many critics thought it was 'goodbye' to the career of Mr Ryan. But how wrong could they be? Towards the end of 1968, Paul had written a marathon five-and-a-half minute song that he gave to arranger, Johnny Arthey to score. Barry's presence was requested in the studio and 'Eloise' was born. The record climbed all the way to number two on the UK charts and ended up selling in excess of three million copies worldwide and topping the charts in 17 countries.

25. LAUGHING FIT TO CRY **David & Jonathan (1966)**

David & Jonathan were in fact Roger Cook and Roger Greenaway and both came from Bristol. They found more success as songwriters than performers. They met while they were members of The Kestrels and whilst on tour decided to try their hand at writing songs together. Their first major success in this capacity was in 1965 with The Fortunes hit, 'You've Got Your Troubles'. Later that year they began recording as David & Jonathan, releasing their first single, 'Laughing Fit To Cry', which, despite receiving it's fair share of airplay, failed to chart.

But they had George Martin as their producer and had strong connections in The Beatles camp. They'd recently sang backing vocals on the Martin-produced hit, 'A Hard days Night' by Peter Sellers, and with the imminent release of The Beatles' *Rubber Soul* album, they decided to cover the song 'Michelle'. Although they managed a respectable top-20 hit both here and in the US with their cover, another group, The Overlanders had the same idea and their version went to number one.

26. FEELIN' SO GOOD (SKOOBY DO) The Archies (1968)

The cartoon characters were squeaky clean and totally innocent. Archie loved Betty, Reggie loved Veronica, Jughead the drummer loved Hot Dog the dog and they all loved the old banger that transported them from Riverdale High to Pop's 'Choklit ' shop. The animated TV series made its television premiere in America on the CBS Network in September, 1968. The cartoon spin-off group's first US release, 'Bang-Shang-A-Lang' reached number 22 on the Hot 100 but the follow-up, 'Feelin' So Good (Skooby Do)' fared less well, only climbing to number 53. Neither made any impact on the British record-buying public. Don Kirshner, creator of the group, had been given a song called 'Sugar Sugar', some years earlier by composer Andy Kim for another of his acts, The Monkees, who were at the height of their musical rebelliousness and who dismissed it without further thought. So Kirshner dug out the demo and recorded it for a follow-up for The Archies. It topped the American charts for four weeks but in the UK it remained at number one for a staggering eight weeks, the longest period at the top of the charts since 1962, when The Shadows equalled it with 'Wonderful Land'.

27. I GET SO EXCITED The Equals (1968)

The group were formed in 1965 by Eddie Grant who, at that time, was supporting a head of blonde hair. The rest of the group consisted of twin brothers Derv and Lincoln Gordon as well as John Hall and Pat Lloyd. Towards the end of 1966, the group released their first single, 'Hold Me Closer', which failed to chart in the UK and although they found success in Europe it wasn't until 1968 that they released this single, which just missed out on becoming a top-40 hit. In Europe, their first single, 'Hold Me Closer', had been flipped and the original B-side, 'Baby Come Back' became the played track due to club DJs finding it a better song. The group's UK label, President, decided it would be worth following suit and re-issued the record plugging the other side. The ploy paid off and The Equals topped the UK charts as well as being number one in several other countries.

28. THE GIRL ON THE FLOOR ABOVE John Leyton (1960)

After landing the role of Ginger in the TV series *Biggles*, John's manager, Robert Stigwood was keen to secure him a recording contract. He arranged an audition with Pye but they turned him down. John was then taken to meet Joe Meek for his next audition, which resulted in him recording a cover of Ray Peterson's American hit 'Tell Laura I Love Her' that was released on the fledging Top Rank label. Unfortunately the label was purchased by EMI, who already had a version of the song released by Ricky Valence and so John's recording was buried. Meek didn't lose heart and recorded another single with John, 'The Girl On The Floor Above', but that too failed to make an impact.

It was his next release that wouldn't be so easily forgotten. Meek and Stigwood were determined John's third release would be a hit and commissioned up-and-coming song writer Geoff Goddard to write him a song. Passing Goddard the instructions on a Friday, the song was delivered the following Monday. The Outlaws were the backing band on 'Johnny Remember Me' with the wordless backing vocals being provided by trained singer, Lissa Gray. John had his doubts about the song, especially disliking the title and further complications arose when the finished record was presented to EMI who objected to a line in the lyric, 'The girl I loved died a year ago' on the grounds that it would be considered too morbid. So they had to go back into the studio and amend it to 'The girl I loved and lost a year ago'. But, despite the change, many music programmes still refused to play the disc. At this time, John had landed a part in the TV soap, *Harper's West One* where he performed the song on three occasions, helping it on its way to the top of the charts.

29. WOMAN, WOMAN The Union Gap (1967)

When Gary Puckett left college, he joined a band called The Outcasts who in 1966 toured parts of America. Then he formed Gary and The Remarkables before meeting Dick Badger, who became their manager and renamed them The Union Gap after a city near where Gary was born, in Minnesota. Kitting themselves out with Union Army-style uniforms they then recorded a demo tape that they played to CBS Records and producer and writer Jerry Fuller signed them to the label.

They recorded their first single, 'Woman, Woman', written by Jim Glaser and Jimmy Payne, in August, 1967 giving them their first American hit. In the UK, the single vanished without trace but success was just around the corner. The follow-up single, 'Young Girl', was written by Jerry Fuller and was subject to much controversy at the time as it told of underage romance. However, this didn't seem to stop the

Dressed as Union Army soldiers, The Union Gap had hits with 'Woman, Woman' and 'Young Girl'

media getting behind the record and soon the group found themselves topping the charts.

30. ROCKIN' LITTLE ANGEL **The Viscounts (1960)**

Don Paul, Gordon Mills and Ronnie Wells first met as part of the eight-piece Morton Fraser Harmonica Gang, a variety act that toured the world and made constant TV appearances. The three became friends and one day, flying back from Dublin in a Viscount plane, decided that would be the name of the group they were planning to form. Paul wrote to Larry Parnes requesting an audition, not expecting to get a reply. He was amazed when he received a phone call and an appointment. Within a week, they were appearing on the bill at the Kingston Odeon with Billy Fury and Marty Wilde. Parnes secured them a recording contract with Pye and gave them an American rockabilly hit, 'Rockin' Little Angel' by Ray Smith, to learn in time for their first recording session. It was released as their debut single in January, 1960.

Despite reasonable airplay and an appearance on *Saturday Club*, the record failed to sell in any significant quantities. But they need not have worried as record number two would be released eight months later. It was another old song first recorded by Paul Chaplain and The Bell Notes, 'Short'nin' Bread'. Originally planned as the B-side, it was swapped with the track 'Fee-Fi-Fo-Fum' at the very last minute – probably a very wise decision, as the record climbed to number 16, giving The Viscounts their first taste of chart success.

31. WHAT MORE DO YOU WANT The Ivy League (1965)

The Ivy League were formed by John Carter and Ken Lewis after they ended their stint as part of Carter-Lewis and The Southerners. They added Perry Ford to make a trio. In 1965 they signed a recording contract with Pye's Piccadilly label, releasing their first single, 'What More Do You Want', which generated some airplay and an appearance on *Ready Steady Go*. The record failed to chart, resulting in Carter and Lewis deciding to concentrate on writing songs for other artists. One of the songs they wrote was 'Funny How Love Can Be', which they played to labelmates The Rocking Berries, who jumped at the prospect of recording it for their next release. The Ivy League's manager, Terry Kennedy, listened once again to the original demo and decided it should be the group's next release. So he was left with the unenviable task of persuading John Schroeder at Pye not to release the Berries version and allow his group to re-cut it. Reluctantly John agreed and The Ivy League achieved their first hit. The Rockin' Berries released 'He's In Town' instead and also had a hit: to show there were no hard feelings, they still included 'Funny How Love Can Be' on their album.

32. COCK-A-HOOP Manfred Mann (1963)

Originally named The Mann-Hugg Blues Band, Manfred Mann were formed in London in 1962 and were signed to EMI's HMV label the following year. Their first single, 'Why Should We Not', went almost unnoticed but the follow up, 'Cock-A-Hoop', gained a certain amount of media interest – though not enough to put it into the charts. It was released on 25 October, 1963, just two and a half months before the record that propelled them to stardom was issued.

Unperturbed by the lack of success, the group set about finding a song for their next single and were asked by the producers of ITV's top pop show, *Ready Steady Go* to provide a new theme tune for the series. They responded with the energetic '5-4-3-2-1' which, with the help of weekly TV exposure, climbed to number five in the UK charts. Shortly after it was recorded, bass player Dave Richmond decided to leave the group, being replaced by Tom McGuinness, the first of many line-up changes.

33. LOVE WALKED IN Matt Monro (1960)

In 1957, pianist Winifred Atwell heard Matt singing and suggested to her own recording company, Decca, that they sign him. Although he cut some fine tracks, he found little success and was dropped. He was given a new contract with Fontana in 1958, but still that hit record eluded him. His lucky break came when EMI producer George Martin asked him to make a demo disc for Peter Sellers to use as a guide to copying a voice in the style of Frank Sinatra for his forthcoming album, *Songs for Swinging Sellers*. George knew he had a talent on his hands and signed him to Parlophone. His debut for the label was the George and Ira Gershwin song, *Love Walked In*, first featured in the 1938 movie, *The Goldwyn Follies* – the final movie score by George before his death on 11 July, 1937. Once again, the record failed.

Not to be phased by his first recording with Matt, George Martin decided to have one further attempt to find him a hit. He had just been brought a song called 'Portrait Of My Love', written by Cyril Ornadel and David West, the latter being a pseudonym for Norman Newell. With a magnificent arrangement by Johnnie Spence, Martin's gamble paid off and Matt Monro's career had been well and truly launched.

34. STICKS AND STONES Ray Charles (1960) US No 40

In 1947, Ray moved from Florida to Seattle, where he began recording as The Maxin Trio with guitarist, Gossady McGhee and bassist Milton Garrett. They achieved their first hit in the States in 1949 with 'Confessin' The Blues'. In 1951 Charles released his first record under his own name and the following year he signed to Atlantic with many of his releases making the R&B charts. In 1957, his first crossover record into the pop charts was 'Swanee River Rock', but it was in 1959 he finally made the American top 10 with his classic, 'What'd I Say'. With his contract coming to an end, he was offered a lucrative deal with ABC-Paramount that Atlantic were unable to match and in 1960 he was back on the charts with 'Sticks And Stones'.

Still no breakthrough in the UK, but that was just about to change. Ray's regular chauffeur, Tommy Brown suggested to him that he should record Hoagy Carmichael's 1930 standard, 'Georgia On My Mind' as he was always singing it in the back of the car. Ray liked the idea and asked Ralph Burns, Woody Herman's pianist, to come up with an arrangement. The song was recorded in four takes and gave him his first American number one and debut British hit – as well as winning two Grammys for 'Best Male Performance' and 'Best Performance by a Pop Single Artist'.

35. LOSE YOUR MONEY The Moody Blues (1964)

El Riot and The Rebels were one of Birmingham's most popular skiffle groups in the early Sixties but broke up after failing an audition for EMI Records. Ray Thomas and Mike Pinder formed a new group, The Krew Cats, and went off to seek work in Germany. On their return they teamed up with Denny Laine, Graham Edge and Clint Warwick, calling themselves The M&B Five as they were getting lots of work from Mitchells and Butlers pubs. But when the brewery decided not to sponsor them, they became The Moody Blues, signing to Decca and releasing their first single, a Mike Pinder song, 'Lose Your Money'. That's exactly what Decca did. But they decided to give them another chance with the release of the cover of the Bessie Banks original, 'Go Now', written by her then husband Larry.

This was the group's second single and within weeks of its release, it went to number one. Denny Laine discovered the song when going through a caseload of singles sent from America to his friend and journalist, James Hamilton. He immediately informed the rest of the group that this was a song he really wanted to cover.

36. LONG LONESOME ROAD Shocking Blue (1969)

Our research points to the fact that just prior to the release of this single a song, 'Send Me A Postcard', was recorded as a demo and only ever released as a single in the UK on the small Olga label. Original copies in mint condition now fetch around £60. 'Long Lonesome Road', has often mistakenly been titled on various compilation labels as 'Long And Lonesome Road', but either way, this was the record the Dutch group released prior to them making the charts. 'Venus', their big hit, became the biggest-selling single to originate in Holland and the first Dutch song to top the American charts: it was also number one in Belgium, Spain, France, Italy and Germany. Robbie van Leeuwen, the group's guitarist who wrote 'Venus', tried desperately to come up with another song to match their international hit but his failure to do so led him to become so depressed, it brought about quarrels within the group and they all decided to go their own separate ways in 1974. At the end of 1984, they decided to reunite for two concerts.

37. ALL I WANT Dave Dee, Dozy, Beaky, Mick & Tich (1965)

Written by Ken Howard and Alan Blaikley, who discovered the group when they were known as Dave Dee and The Bostons and were supporting The Honeycombs, this was their second single release, the follow up to their debut called 'No Time'. Both failed to chart. However it was their third single, also written by Howard and Blaikley that gave them their first taste of chart success: 'You Make It Move' broke into the top 40 in January, 1966 and begun a run of 13 consecutive chart entries.

38. CHAINED Marvin Gaye (1968) *US No 32*

Let's be fair, Marvin Gaye had made the UK top 40 before his big hit singing duets with both Kim Weston and Tammi Terrell. He'd also had two records that hung around just outside the top 40 with 'How Sweet It Is' in 1964 and 'Little Darlin'' in 1966. In America he'd already achieved a string of solo hits including this 1968 Frank Wilson written-and-produced track, 'Chained'. In the UK, it was the one before the hit. Producer, singer and songwriter, Barrett Strong had the phrase, 'I Heard It Through The Grapevine' going around in his head while working in Chicago and, on his return to Detroit, he got together with Norman Whitfield and completed the song that was first introduced to us in 1967 by Gladys Knight & The Pips. Whitfield also produced a version by Smokey Robinson & The Miracles that ended up gathering dust in the vaults. He then recorded it with Marvin, but the powers that be at Motown rejected it for a single in favour of the old-sounding, 'Your Unchanging Love'.

Whitfield went back to the song, recording versions with Bobby Taylor, The Temptations and Gladys Knight but he wouldn't let go of his desire to release Marvin's version. When he was looking for a couple of songs to complete his album, *In The Groove*, it was added to the track listing. WVON Radio in Chicago played 'Grapevine' off the album and the phone lines lit up from listeners wanting to get hold of the track. Motown were finally persuaded to release it as a single and to everyone's surprise, including Marvin's, it became the label's biggest selling record in their history.

39. HOT CHOCOLATE CRAZY Eden Kane (1961)

Richard Graham Sarstedt, older brother of both Peter and Clive, released his first single for Pye in 1961, which was picked up as the theme music to a Radio Luxembourg record show called 'Hot Chocolate Time'. Despite the constant plays, the record failed to chart, Pye Records dropped him from the label and he went and signed to Decca. Songwriter Johnny Worth was impressed when he saw Eden Kane perform as an Elvis Presley impersonator, as he had more appeal than most of the others with his striking good looks, his white suit and his stage presence. Worth played 'Well I Ask You' to Eden, who wasn't particularly struck with the song but his management team thought otherwise and persuaded him to record it – resulting in his first hit and a number-one record.

40. STRONG LOVE The Spencer Davis Group (1965)

The group were originally called The Rhythm And Blues Quartet but changed their name when they signed with Chris Blackwell, whose product at the time was released on the Fontana label. Their first release was a cover of John Lee Hooker's 'Dimples' but it failed to set the world on fire. They followed it with 'I Can't Stand It', a cover of an American single by The Soul Sisters. This single cracked the top 50 at number 47, as did their next release, 'Every Little Bit Hurts', reaching number 41. Then came 'Strong Love', which also reached number 44. The view was then that a record isn't really considered a hit until it breaks into the top 40 and The Spencer Davis group were just one record away. They finally broke through with a song that had been written by one of Chris Blackwell's reggae acts, Jackie Edwards. He had written and performed it with a ska beat but the Spencer Davis Group turned it into a pounding rocker and it became the first new number one in 1966.

41. I'VE GOT TO LEARN TO FORGET Susan Maughan (1962)

In 1960, whilst working as a vocalist with the Ronnie Hancox band, Susan made her first record, an EP of songs from the musical *Oliver* with actor, David Kossoff. The following year she was signed to the Philips label and was also recruited as the female vocalist in the Ray Ellington Quartet, who were best known for providing musical interludes in *The Goon Show*. Susan's first solo release was 'Mama Do The Twist', creating sufficient interest for the label to record two further singles, 'Baby Doll' and 'I've Got To Learn To Forget', neither creating much interest. But fortunately the bosses at Philips decided to give Susan one more chance. Record producer Johnny Franz suggested Susan should record a cover of a proven American hit by New York newcomer, Marcie Blaine, and she agreed it had potential of giving her that elusive hit. 'Bobby's Girl' entered the UK charts on

Susan Maughan

October 11 1962, the same week The Beatles made their chart debut with 'Love Me Do'. She outsold the Fab Four's first hit.

42. THE MULBERRY BUSH
The Dave Clark Five (1963)

The group released four singles before they finally made the charts. In 1962, they released their debut on the Ember label, an instrumental called 'Chaquita' that gathered few sales. They then released a further single on Piccadilly, another instrumental, 'First Love', but still little recognition came their way. Their next move was a lengthy association with EMI, signing to their Columbia label and releasing their first vocal single for the company, 'I Knew it All The Time', to no chart success. Little did they know they were one record away from making the charts when they followed it with a song based on the children's nursery rhyme,

'The Mulberry Bush'. It gathered some media interest and a little airplay but still that elusive hit evaded them. So to follow up 'The Mulberry Bush', it was decided to cover an American hit that was climbing the charts in The States, 'Do You Love Me' by The Contours. The decision was the right one, giving the group their first taste of chart success. Unfortunately, over at Decca records, Brian Poole and The Tremeloes had the same idea and their version went to number one. However, The Dave Clark Five were on the map and their next release, 'Glad All Over' was also a chart-topper.

43. ROOM ENOUGH FOR YOU AND ME The Overlanders (1965)

Taking their name from an old Australian folk song, The Overlanders formed in 1963 as a trio. Heavily influenced by The Kingston Trio and The Four Freshmen, they relied heavily on American folk and country music for their material. Signed to Pye Records, they were assigned to Tony Hatch as their recording manager. Their first taste of success came in 1964 when their cover of Chad and Jeremy's 'Yesterday's Gone' made a brief appearance in the American Hot 100 charts at number 75. Towards the end of 1965, they released their ninth single on Pye, 'Room Enough For You And Me' without so much of a sniff of a hit. But the wait was nearly over. Pye and the group were determined to have a hit, so drastic measures were called for. Expanding to a quintet, they were able to progress from their folk roots to more mainstream pop and all they needed from this point was a hit song. Help was at hand with the release of a new Beatles album, *Rubber Soul* in December, 1965. There was a mighty scramble by record labels to get their hands on advance copies in order to cover the songs with their acts. The Overlanders were quickest off the mark with their version of 'Michelle' arriving in record stores within four weeks of the album's release. Two weeks later it was topping the UK charts, giving them that hard-earned but sole hit of their career.

44. DO-WACKA-DO **Roger Miller (1964)** *US No 31*

Roger Miller recorded his first material for RCA in 1957 following a disastrous meeting with the legendary Chet Atkins who asked him at his audition, where was his guitar, to which he replied he didn't own one. Atkins lent him his own but was he was turned down by the label but was signed by Mercury with little success. He then recorded a couple of duets with both Donny Young and Justin Tubb for Decca, during which time he was establishing himself as a songwriter. He then returned to RCA and on this occasion, secured a contract but still the hits eluded him. In 1964, he was re-signed by Mercury to record an album of novelty songs that produced his first Stateside hit, 'Dang Me', followed by 'Chug-A-Lug', and then the less successful, 'Do-Wacka-Do', none of which made any impact on the British charts. But things were about to change. Towards the end of 1964, Roger was driving home from a gig when he passed a sign that read, 'Trailers For Sale Or Rent'. He couldn't get that line out of his head, and by the time he'd reached his destination, he'd all but completed the song, 'King Of The Road', giving him an American top five hit and his first taste of success in Britain, where the record topped the charts and won him five Grammy awards.

45. IN MY LONELY ROOM **Martha & The Vandellas (1964)**

In America, the girls had already achieved two major hits there with 'Heat Wave' and 'Quicksand'. In the UK it was a completely different story. Although an original mint copy of this single will fetch around £150, none of their earlier records made any impact on the charts and this single, written by Holland, Dozier and Holland only just made the US top 50, reaching number 44. They needn't have worried though, as a big international hit was just around the corner. With the relative failure of 'In My Lonely Room', Motown records made the decision to change producers and writers for their next release and William 'Mickey' Stevenson was allocated the job of coming up with a big hit. Together with Marvin Gaye and Ivy Joe Hunter, they delivered 'Dancing In The Street' and although it gave the group their first British taste of chart success, it wasn't until 1969 when the record was re-issued that it climbed all the way to number four.

46. LOOK HOMEWARD ANGEL The Fortunes (1964)

The Birmingham-based band were formed in 1963 as The Cliftones and managed by pirate radio entrepreneur, Reg Calvert. Their first single was a cover of The Jamies' original, 'Summertime, Summertime', followed by 'Caroline', which was selected as the theme song for the successful radio station and just failed to make the charts. Their next single, 'I Look Like You' went almost unnoticed, as did their distinctive revival of Johnny Ray's 'Look Homeward Angel', but success was just around the corner. They were seriously considering calling it a day. However, good fortune came their way via songwriters Roger Cook and Roger Greenaway who presented the quintet with 'You've Got Your Troubles', giving both band and composers their first smash hit both in the UK and in America.

47. DO YOU WANT ME TO The Four Pennies (1964)

Having won a talent contest run by Frankie Vaughan, the Four Pennies gained an appearance on television and a recording test with Philips Records. They recorded three songs on that first session, all of which were their own compositions. One of the songs became their first single, 'Do You Want Me To' with the B-side being 'Miss Bad Daddy'. The record was released to a fair amount of interest and just missed out on becoming a top-40 hit when it peaked at number 47, but real success wasn't far away. For their next single, the group returned to the studio and cut another of their own songs, 'Tell Me Girl (What Are You Gonna Do)' which was released in March, 1964, with the third song they recorded on the first session, 'Juliet' on the B-side. The new single was struggling until a couple of DJs happened to turn the record over and began playing

'Juliet', which led to further airplay and an eventual number one.

48. THE KISSIN' GAME Dion (1961)

Dion had a minor UK success in 1961 with a song called 'Lonely Teenager' but it failed to make the top 40, peaking at number 47. In America, it was a very different story. He'd had several hits with his group, The Belmonts, before achieving solo success with 'Lonely Teenager' reaching number 12. The follow up, 'Havin' Fun', didn't fare so well, only reaching 42 in the Hot 100. Then the one before the big hit on both sides of the Atlantic, 'The Kissin' Game' did even less business, reaching only number 82, resulting in it not being released as a single at all in the UK – it only appeared on a four-track EP. So after two comparative failures in America, it was imperative for Dion to come up with a sensational record for his next release. With his friend, Ernie Maresca, who was in a group called The Regents, they were jamming on a New York street corner by hitting box tops and dustbin lids when they came up with the idea of 'Runaround Sue'. So thrilled with the basic song was he, that he went into the studio a few days later, resulting in his first major UK hit and an American number one.

49. AS LONG AS THERE IS L-O-V-E Jimmy Ruffin (1965)

In 1961, Jimmy was the first act to release a record on Motown's subsidiary label, Miracle, with his own composition, 'Don't Feel Sorry For Me'. The label was short-lived, not helped by its slogan, 'if it's a hit, it's a Miracle'. Jimmy didn't have any further product released until 1964, when he was signed to another new Motown label, Soul, under the supervision of Norman Whitfield who wrote and produced 'Since I've Lost You'. Still without a hit or a release in the UK, the following year he was put to work with Smokey Robinson, resulting in another failing single. But little did he know that success was just around the corner. His next release was a song was written by Jimmy Dean, Paul Riser and William Witherspoon, who had The Motown Spinners in mind to record it. However, Ruffin was walking past the music room where the writers were putting finishing touches to the song and overheard it. He rushed in, begging the team to allow him the chance to sing it, relating to the anguished lyric about heartbreak. Originally there was a spoken intro but in the final mix, the words were omitted. This was Ruffin's only American top-10 hit and first UK release, reaching number four in 1974.

THEY CALL IT THE BLUES

Being a big fan of the blues I often include a record or two from that genre. Here are 24 examples of those that have been played on the show.

1. BABY SCRATCH MY BACK Slim Harpo (1966)

He was born James Moore in Louisiana and, as an orphaned teenager, went to work as a stevedore in New Orleans. He was obsessed with the blues, mesmerised by the sounds of Little Walter and Junior Parker and, in the mid-Fifties, he found himself playing with top bluesman Lightnin' Slim, who in turn helped him secure a recording contract. The first thing that record label boss, Jay Miller, did was to change his name, taking Slim as a first name and, as a fan of The Marx Brothers, chose the surname of Harpo. His first release, 'I'm A King Bee' never made the charts, but gained huge critical acclaim and it wasn't until 1966 that Slim found the really big crossover record, by adapting a simple dance tune, 'The Scratch', into 'Baby Scratch My Back' – giving him his only ever American top-20 hit.

2. HEARTBREAK (IT'S HURTIN'ME)
Jon Thomas & His Orchestra (1960) *US No 48*

The little heralded John C Thomas was born in Mississippi on February 21, 1918. His family moved to Cincinnati three years later where he grew up and learned to play piano at a church school from piano rolls. He studied voice training at the Cosmopolitan School of Music run by black music legend Artie Matthews, reportedly being the first to publish a blues song in 1912 even predating WC Handy. He formed his own quartet in 1955 and became a staff session player for King Records, working with the likes of Little Willie John and Titus Turner. In May 1960 he was invited to appear on the top -rated TV Show *American Bandstand*, presented by Dick Clark; a month later this single broke into the Billboard Hot 100.

3. IT'S A MAN DOWN THERE Duster Bennett (1968)

Tony 'Duster' Bennett was signed to the Blue Horizon label as a direct tip-off from Peter Green of Fleetwood Mac, who can be heard playing guitar on this track. Label boss Mike Vernon went along to see Bennett play and immediately decided to sign him up. Bennett wanted to release one of his own songs, 'Hard To Resist', as his first single. After several attempts to record it, the end result was unsatisfactory to everyone. Then Mike hit on the idea of covering an old G.L Crockett song, 'It's A Man Down There', which proved more pleasing to all concerned.

4. NEED YOUR LOVE SO BAD Fleetwood Mac (1968) *UK No 31*

Originally written and recorded by Little Willie John in 1960, this became the original Fleetwood Mac's second UK top-40 hit, following in the footsteps of Peter Green's own song, 'Black Magic Woman', later to be successfully covered by Santana. Little did they know that they were one record away from their biggest hit, the chart-topping 'Albatross'.

5. HOW LOW IS LOW Harmonica Fats (1962)

During the Sixties the blues were flourishing in America, with a seemingly unlimited amount of lesser-known artists earning a decent wage. This track by Harmonica Fats found a sound that more than resembles his mentor and namesake, Fats Domino. It's worth noting that the arrangement was by jazzman Shorty Rogers who later worked on an album with ex-Canned Heat guitarist, Harvey 'The Snake' Mandel.

6. BLUE SHADOWS B.B. King (1967)

B.B was born on 16th September, 1925, in Indianola Mississippi; his cousin was bluesman Bukka White, who helped him get started as a performer. His first major break happened when he landed a spot on one of America's first black stations, WDIA, promoting a pick-me-up tonic, Pep-Ti-Kon. By Spring 1949 his popularity had risen and he was selected to present the afternoon show, where he was nicknamed by his audience 'Swinging Black Boy', thus the name, B.B. A year later he met the Biharis Brothers who were about to launch a new blues label, RPM, and were keen to sign King. They cut some songs at Sam Phillips' Sun studios but fell out with Phillips and had to make do with portable recording equipment in a rented room at the local YMCA. One of the tracks recorded there was '3 O'Clock Blues', which became his first hit, reaching number one on the Billboard R&B charts in 1951.

7. HIDDEN CHARMS Howlin' Wolf (1963)

Written by Willie Dixon and featuring Hubert Sumlin, who was

Wolf's guitarist for over 23 years. Wolf was born Chester Alexander Burnett in Mississippi. He began performing in the late Twenties before meeting Sonny Boy Williamson who taught him the harmonica. It was country bluesman Charlie Patton who helped him develop his gutteral 'howlin' style and he changed his name to Howlin' Wolf before serving in the Army during World War II. On his discharge, he relocated to West Memphis, working as a DJ for a local radio station during which time he formed his own band and was soon to be signed to the Chess label, where he remained for the rest of his life.

8. SCREAMIN' The Paul Butterfield Blues Band (1965)

Taken from their self-titled 1965 debut album, the piece was composed by Mike Bloomfield, who had only recently joined the band that had recently won so much media attention when they backed Bob Dylan on his first electric rock'n'roll performance at the Newport Folk Festival. Elektra records pressed 10,000 copies of their first album but producer Paul Rothchild then decided the product wasn't good enough and forced the label to withdraw all copies. He claimed that if he recorded a week's worth of their live shows, he would come up with a far superior product. He was mistaken and the record company were forced to finance a third set of recordings, which finally surfaced in October 1965.

9. TWO FOR THE PRICE OF ONE
Larry Williams & Johnny Guitar Watson (1967)

Both artists had come to California in the mid-Sixties and became close friends and label mates, recording for the Okeh label. They decided it would be a great idea to record an album together resulting in *Two For The Price Of One*. Sadly Larry William's post '67 activities led to a criminal record and in 1977, there was an incident where he tried to shoot Little Richard over an outstanding debt. Three years later, he himself was found dead from a gunshot wound in his L.A home, aged just 44.

10. COUNTRY LINE SPECIAL
Cyril Davies & His Rhythm & Blues All Stars (1963)

This was the first single release by Cyril Davies and His All Stars. Cyril

Memphis Slim: a master of blues and boogie piano. There may have been a fool in town, but it sure wasn't Slim

had previously been part of Blues Incorporated with Alexis Korner and as the resident band at the popular G Club on Ealing Broadway. They offered musical credibility but lacked teen appeal. He left the band in 1962 in order to form his own Allstars with Long John Baldry, to play Chicago-style interpretations of R&B with occasional members Nicky Hopkins and Jeff Beck. Tragically the band proved to be short-lived when in early 1964, Davies died from leukaemia. After which Baldry took the remnants of the group to form his own Hoochie Coochie Men.

11. THERE'S A FOOL IN TOWN Memphis Slim (1969)

Memphis Slim took up residency in Paris in the early Sixties but would take the occasional trip back to his homeland of Memphis. During the summers of 1965 and 1967 when he returned home, he recorded two albums. The American Jubilee label, not known for blues music at all but for quirky products such as radio bloopers and organ music, released some of the tracks. Essentially, producer Clyde Otis, a good businessman, sold an album's worth of tracks to the company. However, the albums finally gained an official release of sorts in 1969 on an equally quirky British independent label, Beacon.

12. PARCHMENT FARM John Mayall with Eric Clapton (1966)

Two of the most dedicated blues musicians in the country, together with John McVie and Hughie Flint made up John Mayall's Bluesbreakers for the legendary 1966 album that subsequently was known as the *Beano Album*, as the sleeve depicts the four of them sitting in front of a wall with Clapton reading the *Beano* comic. Apart from being considered one of the most overall influential albums in blues-rock history, it was one of the first occasions anyone heard a Les Paul Gibson guitar played through a Marshall amplifier. Clapton's sensational playing inspired graffiti appearing on the streets of London declaring, 'Clapton Is God' at the time of the album's release. Written by Mose Allison, 'Parchment Farm' is about the Mississippi State Penitentiary known as Parchment Farm, a hard-time prison because of its strict regime, which was later reassessed and overhauled.

13. BORN UNDER A BAD SIGN Albert King (1967)

Written by Booker T Jones and William Bell, this was the title track of the first album that Albert King recorded for the mighty Stax label in 1967. The song has since become a blues classic covered by many top artists, not least of all Eric Clapton who firstly covered it with Cream on their 1968 album *Wheels Of Fire*. King himself was six-foot four inches tall and weighed over 250 pounds. He was left-handed and taught himself to play the guitar upside down, so he could use instruments built for right-handed players.

14. TRAIN TO NOWHERE Savoy Brown (1968)

Three days to record a single was a remarkably long time to spend in the studios by anyone's standards in the Sixties, but that was the case when Savoy Brown recorded 'Train To Nowhere' and 'Tolling Bells'. The former took the better part of 48 hours to complete, with additional musicians being utilized in the shape of no fewer than five trombonists and producer, Mike Vernon, adding extra percussion. The record was rushed released on 1 November, 1968 but failed to make any impact on the charts despite all the band's touring – with the band's name plastered up at a venue almost every night of the week.

15. MY BACK SCRATCHER Frank Frost (1966)

Frank was born in Auvergne, Arkansas and was hailed as one of the foremost harmonica players of his generation. However, he began by playing piano as a young boy and moved to St Louis aged 15 where he gained session work as a guitarist. He learned to play harmonica from Sonny Boy Williamson and whilst playing with guitarist, Big Jack Johnson, attracted the attention of Sam Phillips, the founder of Sun Records, who introduced him to Scotty Moore (guitarist on dozens of Elvis Presley hits), resulting in several recordings of considerable note including this one, 'My Back Scratcher'.

16. HI-HEEL SNEAKERS Tommy Tucker (1964) *US No 11/UK No 23*

Tommy's own composition has been covered by over 200 other performers over the years, including Elvis Presley, Stevie Wonder, John Lee Hooker, Jerry Lee Lewis and The Everly Brothers. Tucker's real name was Robert Higginbotham, and he came from Springfield, Ohio. He gave up the music business at the end of the Sixties. Tucker is also the father of an up-and-coming blues artist, Teeny Tucker (real name Regina Westbrook); and a cousin of his is Joan Higginbotham, an American female astronaut who in 2006 travelled on the spaceship *Discovery*.

17. MY NAME IS MISERY Al King (1967)

Born in Monroe, Louisiana, King travelled to Los Angeles in 1947 and cut his first single in 1951. A couple of years later, he was signed by Johnny Otis to the small Combo label, where he recorded as a solo artist under the name of Al Smith and as a member of The Savoys. Migrating north to the Oakland area at the start of the Sixties, he recorded a version of Lowell Fulson's 'Reconsider Baby' that gained regional popularity and was a stepping stone for his next release, his own song, 'Think Twice Before You Speak' (released on his own label, Flag). He then received a telegram from Sahara Records in New York asking him to ship 2,000 copies of the record, but he was unable to do so as he couldn't afford to press them. They agreed to lease the tape and distribute it properly resulting in a top 40 R&B hit. In 1967, he signed to the Modern label the first session for them produced this track 'My Name Is Misery'.

18. GOING BACK TO MEMPHIS Muddy Waters (1966)

Taken from his 1966 album, *Muddy, Brass And Blues*. The album was initially recorded with Muddy and his band of the time, which included

James Cotton and Otis Spann, then overlaid with a brass section. The arrangements were by Gene Barge and Charles Stepney.

19. YOU DON'T LOVE ME Willie Cobb (1961)

Written by Bo Diddley and first appearing on the B-side of his second single in 1956, 'Diddley Daddy', when it went under the title of 'She's Fine, She's Mine'. The song has also been known variously as 'You Don't Love Me', 'No, No, No' and as an instrumental, 'Shimmy Shimmy Walk'. In 1961, Arkansas native Willie Cobb set foot into a recording studio in Memphis to record his own slightly adapted version of the song for the American Mojo label. Cobb's version became so popular in R&B circles that many people mistakenly assumed he wrote it. In fact, when a reggae version by Dawn Penn made the UK top 10 in 1992, it was Willie's name who appeared on the composer credits. As to whether Bo Diddley received his royalties, it's not known.

20. CHECKIN' UP ON MY BABY Sonny Boy Williamson (1960)

Written by Williamson, the track originally appeared on his album, *The Real Folk Blues* in 1960 and featured Otis Spann on piano, Robert Lockwood Jnr and Luther Tucker on guitars with Fred Below on drums.

One of the blues scene's greatest harmonica players: Sonny Boy Williamson

21. DON'T BE MESSIN' WITH MY BREAD
John Lee Hooker with The Groundhogs (1965)

John Lee Hooker first came to the UK in 1962 as part of the American Folk and Blues tour, when the blues boom was beginning here – thanks largely to the virtually unknown Rolling Stones, The Pretty Things and The Yardbirds. The Groundhogs had a good following too; big fans of Hooker, they had taken their name from a JLH album track.

22. WHO'S CHEATING WHO Little Milton (1965)

Born James Milton Campbell Jnr in the Mississippi Delta town of Inverness and raised by a farmer who also happened to be a local musician. By the age of 12 his was an accomplished guitar player and by 1952 he was playing in local clubs and bars when he caught the attention of Ike Turner, who was talent scouting for Sam Phillips's Sun label.

Although he released a number of records, none created any real success – nor did future releases on a number of other small labels. Feeling let down, he started his own St Louis based Bobbin Records and secured a distribution deal through Chess where he experienced his first taste of regional success with the 1962 release, 'So Mean To Me'. Following a break to tour and manage other acts, he began recording new material and in 1965 released 'We're Gonna Make It', which topped the American R&B charts followed by this, 'Who's Cheating Who' that also became a best seller.

23. YOU BETTER WATCH YOURSELF
George Smith & The Chicago Blues Band (1969)

George Smith & The Chicago Blues Band recorded a track, 'Blues With A Feeling', in 1968 as a tribute to the late blues artist Little Walter Jacobs. Amazingly, it was in the spring of 1968 that George Smith finally got his opportunity to record an album, having played the Los Angeles blues circuit for several years and gained the respect and help of many top names. Otis Spann played piano and Muddy Waters and Luther Johnson helped out on guitar on several of the tracks.

24. I'M GOING TO MAKE MY HOME WHERE I HANG MY HAT
Johnny Copeland (1966)

Born in Louisiana, some of Copeland's Sixties releases billed him as

Johnny Clyde Copland although it's unclear if that was his birth name or just a nickname. Influenced by blues singers he'd heard on the radio such as BB King and Sonny Boy Williamson, he moved to Houston and formed The Dukes of Rhythm, backing up talent that came to play the local venues. After a few bad deals, he finally managed to cut his first record in 1958, 'Rock'n'roll Lilly' for Mercury, but to little interest.

It wasn't until the mid-Sixties that he recorded again, for the independent Golden Eagle label, before signing to Wand in 1965. He recorded a mere seven tracks for them, one of which was his interpretation of Bob Dylan's 'Blowing In The Wind' that was released as a single but quickly withdrawn as attention was being paid to the B-side, 'Dedicated To The Greatest' a tribute song to several deceased soul greats. The label wanted to turn that into the A-side and have one of Johnny's own songs to which they owned the copyright on the 'B', so the stunning 'I'm Gonna Make My Home Where I Hang My Hat' was included on the re-issue.

TV AND RADIO THEMES

Here we look at a selection of TV and a few radio themes that became popular in the Sixties. In most cases the original version of the themes have been included.

1. SATURDAY JUMP **The Midnight Shift (1966)**

The theme music to *Saturday Club*, which was originally recorded and featured on the programme by Humphrey Lyttleton's Band as the 'New Saturday Jump' and credited to Eddie James as composer – which many believe to have been a pseudonym for the show's producer, Jimmy Grant. In 1966 a more up-to-date arrangement of the theme was recorded by session men calling themselves The Midnight Shift and became the replacement version for the programme.

2. MARCH FROM A LITTLE SUITE **Trevor Duncan (1962)**

Set around a small village in Scotland during the late Twenties, *Dr Finlay's Casebook*, ran from 1962–1971 starring Andrew Cruikshank as the grumpy Dr Cameron and Bill Simpson as Dr Finlay, with Barbara Mullen as the no-nonsense housekeeper, Janet.

3. I SPY **Earle Hagen (1967)**

This espionage series, which ran from 1967 to 1969 became the first major American TV series to co-star a black actor, Bill Cosby, who played agent Alexander Scott alongside a white actor, Robert Culp, who was agent Kelly Robinson. The pair travelled all over the world disguised as a tennis star and his coach, with Cosby as the coach, winning for himself three Emmys for his role. The theme music was composed by Earle Hagen, best remembered for his composition 'Harlem Nocturne'.

4. THE POWER GAME **Cyril Stapleton & His Orchestra (1966)**

In 1963 a nailbiting drama series taking in all aspects of the aviation industry, from the boardroom to the workshop floor, hit our television screens under the title of *The Plane Makers*. However, it wasn't until 1965 when it reappeared as *The Power Game*, that it really captured the public's imagination. Featuring the ruthless character John Wilder, played by Patrick Wymark, fighting his way into power, the series co-starred Barbara Murray as Lady Wilder, Clifford Evans as Caswell Bligh and Peter Barkworth Caswell's son, Kenneth.

5. 77 SUNSET STRIP Warren Barker & His Orchestra (1960)
The series first started in America in 1958 but only came to the UK two years later and ran until 1964. The stories were based at the titular swanky Hollywood address and featured Efram Zimbalist Jnr as Stuart Bailey, Roger Smith as Jeff Spencer and the jive-talking Kookie – the lot attendant at the next door diner – played by Eddie Byrnes.

6. GURNEY SLADE The Max Harris Group (1960)
The short-lived series with the more popular theme tune began in 1960 starring Anthony Newley as an over-imaginative young man finding himself in strange situations, talking to trees and fantasizing about the ideal woman.

7. THANK YOUR LUCKY STARS
Peter Knight & The Nightriders (1961)
The show started out as a rival to *Juke Box Jury* in the early Sixties on a Saturday evening. Keith Fordyce presented it in the early days, then Brian Matthew took over the job. DJ Don Moss introduced a weekly feature in which youngsters reviewed new releases and gave them marks out of five, bringing to the forefront a young West Midlands girl, Janice Nicholls, who coined the catchphrase, 'I'll Give It Foive'.

8. THEME FROM CROSSROADS Tony Hatch (1965)
The show ran from 1964 to 1988 but always suffered from somewhat poor production values – and the acting standard was considered so low that the TV network decided the weekly output should be reduced from five episodes a week to just three. The Crossroads motel was run by Meg Richardson, played by the late Noele Gordon, who was evidently somewhat accident-prone: getting injured in a bomb explosion, poisoned by an ex-lover, imprisoned for dangerous driving and abandoned at the altar. Her daughter, Jill, played by Jane Rossington had her own share of bad luck: married three times (once to a bigamist), having a baby by her stepbrother, becoming a drug addict, then an alcoholic, having two miscarriages and a nervous breakdown… and that was just episode one!

9. BATMAN THEME Neal Hefti (1966) *US No 35*

Hefti gained early recognition as an arranger for Woody Herman, Harry James and Count Basie before making a name for himself as composer of top TV and movie themes including 'The Odd Couple', 'Barefoot In The Park and probably his most famous, 'Batman Theme'. The TV series ran for 120 episodes and included cameo appearances by many top stars including Joan Collins, Eartha Kitt, Tallulah Bankhead (in her final

Neal Hefti: the jazz arranger who was the 'Bruce Wayne' behind the Batman TV theme

screen appearance) and in 1967, appearing as 'Pussycat' and singing 'California Nights', Lesley Gore. The series starred Adam West and Burt Ward and was such a success when it was launched that there was a concerted rush by many record companies to get a version of the theme into the music stores. Hefti's original had to share shelf space with other versions including Link Wray's, Al Caiola's, Jan and Dean's and The Marketts'.

10. AQUA MARINA Gary Miller (1964)

Sung over the closing credits of *Stingray*, which was Gerry and Sylvia Anderson's third string-puppet production following on from the success of *Supercar* and *Fireball XL5*. The stories were set in the twenty-first century and the crew was commanded by Captain Roy Tempest, voiced by Don Mason, with help from his first mate Phones, voice by Robert Easton, and of course the gorgeous looking underwater mermaid Marina, voiced by co-creator, Sylvia Anderson. She was mute due to a vow of silence but made herself understood by her, ahem, 'body language'. It was thought that she was probably modelled on Brigitte Bardot. The organisation behind the sub and its crew was the World Aquanaut Security Patrol headed by Commander Shore voiced by Ray Barrett and his daughter, Atlanta (Lois Maxwell). The series ran from 1964–1965 and a total of 39 adventures were made.

11. DOCTOR IN THE HOUSE Alan Tew & His Orchestra (1969)

Based on the popular *Doctor* series of books by Richard Gordon, the TV programme went under several different titles including *Doctor At Large* and *Doctor In Charge*, ran for nearly 10 years beginning in 1969. The original series starred Barry Evans as medical student, Michael Upton and Ernest Clark as Professor Loftus, working at the famous St Swithin's Hospital. George Leyton and Geoffrey Davies, Robin Nedwell, Martin Shaw and Jonathan Lynn also appeared as students.

12. A MAN IN A SUITCASE Ron Grainer & His Orchestra (1967)

The series ran from 1967–68 and starred Richard Bradford as ex-CIA agent McGill, who became a troubleshooter for hire. It's theme was by Ron Grainer, whose best-known piece of music is probably the *Doctor Who* theme, memorably realised by the BBC Radiophonic Workshop.

13. EMERGENCY WARD 10 (SILKS AND SATINS) Peter Yorke (1957)

The series ran from 1957 until 1967 and was ITV's first long-running, twice weekly soap opera, following the lives of both the doctors and nurses as well as the patients of The Oxbridge General Hospital. Created by writer Tessa Diamond, it started out as *Calling Nurse Roberts*, a six-week serial about a probationary nurse that became so popular that the TV network broadened the format, changed the title and then the series constantly topped the ratings. Many famous stars appeared during its long run, including Jill Browne, Desmond Carrington, John Alderton Ray Barrett and Charles Tingwell. Lou Grade who was the head of ITV and was responsible for finally cancelling the show in 1967 later claimed that it was one of his biggest mistakes of his life.

14. THEME FROM Z CARS
Johnny Keating & His Orchestra (1962) *UK No 8*

Considered one of the finest police drama series of the Sixties, its original cast included Jeremy Kemp as PC Steele, James Ellis as PC

Bert Lynch and Brian Blessed as PC Fancy Smith, who were joined by Stratford Johns as Detective Chief Inspector Barlow and Frank Windsor as Detective Sergeant John Watt.

15. MISSION: IMPOSSIBLE Lalo Schifrin (1968)

The series ran in America from 1966 to 1973, thrilling us with the adventures of the Impossible Mission Taskforce (IMF), a team of government spies and specialists who were assigned 'impossible missions' by the unseen 'Secretary'. Although the cast varied over the years, the main characters included The Team Leader (Dan Briggs the first season, then Jim Phelps for the other six), The Techno-Wizard (Barney Collier), The Strongman (Willy Armitage), The Master of Disguise (first Rollin Hand, then The Amazing Paris), and The Femme Fatale (Cinnamon Carter, Casey, Dana Lambert, and Mimi Davis). The series is probably best remembered for its opening theme, its leader's selection of mission agents from a dossier, and the intricate use of disguises and a typical 'mask pull off' reveal scene near the end of most episodes. *Mission:Impossible* was brought to the cinema screens in 1990 as a star vehicle for Tom Cruise.

16. HIT AND MISS The John Barry Seven Plus Four (1960) *UK No 10*

The theme form the TV series *Juke Box Jury*, which ran from 1959–1967, presented by David Jacobs. Originally screened on a Monday but soon moved to Saturday evenings. A later version of the theme was introduced to the show from Ted Heath and his Orchestra.

17. IRONSIDE Quincy Jones & His Orchestra (1967)

Wheelchair-bound Robert Ironside, played by Raymond Burr, was a former cop wounded in the line of duty and kept on by the San Francisco police force as a consultant. The programme's theme was performed by the legendary jazz and soul arranger, Quincy Jones.

18. THE MUNSTERS THEME Jack Marshall (1964)

Built in the mid-Forties, the creepy 'Munster House' still stands on Colonial Street on the back lot of California's Universal Studios, though it has since been renovated and bares little resemblance to its original eerie past. The show starred Fred Gwynne as Herman (who worked at the Gateman, Goodman and Grave Funeral home) to provide for his family: wife Lily, played by Yvonne De Carlo, Butch Patrick as his werewolf son Eddie, Beverley Owen as niece Marilyn and Al Lewis as Grandpa. The series ran on BBC TV in the UK first from 1965 to 1971 and was regularly repeated.

19. BONANZA THEME Al Caiola & His Orchestra (1961)

The series began in 1960 and ran for several seasons, telling stories set on the Ponderosa Ranch near Virginia City during the 1860s. It starred Lorne Greene as father Ben Cartwright with his sons Adam, Hoss and Little Joe who was played by Michael Landon.

20. THEME FROM BEN CASEY Valjean (1962) US No 28

To Rival BBC's *Dr Kildare* screenings, ITV bought in the American medical series *Ben Casey*, which propelled actor Vince Edwards to stardom. The series was made by Bing Crosby's production company and several episodes were directed by the then-unknown Sydney Pollack. Ben Casey was a rebel neurosurgeon at County General Hospital, routinely risking the sack to save his patients. Only older and wiser Dr David Zorba, played by Sam Jaffe provided a stabilizing influence. He also spoke the show's famous opening line: 'Man, woman, birth, death, infinity'.

This version of the theme, by Valjean, was an American hit for the handsome pianist from Oklahoma. To make sure he wasn't putting all his TV medical drama eggs in one basket, the B-side actually featured the 'Dr Kildare Theme'.

21. THEME FROM THE AVENGERS
Laurie Johnson & His Orchestra (1965)

The series started out in 1961 starring Ian Hendry as Dr David Keel and Patrick McNee as agent John Steed. The following year, Hendry departed and Honor Blackman, clad in leather, made her entrance as Cathy Gale. The show hit its peak in 1965 when Diana Rigg became Steed's new partner, Emma Peel.

22. DEPARTMENT S Edwin Astley & His Orchestra (1969)

The series about counter-espionage began in 1969 with three Interpol-connected agents: Jason King played by Peter Wyngarde, Stewart Sullivan played by Joel Fabrini and agent Annabelle Hurst, played by Rosemary Nicols. They worked together and separately, solving murder and other mysteries.

23. OLD NED Ron Grainer & His Orchestra (1962)

The theme from *Steptoe And Son*. This show started out as a one-off comedy in the BBC TV series *Comedy Playhouse* in 1962. It was so popular that an entire series was commissioned for the same year. It featured two rag-and-bone men, a father and son played by Wilfred Brambell as Albert and Harry H Corbett as Harold. They made 20 episodes between 1962 and 1972 and two spin-off full-length movies were released to the cinema circuit. NBC in The States were so impressed with the series that they bought the rights and made a version for American television under the title of *Sanford And Son*, whilst Dutch television translated it into *Stiefbeen en Zoon*.

24. CANDID CAMERA THEME (I'VE GOT YOU COVERED)
Bill Bramwell (1960)

The theme tune to the popular TV series of the Sixties, presented by Jonathan Routh, in which the production team would hide cameras in order to film members of the public performing mad things, induced by the programme. Composed by Bill Bramwell, whose real name was Roger, features Johnny Scott on piccolo. The piece is actually called, *I've Got You Covered*.

25. THE MAN FROM U.N.C.L.E
Hugo Montenegro & His Orchestra (1965)

Inspired by the cinema success of James Bond, American TV channel NBC invited Ian Fleming to devise a spy series for television. The result was *The Man From U.N.C.L.E*, which stood for United Nations Command for Law Enforcement. Originally titled, *Solo* after the character Napoleon Solo played by Robert Vaughn, the U.N.C.L.E. offices were situated behind a secret wall at the back of a New York dry cleaners. The series also starred British actor David McCullum, who played agent Ilya Kuryakin and Leo G Carroll as Mr Alexander Waverly, the head of the organisation. Their main objective was to crush an international crime syndicate known as THRUSH.

26. LIGHT FLIGHT The Pentangle (1969)

Used as the theme to the TV series *Take Three Girls* about the adventures of three single girls who shared a flat in London. Liza Goddard played the posh cellist, Victoria; Angela Down was the cockney art student Avril; and Susan Jameson played an aspiring actress, Kate. The second series found Victoria with two new flatmates in the shape of Barra Grant, an American psychology graduate and Carolyn Seymore, an ambitious young journalist. Eleven years later, BBC 2 brought back the series with the original cast for a further four episodes as *Take Three Women'*, keeping the theme music from the original series.

27. NO HIDING PLACE Laurie Johnson & His Orchestra (1960)

The TV series began in 1959 but the theme music wasn't made available on disc until the following year. *No Hiding Place* ran through 236 hour-long cases until 1967, starring Raymond Francis as Chief Detective Superintendent Francis Lockhart with the TV series growing out of two previous series, *Murder Bag* and *Crime Sheet*.

28. TAXI The Robinson Crew (1963)

This was a British production, long before the successful American series of the same name that starred Danny De Vito. Written and created by *Dixon Of Dock Green* deviser, Ted Willis, it featured Sidney James as London taxi driver Sid Stone, who spent most of his working life getting involved in other people's problems. The theme music was written by Harry Robinson and Bunny Lewis.

29. SOFTLY SOFTLY London Waits (1966)

This series ran on BBC TV from 1966 to 1970 and was a spin off from *Z Cars*: it again starred Stratford Johns as Detective Chief Inspector Barlow, later joined by Frank Windsor as Inspector Watts. In 1971, there was even a spin-off from *Softly Softly*, when Stratford Johns was cast in the same role for *Barlow At Large*, where he was transferred to the Home Office and into the world of diplomacy and political intrigue.

30. THE UNTOUCHABLES Nelson Riddle & His Orchestra (1959)

The series ran from 1959 until 1963 and was based on the 1947 novel by Eliot Ness and Oscar Fraley. *The Untouchables* was the first drama series to be produced by Desilu Productions, the company owned by Lucille Ball and her then-husband, Desi Arnez. The series focussed on a greatly exaggerated version of the real-life Eliot Ness, played by Robert Stack, and his group of agents who had been labelled by the media as

'The Untouchables' in their constant battle against organised crime. The Capone family brought a million-dollar lawsuit against the production company, claiming they had used a Capone likeness for financial gain.

31. THIS IS YOUR LIFE Laurie Johnson & His Orchestra (1969)

The series *This Is Your Life* was first screened in the UK by The BBC from 1955 until 1964, with presenter Eamonn Andrews. The show would surprise people in the public eye by presenting them with the big red book that contained their life history – which would be displayed to the television audience. The show was revived by Thames television for the ITV network in 1969 and it ran well into the Nineties with presenter Michael Aspel. In 1994, the programme returned to the BBC after nearly 30 years. This theme was recorded by the composer, Laurie Johnson in 1969.

32. CAPTAIN SCARLET The Barry Gray Orchestra (1967)

Originally screened in September 1967, *Captain Scarlet And The Mysterons* was Gerry Anderson's follow-up series to the hugely successful *Thunderbirds*. Set in the year 2065, the good captain protected the world against evil campaigns launched by the mysterious Mysterons. Indestructible, he could survive car crashes,

missiles and bullets and his voice was supplied by Francis Matthews. Other regular characters were voiced by such stars as Paul Maxwell, Cy Grant, Charles Tingwell and Liz Morgan.

33. UP THE JUNCTION Manfred Mann (1968)

This is the title song from the one-off TV drama starring Dennis Waterman and Suzy Kendall, about the abrasiveness of the society of Clapham in south-west London – now distinctly posher than it was then. Written by Nell Dunn and directed by Ken Loach and watched by an audience of 10 million, it provoked over 400 complaints to the BBC mainly over its bad language and provoking sexual promiscuity, thus contributing to a national debate on the subject of abortion. The original soundtrack album now changes hands for over £50.

34. THE BALLAD OF JED CLAMPETT
Lester Flatt, Earl Scruggs & Jerry Scoggins (1964)

Jerry Scoggins was once a backing singer for legendary country star Gene Autry. This classic American comedy series told the adventures of The Clampett family, who struck oil in their backyard of their Ozark ranch then relocated to the high life of Los Angeles. Their attempts at the high life brought constant difficulties as they had little idea about what to do with all the mod cons that $25 million could buy – finding it difficult to differentiate between a dishwasher and a television set, for instance. Jed Clampett was played by Buddy Ebsen; his animal-loving daughter, Elly May Clampett, was Donna Douglas; and Granny, who had the most trouble with all the domestic machinery, was played by Irene Ryan. The series ran from 1964 until 1970.

35. 5-4-3-2-1 Manfred Mann (1964)

In 1963, ITV were planning to launch a new pop show to rival BBC's *Top Of The Pops* and the producers approached Mike Hugg, Manfred Mann and Paul Jones to write a theme tune for their prestigious 'Ready Steady Go'. The song was accepted and the group recorded two different versions, one for the show and the other for a commercial release as a single. Having the song played every Friday evening resulted in them achieving their first British hit.

36. THEME FROM THE MONKEES The Monkees (1966)

The theme song that was used for the opening and closing credits of the TV series *The Monkees* every week during 1966 and 67, it was for some reason never released as a single during the Sixties. The series was about the adventures of the artificially created group The Monkees, and their misadventures on the road. Stephen Stills and Charles Manson were amongst over 400 applicants to join the all-singing, all-acting group and were auditioned by the producers before they settled on Mickey Dolenz, Davy Jones, Mike Nesmith and Peter Tork. Initially the group mainly contributed just vocals to the songs they performed, as most of them didn't play a musical instrument. Despite that, 'The Monkees' won an Emmy in 1966 for Outstanding Comedy series.

37. SATURDAY NIGHT BEAT Ted Heath & His Music (1962)

On The Braden Beat was a forerunner to That's Life and Watchdog – one of the first British topical consumer affairs programmes – and was presented by Canadian actor, Bernard Braden. ATV's late-night Saturday show ran from 1962 until 1967 and delved into problems facing the average man in the street brought about by big companies.

38. RAWHIDE Frankie Laine (1960) UK No 6

Not a success in America, despite being the theme song from the popular TV series of the same time, starring Clint Eastwood as Rowdy Yates. Frankie Laine actually made a guest appearance in one episode of the series. He died in hospital aged 93 on 7 February, 2007, following a heart attack.

39. THEME ONE The George Martin Orchestra (1967)

The George Martin Orchestra was made up of top session musicians that varied from recording to recording, but always had George at the helm. There were several EPs and albums recorded, many of them overlooked. 'Theme One', was commissioned by the BBC to launch the opening of Radio 1 in September, 1967. The track was issued as a single and used to open and close the station for the first couple of years of its broadcasting.

40. SUCU SUCU Laurie Johnson & His Orchestra (1961) UK No 9

London-born Laurie Johnson studied at The Royal College Of Music and went on to become one of the finest British composers of cult TV themes and incidental scores for TV and films. He started composing for TV in 1959, beginning with the title music to the ITV series, No Hiding Place then, two years later, was commissioned to supply the music for another television series about a British Intelligence agent named Peter Dallis, who assists the Argentinian authorities in fighting organised crime. The series was called Top Secret and the theme music became a top-10 hit with the title, 'Sucu Sucu'.

REGGAE, SKA AND BLUE BEAT

A popular musical culture that sprang out into the world from Jamaica in the Sixties, strongly influenced by calypso music along with jazz and rhythm and blues. Here are a handful of perfect examples of the irresistible skanking rhythms of reggae and its musical brethren.

1. 54-46 WAS MY NUMBER The Maytals (1968)

Written by Fred 'Toots' Hibbert and famous reggae record producer Leslie Kong, this was one of the first reggae records to receive widespread recognition outside Jamaica and is still considered to be one of the defining songs of the reggae genre. The song was inspired by Toots' time in jail for possession of illegal substances and 54-46 was his prison ID number. He later revealed during an interview that he had actually made up the number and the story about being in prison in order to gain publicity for the record and was innocent of the drug charges, claiming he was set-up. The song was covered and released as a single in 1983 by British reggae band Aswad.

2. THE ISRAELITES Desmond Dekker & The Aces (1969) *UK No 1*

After three weeks at the top of the charts, 'I Heard it Through The Grapevine' by Marvin Gaye gave way to Desmond Dekker & The Aces but it only managed to hold onto pole position for one week before surrendering to The Beatles' 'Get Back', which remained at number one for six weeks. Dekker re-recorded 'The Israelites' in 1975 and the new version made it to number 10. The follow-up was 'It Miek', which is Jamaican for 'that's why' or 'that is the reason'. Dekker died of a heart attack on May 27, 2005, aged 64, and was one of the first Jamaican vocalists to make a significant impact on the charts outside the land of his birth.

3. RIVERS OF BABYLON The Melodians (1969)

Boney M's version of the song topped the charts in 1978, but it was written by Brent Dowe and Trevor McNaughton of The Melodians. They based it on the biblical hymn, Psalm 137, expressing the yearnings of the enslaved Hebrews in exile following the Babylonian conquest of Jerusalem in 586BC. It was set to music and, in context, fit appropriately into the ongoing contemporary black freedom struggle. The Melodians version later appeared on the soundtrack to the 1972 movie, *The Harder They Come*.

4. IT HURTS Delroy Wilson (1968)

The late Delroy Wilson wrote many of the songs he recorded but also had an ear for interpreting American soul songs, both well-known and obscure. On this occasion he settled on a song that had originally been recorded by The Tams in 1965 and which became an American top-40 hit in 1969 for Bill Deal and The Rhondels under the title 'I've Been Hurt'. It had also been recorded by British singer, Guy Darrell, whose version made the charts on re-issue in 1975.

5. AL CAPONE Prince Buster (1967) *UK No 18*

This was a huge club hit during the Sixties, featuring Dennis Campbell and Val Bennett on saxes, Raymond Harper and Baba Brooks on trumpets with Junior Nelson on trombone, and Ernest Ranglin on guitar and bass. The track later inspired the first hit by the group Madness, who made their chart debut in 1979 with 'The Prince', a tribute to Prince Buster who also re-recorded a version of 'Al Capone' in 1969 for his album *The Outlaw*.

6. LONG SHOT KICK DE BUCKET The Pioneers (1969) *UK No 21*

Originally formed in the early Sixties, The Pioneers became one of Jamaica's most successful acts during the latter half of the decade, recording a series of hits with producers Leslie Kong and Joe Gibbs, the most notable being 'Long Shot Kick De Bucket', a song written in homage to a well-known veteran racehorse whose sudden demise came during the last of his 202 races. Mourned by the racing world, the annual 'Long Shot Trophy' was established in the horse's memory and the less sensitive tribute came via this single.

7. HOUSEWIVES CHOICE Derrick & Patsy (1962)

At the time this single hit number one, Derrick Morgan had six other records in the top 10 in Jamaica. He would normally receive a flat payment for each record he made, a clear incentive to record as many songs as possible and work with different record producers. When this track started being played by the local radio stations, it was called 'You Don't Know How Much I Love You', and it garnered so many requests from housewives that producer Lesley Kong decided to rename it. Blue Beat star Prince Buster considered the sax solo to have been copied from one of his records and began an unresolved musical feud with Derrick, accusing him of stealing his ideas.

8. LONESOME TRAVELLER Laurel Aitken (1966)

Track two on the ultra-rare album *Ska With Laurel* – even the artist didn't own a copy. At his home in Leicester, Laurel Aitken managed to find the sleeve but the vinyl had long since disappeared. For the last 20 years it has been one of the most sought-after ska albums with occasional copies turning up in auction for around £300. Dubbed 'The Godfather Of Ska', Laurel Aitken was the man who recorded the very first ska record.

9. MY CONVERSATION The Uniques (1968)

This was one of several tracks that provided a fascinating insight into the changing sound of Jamaican music. The Uniques' lead singer, Slim Smith, has been described as one of the greatest singers to emerge from the ska era. He died in 1973 when, unable to gain entry to his parents' house, he broke a window, badly lacerating his arm, and he bled to death before he could receive treatment. Legendary Jamaican record producer Bunny Lee was responsible for what has become a classic track amongst reggae music fans. Co-written by Smith, Lloyd Charmers helped out on its backing vocals and Bobby Aitken and the Carab Beats were the musicians. The track was more recently featured in 'Everybody Hates Hugo', the fourth episode of the second series of the TV series *Lost*.

10. KING OF KINGS
Ezz Reco & The Launchers with Boysie Grant (1964)

The song is credited to the composing talents of James Cliff, who we believe to be none other than the legendary Jimmy Cliff. The single was labelled as the first ska single to have been released in the UK. Emmanuel Rodriguez, one of the most gifted trombonists working in the early years of Jamaican music, came to settle in the UK in 1961 where he worked as a session musician for many top stars including Georgie Fame. He released several singles and albums under his own name throughout the Sixties and in 1964 he recorded this single under the name of Ezz Reco, with Boysie Grant on vocals spending several weeks just outside the top 40, peaking at number 44.

11. THE RUSSIANS ARE COMING (TAKE FIVE) Val Bennett (1968)

Val Bennett was a Jamaican tenor saxophonist and a jazz and roots reggae musician, who began his career in the 1940s when he formed his own orchestra. Ernest Ranglin began his career with it. Performing regularly at The Colony Club for foreign visitors in their native country, but they also toured abroad – including in Haiti where they learned about the dance 'The Merengue', which they featured in their act on their return to Jamaica. In the Sixties, Bennett became a regular member of Prince Buster's band, playing on many of his best-known recordings including 'Al Capone'. In the late-Sixties he joined Bunny Lee's All Stars before recording this, one of his most memorable tracks, a cover of the Dave Brubeck hit 'Take Five', which he called 'The Russians Are Coming'.

12. PRESSURE DROP Toots & The Maytals (1969)

Toots is Toots Hibbert, who formed The Maytals in 1962 in Jamaica, releasing their debut single, 'Hallelujah', giving them a local hit. Further successes followed and their reputation spread across the West Indies. They then linked up with Prince Buster who was enjoying an International hit with 'Al Capone'; together they produced some of the best records of the ska era. Towards the end of the Sixties, they began working with top reggae producer, Leslie Kong, coming up with 'Do The Reggay', the first record to use the word reggae (albeit with a different spelling). In 1969 they released the classic dance-floor giant, 'Pressure Drop', one of the all-time great reggae songs.

13. SOON YOU'LL BE GONE The Blues Busters (1964)

The Blues Busters were Philip James and Lloyd Campbell, who became one of the best and soulful vocal duos in the great era of Jamaican ska and blue beat. Formed in 1960, they initially worked in local cabaret shows put on for tourists, but got their big break when they were invited to support Sam Cooke on his tour of the island. This led to a recording contract, a number of soul and reggae cover versions and a few minor

Frederick 'Toots' Hibbert (centre) and the Maytals

hits. They continued to record well into the Eighties, by which time they had released several albums, one of which was a tribute to Sam Cooke.

14. THE LIQUIDATOR The Harry J All Stars (1969) *UK No 9*

The musicians used by Harry Johnson later formed the core of reggae groups The Upsetters and, later, Bob Marley's Wailers. The group's drummer Carlton Bennett believes the track was originally recorded as a song by Tony Scott, 'What Am I To Do', but after buying the rights, Harry made a deal with Trojan records, removed the vocal and released it as The Harry J All Stars.

15. THE BLUE BEAT The Beazers (1964)

By 1964, Blue Beat music was sweeping through London, and Chris Blackwell at Island records had brought Millie Small over from Jamaica to record 'My Boy Lollipop'. Meanwhile, over at Decca, instead of importing musicians they employed Chris Farlowe and The Thunderbirds to record two songs with a ska rhythm. The single 'The Blue Beat' was released some months before the general public had fully latched onto this style of music. However, due to contractual reasons, the record was released under the name The Beazers, although every London blues and soul fan knew the voice belonged to Farlowe. Despite the record becoming a floor filler, it failed to make the national charts.

16. MIX IT UP The Kingstonians (1968)

The group were formed in 1966 by Jackie Bernard and recorded a number of notable rocksteady tracks with their producer, JJ Johnson, before cutting 'Mix It Up'. They continued working and recording well into the Seventies, working with a number of different producers, including Derrick Harriott, with whom they had a big hit in Jamaica with 'Sufferer'.

17. BROKEN HEART The Locomotive (1967)

This was the group's first single, released on CBS's Sixties soul label, Direction, while The Locomotive's version of 'A Message To You Rudi' was on the B-side. The song later became a top-10 hit in 1979 for The Specials, featuring Rico. The band first called themselves The Kansas City Seven but after several changes to their personnel, they became The Locomotive. In 1967, keyboard player Norman Haynes joined the band; he had a strong interest in ska and Blue Beat music,

Derrick Morgan was the first act to occupy all the top seven places in the Jamaican top 10

having worked in a record shop in a part of Birmingham with a large West Indian population. His talent was soon put to the test when they recorded this song of his for their first release.

18. LEAVE HER ALONE Derrick Morgan (1963)

Sounding remarkably like the tune 'Tom Hark', this is Derrick's own composition and was produced by the legendary Lesley Kong who, in his lifetime, was responsible for so many successful reggae and ska recordings. Morgan, who worked with many fellow Jamaican stars including Desmond Dekker, Jimmy Cliff and Bob Marley, entered a local talent contest in 1957, winning with a rousing impression of Little Richard. This led to him being booked to perform around the island with the comedy duo Bim and Bam. In 1959 he was signed to the small Treasure Isle label and the following year became the first artist to achieve all of the top seven positions on the Jamaican charts.

Soon after this came the breakout of the legendary rivalry between Morgan and Prince Buster, who accused Morgan of stealing his ideas. Buster then released 'Blackhead Chiney Man', chiding Morgan with that sarcastic putdown of, 'I did not know your parents were from Hong Kong', a clear swipe at Kong. Morgan returned with the classic 'Blazing Fire', in which he warns Buster to 'Live and let others live, and your days will be much longer/You said it. Now it's the Blazing Fire'. Buster shot back with 'Watch It Blackhead', which Morgan countered with, 'No Raise No Praise' and 'Still Insist'. Followers of both artists often clashed, and eventually the government had to step in with a staged photo-opportunity depicting the rivals as 'friends'.

19. GOING BACK TO MY HOME TOWN **Hal Paige & The Wailers (1960)**
Hal Paige's recording career dates back to the early Fifties when he recorded for the American Old Town label, but this was the second of two singles he cut for Bobby Robinson's Fury label, whose artists roster at the time included Wilbert Harrison, Lee Dorsey and Gladys Knight & The Pips. This R&B record, with more than a hint of ska, was picked up in the UK by the independent Melodisc and became a floor filler around the clubs, largely due to Britain's growing population of Jamaican immigrants. The record even became a minor hit, peaking at number 50: its success helped signal the beginning of Blue Beat.

20. TONK GAME **Hank Marr (1960)**
Based in Columbus, Ohio, Hank Marr was a leading organist signed to the American King label, for whom he recorded several influential instrumental tracks including his own composition, 'Tonk Game' which became so popular in the UK amongst Britain's Jamaican population that it was picked up and released on the Bluebeat label that specialised in reggae and ska.

21. REGGAE IN YOUR JEGGAE **Dandy Livingstone (1969)**
Born Robert Livingstone Thompson in Kingston, Jamaica, Dandy moved to the UK in 1958 at the age of 15. In 1964, London-based record label Carnival were looking for a Jamaican vocal duo and Livingstone fitted the bill – by double-tracking his own voice and releasing records under the name of Sugar and Dandy. One of the singles, 'What A Life', sold in excess of 25,000 copies, giving Dandy his first taste of success. In 1968, he formed a real duo with Audrey Hall – Dandy and Audrey – producing theirs and other artists' records. He then signed to Trojan, releasing two albums before setting up his own Down Town label, releasing several singles including this self penned 'Reggae In Your Jeggae'.

22. YOU GOT SOUL **Johnny Nash (1969)** *UK No 6*
Johnny Nash was born John Lester Nash, Jr, in Houston, Texas and is of African-American descent: one of the first non-Jamaican singers to record reggae music in Kingston, Jamaica, where he had several hits

in the Sixties. Whilst over there, he met up with the struggling Bob Marley & The Wailers and financed their early recording sessions, none of which were successful. But Nash himself later recorded several of Marley's songs. 'You Got Soul' was Johnny's own composition and the follow-up to his debut UK top-10 hit, 'Hold Me Tight'.

23. BEHOLD The Blues Busters (1962)

Back Beat Records was founded in Jamaica in 1959 by Chris Blackwell and Graeme Goodall with £1000, to market their Afro-Caribbean products. Discovering he was selling more records in England, he set up headquarters in London in 1962. That year, he released singles by Jimmy Cliff, Derrick Morgan, Wilfred Jackie Edwards and vocal duo The Blue Busters, who were Philip James and Lloyd Campbell. One of the most consistently popular Jamaican acts of the Sixties, they went on to work with Sam Cooke.

24. BONANZA SKA
Carlos Malcolm & His Afro Jamaican Rhythms (1964)

The Bonanza theme was composed by the legendary Jay Livingston with Ray Evans and was orchestrated by David Rose. Carlos Malcolm & His Afro Jamaican Rhythms decided to take the piece and give it a ska arrangement. Carlos was born in Panama to Jamaican parents, where his father became a prominent businessman and also taught his son to play the trombone – recognising his natural gift for writing and arranging music. In 1963 Eon Productions went to Jamaica to film the first James Bond movie, *Dr No*, and employed Carlos to write the incidental tropical music for the film. The following year Carlos formed The Afro Jamaican Rhythms, which included Boris Gardiner, and enjoyed a massive hit in the Caribbean with this 'Bonanza Ska'.

25. SU, SU, SU The Soul Directions (1969)

This ultra-rare reggae record was released in 1969 on the Attack label and a copy once fetched £375 at a record auction. There is almost no information about the group although there have been rumours that they were the more successful Pioneers playing under another name. The record was produced by Byron Lee at his Dynamic Sounds Studios in Jamaica, which had the reputation of being the best-equipped studio in the Caribbean.

TURNTABLE HITS

A collection of 60 songs you may well know, but which never managed to make it into the UK charts.

1. CRAISE FINTON KIRK Johnnie Young (1967)

Written by Barry and Robin Gibb, this cover from their debut album *The Bee Gees First* is one of the records most consistently found on collectors' most-wanted lists. Born John De Jong, in Australia, he trained to become a DJ on Perth Radio and began singing with local band The Nomads, who scored a number-one hit down under in 1966 with a double A-side, 'Step Back' and 'Cara Lyn'. The following year, he travelled to the UK where he recorded this track, and in 1969 wrote Herman's Hermits' final hit of the Sixties, 'Here Comes The Star'.

2. A TOUCH OF VELVET – A STING OF BRASS Mood Mosaic (1966)

Featuring the voices of The Ladybirds, this track was once used by Dave Lee Travis as his signature theme. It was written and produced by Mark Wirtz, who is probably best remembered for his production of Keith West's *Excerpt From A Teenage Opera*.

3. GRAZING IN THE GRASS Friends Of Distinction (1969)

Friends of Distinction were performing in the soul and jazz clubs of Hollywood, where they were discovered by American football legend Jim Brown. Brown convinced RCA records to sign them. This, their first US hit, was a vocal version of the Hugh Masekela classic.

4. LIKE TO GET TO KNOW YOU Spanky & Our Gang (1967)

This became the fourth and final US top-40 hit for Spanky & Our Gang, led by Elaine McFarlane. Elaine once waited on tables at The Rising Moon nightclub in Chicago, which is where she met the three other members of the group. They headed off to New York and signed a recording contract with Mercury. 'Like To Get To Know You' was written in just one day by Stuart Scharf, their producer, as 'a filler' for an album but, when they heard the finished record, decided quite rightly to issue it as a single.

5. WOLVERTON MOUNTAIN Claude King (1962)

King was a natural athlete and was once offered a baseball scholarship to the University of Idaho in Moscow, but instead bought a guitar from a farmer for 50 cents. The song is based on a real character, Clifton Clowers, who lived on the actual mountain in Arkansas.

6. SOMEONE OUT THERE The Flirtations (1968)

The group were formed in South Carolina in 1962 by sisters Earnestine, Shirley and Betty Pearce and with a fourth member, their friend Lestine Johnson, called themselves The Gypsies. In 1964 they secured a record deal with the American Old Town label, releasing several singles, with 'Jerk It' getting a UK release in 1965. Soon after, Lestine left the group and was replaced by the dynamic Viola Milups. Shortly after, this was followed by the departure of Betty. Now a trio, the girls had changed the group's name to The Flirtations. By 1967, the girls had packed their bags and headed for Britain, where they met Wayne Bickerton. Bickerton was writing and producing for the Deram label and wanted to record some songs with them that he had written with his business partner, Tony Waddington. Their first release for the label, however, was a cover of an American single by Candy & The Kisses, 'Someone Out There'.

7. TIME OF THE SEASON The Zombies (1968)

The Zombies were getting frustrated by their lack of success in the UK, and in 1967, after the completion of their album *Odyssey And Oracle*, decided to call it a day and split up. The following year, the closing track on the album *Time Of The Season* was released as a single in The States and, to everyone's surprise, became a massive hit. Despite enormous pressures put on the group by their management and record company, the original line-up refused to get back together; so founder member Rod Argent quickly assembled a new band to promote the single.

8. PER-SO-NALLY Bobby Paris (1968)

This track – by a singer everyone presumed was black but was a white man born to an American mother and a Puerto Rican father – became a Northern Soul anthem.

9. NEVERTHELESS Eclection (1968)

Eclection – who decided on their name because of their diverse

Martha & The Vandellas: Martha got her lucky break after working as a secretary at Motown

backgrounds – consisted of a Canadian, two Australians, a Norwegian and, later on, an Englishman. Their first big professional appearance was at The Royal Festival Hall where they were support act to Tom Paxton. Their only album was released in 1968, and by 1969 they had disbanded.

10. QUICKSAND Martha & The Vandellas (1963)

Originally formed in 1960 as The Del-Phis, Martha & The Vandellas were one of dozens of female groups operating out of Detroit. They were offered the opportunity to record a one-off single for Motown, where Martha had been working a s a secretary. They released it on one of the label's smaller subsidiaries, Mel-o-dy, under the name of The Vels. In 1960, they were given a second chance, cutting a song called 'I'll Have to Let Him Go', which was originally intended for Mary Wells. Renamed Martha & The Vandellas, the group had a string of hits in the US in the Sixties. They disbanded in 1969, only to re-form in 1971 with Martha, her sister Lois Reeves and Sandra Tilley. The following year, Martha decided to embark on a solo career.

11. I GUESS THE LORD MUST BE IN NEW YORK CITY Nilsson (1969)

The track was considered for the theme song to the movie *Midnight Cowboy* but lost out to 'Everybody's Talkin'', which was also recorded by Harry Nilsson but written by Fred Neil.

12. MAMA SAID The Shirelles (1961)

The girls met and formed The Poquellos (Spanish for 'little birds') whilst at high school (where Joey Dee, later of 'The Peppermint Twist' fame, was also a pupil). Unhappy with their name, they needed to come up with a new one for the release their first single in 1958. On their way to the studio, they mused over a variety of suggestions, finally settling on The Shirelles. They became the first female group to top the American charts, with 'Will You Love Me Tomorrow' in 1961.

13. SOLITARY MAN Neil Diamond (1966)

Although only a minor hit, this was Diamond's first American chart entry as a performer. He attended the same school in Brooklyn as Neil Sedaka, and began writing songs in his teens. He made his first record in 1960 for a small independent label, Duel. His first success as a composer was the 1965 US hit for Jay and The Americans, 'Sunday And Me'.

14. PINOCCHIO Boz (1966)

Raymond 'Boz' Burrell formed a band in the Sixties called The Boz People and released several singles for EMI's Columbia label, including a version of Bob Dylan's 'I Shall Be Released'. In 1970, Robert Fripp persuaded him to become the lead vocalist in the newly-formed King Crimson, and also taught him to play bass.

A year later, after recording one album with the group, he left to join Bad Company. He worked with Bad Company on and off for many years, including taking part in a successful reunion tour in 1999. Boz passed away on 21st September 2006.

15. INCENSE AND PEPPERMINTS Strawberry Alarm Clock (1967)

The band were originally named Thee Sixpence, but because two other groups turned up with similar names, they blindly stuck a pin into the top-20 chart of the week and landed on 'Strawberry Fields Forever' by The Beatles. This is how they settled on the name Strawberry Alarm Clock. 'Incense And Peppermints' was intended as the B-side to one of their own songs.

Because they weren't overly concerned about this song, they asked one of their friends, who happened to be observing the recording, to sing vocals. Once the single became a hit, the 'friend' had disappeared without trace; so their drummer, Randy Seol, was forced to sing the song at live gigs, as his voice was the closest to that of their 'friend'. Randy, as well as this unusual vocal role, also had a gimmick of playing the bongos with his hands on fire.

16. UNDER THE BOARDWALK The Drifters (1964)

The song was written by up-and-coming composers Artie Resnick and Kenny Young, who were signed to Bobby Darin's publishing company. However, the recording nearly didn't take place. One of the group's lead singers, Rudy Lewis, was found dead in his hotel room from an overdose of narcotics the night before the session. The song was written for him and arranged in his key. Johnny Moore, their other lead vocalist at the time, stepped in and recorded the vocal for this American top-10 hit.

17. PENTECOST HOTEL Nirvana (1967)

The six-piece group, led by Patrick Campbell-Lyons from Ireland, were involved in a lawsuit over their name in the Nineties after the success of Kurt Cobain's successful band. The argument was settled and resulted in the original Nirvana recording a cover of the other Nirvana's 'Lithium' for a 1996 album of previously un-issued material.

18. TAR AND CEMENT Verdelle Smith (1966)

This single by Verdelle, a black soul singer born in Florida, became a number one in Australia. Afterwards, however, this singer disappeared from view. The song was originally recorded by Italian singer Adriano Celentano as 'Il Ragazzo Della Via Gluck', which translated to 'The Boy From Gluck Street'. The song was also translated into 18 other languages, including a French version by François Hardy.

19. SOCIETY'S CHILD Janis Ian (1967)

Born Janis Eddy Fink in Brooklyn, New York, Janis wrote this song about interracial romance in 1965 when she was only 14. Its first appearance was as a poem in underground folk magazine *Broadside*, in which she was billed as Blind Girl Grunt (Bob Dylan was Blind Boy Grunt). Janis was later introduced to record producer Shadow Morton, most known for The Shangri-Las' hits. As she walked into his office to audition, he was sitting with his cowboy boots on his desk and wearing sunglasses with a hat pulled over his head, reading a newspaper. He told her to sing but Janis was aware he wasn't listening so, when she had finished, she pulled out a cigarette lighter from her bag, set fire to his newspaper and left.

A short time later he realised his paper was on fire, put it out in the waste bin and chased after Janis, calling her back into his office, this time giving her his undivided attention. A few weeks later they were in the studio recording 'Society's Child'.

No fewer than 22 record companies turned down 'Society's Child', as they were concerned about the lyrical content about interracial romance performed by a teenager. Finally Verve took a chance and signed her, but for a while were still reluctant to release the track as a single. When it was finally issued, few DJs would touch it – until Leonard Bernstein took an interest in the song and invited Janis to perform it on his TV programme *Inside Pop*, giving the record the boost it needed.

20. RINKY DINK Dave 'Baby' Cortez (1962)

Born David Cortez Clowney in Detroit, Michigan, this artist began playing organ and singing with doo wop vocal group The Pearls and later with the Valentines. He became known as a session keyboard player and made his first solo record in 1956 under the name of David Clooney.

21. DAYS OF PEARLY SPENCER David McWilliams (1967)

One of the most played singles of 1967 to fail to make the charts was by Belfast-born David McWilliams. McWilliams began playing guitar and writing songs in his early teens and in 1963 he started a local dance group, The Coral Showband, before sending some demos of his material to Philip Solomon (who had previously managed The Bachelors and Them). McWilliams secured a deal with CBS in 1966, releasing the unsuccessful 'God And My Country', before being signed to the newly-formed Major Minor label. His debut album was arranged and produced by Mike Leander, and made the UK's top-40 album charts. A second album quickly followed and that too reached the top 40 (at number 23). It featured the track 'The Days Of Pearly Spencer' that was released as a single. This track, although a huge international hit selling over a million copies, failed to chart in the UK. However a 1992 cover by Marc Almond, who added some extra lyrics, reached number four in the UK.

22. GIRL WATCHER The O'Kaysions (1968)

The O'Kaysions were a white rock band from North Carolina who first formed as The Kays. 'Girl Watcher' was their only major American hit, although they did reach the lower regions of the charts with the follow up, 'Love Machine'. In 1987, 'Girl Watcher' was reworked in The States as 'I'm A Wheel Watcher', to promote the TV game show *Wheel Of Fortune*. As far as we know, the group are still performing with a different line-up, with only guitarist Wayne Pittman remaining from the original band.

23. BABY WORKOUT Jackie Wilson (1963)

Jackie was born in Detroit, Michigan, and as a youngster was forever in trouble as a member of a rough gang called The Shakers. Sentenced to juvenile detention twice, he dropped out of school at the age of 15 and took up boxing, winning Detroit's Golden Gloves award at the age of 16. The following year he was married and soon became a father, leading to his decision to give up boxing in favour of a career as a singer. He formed his first group with a close relative, Levi Stubbs, who later became the leading light in The Four Tops. He then joined a group called The Thrillers that evolved into The Royals and, later, the legendary R&B group The Midnighters. He then replaced Clyde McPhatter in The Dominoes and, in 1957, launched his solo career when he signed to the Brunswick label and released his first single, 'Reet Petite', leading on to a string of American hits.

24. YOU BETTER MOVE ON Arthur Alexander (1962)

Arthur's family came from Florence, Alabama, and his father, Arthur Senior, was a blues singer who performed in local clubs. His mother taught him to sing gospel songs, which led to him joining a group called The Heartstrings whilst still at high school. They made several

Arthur Alexander, a gifted R&B singer, had hits that were covered by both The Beatles and The Stones

TV appearances but failed to obtain a recording deal. He then met up with the Stafford family who owned a music publishing company. They encouraged Arthur's songwriting and financed his first recordings, which they sold to Judd Phillips, brother of Sam, for his Judd label. His first record was issued under the name of June Alexander – 'June' being his nickname for Junior. The single escaped rather than being released, barely selling a single copy; but it didn't discourage The Staffords and they bankrolled another session that included 'You Better Move On'. They took the tapes to record companies in Nashville but found no takers. Finally they played it to local DJ Noel Ball, who fell in love with the song and played it to Dot Records president, Randy Wood, who jumped at the opportunity of purchasing the rights. It was released at the end of 1961 and a few months later had sold over 800,000 copies. The song was subsequently covered by The Rolling Stones on their 1965 album *December's Children*.

25. LITTLE BOXES Pete Seeger (1964)

This is one of those songs that everybody knows but never became a major hit. It was recorded live at New York's Carnegie Hall on 8th June, 1963, at a concert given by the legendary folk singer Pete Seeger. Pete had formed The Almanac Singers with Woody Guthrie in 1940, and then The Weavers in 1948. His list of works as a writer are endless, many adapted from traditional folk songs, including 'If I Had A Hammer', 'Guantanamera' and 'Where Have All The Flowers Gone'. In 1993 he was awarded a Grammy for his lifetime achievement in music.

26. HURT SO BAD Little Anthony & The Imperials (1965)

By 1961, the popularity of Little Anthony & The Imperials in America was on the decline so they decided to split and go their separate ways. Anthony signed a solo recording deal with Roulette while The Imperials took on a new lead singer, George Kerr, releasing singles on a variety of labels. Much confusion surrounded their output at this time. Anthony's first release was credited to him and The Imperials when in fact he was backed by session musicians, and another release saw the credits as The Original Group of Anthony & The Imperials, causing a major outcry. Later copies of these releases were credited to simply 'The Imperials'. None of these records did well, and in 1964 they reunited to work alongside writer and producer Teddy Randazzo, who the following year gave them two US top-10 hits, 'Goin' Out Of My Head' and 'Hurt So Bad'.

27. OOH LA LA Normie Rowe (1966)

Normie released a string of singles in his homeland of Australia, where he could be found constantly at the top of the charts, making him one of the most successful solo performers of the mid-Sixties. In 1966, he headed off for London and began recording with the cream of the British session musicians, including Jimmy Page, John Paul Jones and Clem Cattini, with vocal backing by The Breakaways. His most successful record was 'Ooh La LA', which received substantial airplay in the UK. At this time he was still Australia's most popular male star despite being in England, but his career was cut short when he was called up for military service in 1967, ending his pop career as he was unable to recapture the following he enjoyed in the earlier years.

28. YOU TURN ME ON Ian Whitcomb (1965)

This big American hit that failed to make the UK charts was recorded in Dublin, where British-born Whitcomb was studying at Trinity College. At night he played local gigs with his band, Bluesville. In 1965, he achieved a surprise minor hit in America with a song called 'This Sporting Life' and a follow up was called for. He went back into a tiny potting shed of a studio, owned by the late Eamonn Andrews, to record a few more songs. His backing group started jamming and Ian joined in, making up the lyrics as he went along. The end result was this semi-novelty single that was written 'on the wing'.

29. WONDERFUL DREAM The Majors (1962)

Recorded on 20th January, 1962, this was the first big hit record to be written, produced and arranged by Jerry Ragavoy. The single, which was financed by Jerry himself and cost $1200 to record, was turned down by most major record labels on the grounds that it was nothing like anything in the charts. Taking it to Imperial Records, he was offered just $500 for the rights, which he accepted just to get a release. The initial response was poor, but after a few weeks a popular local Philadelphia station picked up on the single, creating a huge buzz, and eventually it became a national hit.

30. KEEP THE BALL ROLLING Jay & The Techniques (1967)

Jay & The Techniques were formed in Allentown, Pennsylvania, during the mid-Sixties by lead singer Jay Proctor. Their biggest

American hit was their debut into the top 10, 'Apples, Peaches, Pumpkin Pie'. 'Keep The Ball Rolling' was the follow-up and their only other single to make the top 20 in The States, although the group continued to work and record well into the Nineties, finally calling it a day in 1996. One piece of interesting trivia: Motown writers and performers Nicky Ashford and Valerie Simpson often worked with them as backing singers.

31. THE LITTLE OLD LADY FROM PASADENA Jan & Dean (1964)

The Little Old Lady was an imaginary character in Pasadena's local folklore. The background to the folklore was as follows: Pasadena was a popular place for couples to retire. When the elderly husband eventually passed away, the widow would be left with the estate – often including a car in the garage that, in most instances, had never been driven by the wife. So the widows were apt to sell the car, and the car salesmen were often spoofed as saying that the previous owner was 'A Little Old Lady From Pasadena'. This story inspired Jan and Dean to write and record this song – but in their case the car turned out to be a Super Stock Dodge and this little old lady not only drives the car but is an unbeaten street racer.

32. SIGN ON THE DOTTED LINE Gene Latter (1969)

Gene had been the lead singer with a Belgium-based group called The Shakespeares but decided to pursue a solo career when the group relocated to Australia. Remaining in England, Gene went on to record several storming British Blue-eyed soul singles, this being one of the most popular and receiving considerable airplay at the time of its release.

33. CRIMSON AND CLOVER Tommy James & The Shondells (1968)

This became Tommy James & The Shondells' tenth American top-40 hit and second number one, following on from 'Hanky Panky' in 1966. Tommy James wrote 'Crimson And Clover' based on his favourite colour and preferred flower. When the record was completed it ran for under two and a half minutes so the engineer spliced together and repeated bits from throughout the song, adding almost another minute to the running time. Careful listening will reveal a couple of less than perfect edits.

34. FIVE O' CLOCK WORLD The Vogues (1965)

The Vogues hailed from Turtle Creek, a suburb of Pittsburgh, and formed as The Val-Aires in the late Fifties whilst at high school, releasing a few doo-wop singles with little success. In 1965, they discovered a Petula Clark single, 'You're The One', that hadn't been released in America and decided to cover it for the small Blue Star label. At this point, they changed their name to The Vogues. The record brought the group to the attention of the bigger Co & Ce label, who bought the rights to the single, taking it to number four in the charts. Looking for a follow-up, they found a song written by Allen Reynolds, who went on to even greater success as the producer of country singer, Garth Brooks.

35. BROWN EYED GIRL Van Morrison (1967)

Although considered one of his career classics, this was never a hit in the UK but made the American top 10. Recorded during his tempestuous period with the Bang label, who irritated him by releasing an album of his first recorded material for them without his permission. He was also annoyed by the fact that they edited 'Brown Eyed Girl' for radio play because it contained the line 'making love in the green grass', believing it too suggestive and splicing in a line from another verse.

36. WE'LL SING IN THE SUNSHINE Gale Garnett (1964)

One of those records we believe was a UK hit but wasn't. Born in New Zealand, Garnett and her family moved to Canada, where she made her singing debut in 1960 at the age of 18. She also made appearances as an actress on TV shows such as *77 Sunset Strip*. In 1964, she scored a massive American hit with 'We'll Sing In The Sunshine', winning a Grammy the following year for Best Folk Recording. She never managed to repeat her music success, but was had some continuing stardom with her work as a TV and movie actress.

37. I DIG ROCK 'N' ROLL MUSIC Peter, Paul & Mary (1967)

This track hails from Peter, Paul & Mary's 1967 album *Album 1700*, a landmark release for the trio. It boasted an exceptional selection of material and benefited from the production work of Phil Ramone, who went on to produce hits for dozens of other acts including Elton John, Billy Joel, Paul Simon and Rod Stewart. 'I Dig Rock'n'Roll Music' was released as a single and was an affectionate send-up of the music of the Flower Power era.

38. YOUNGER GIRL The Critters (1966)

Written by John Sebastian of The Lovin' Spoonful and originally recorded by the group for their debut album *Do You Believe In Magic* – an album on which any song could have been a single. Enter The Critters' producer, Artie Ripp, who was quick to pick up on the potential of 'Younger Girl'. He cut the track with his new group, The Critters, giving them their first of four American Hot 100 hits. The group's career came to a sudden end in 1968 when three key members received their call-up papers and their record company released them from their contract. The two remaining members kept the group going for a further 18 months but by that point the hits had dried up.

39. LIVING ABOVE YOUR HEAD Jay & The Americans (1966)

Jay Traynor sang lead on Jay & The Americans' first US hit, 'She Cried', in 1962, but after a couple of less successful releases he quit and was replaced by David Black – who agreed to adopt the name Jay. With their new singer in place, they returned to the charts in 1963 with a song originally meant for The Drifters, 'Only In America'. Several further hits followed and in 1966 they recorded 'Living Above Your Head', a track that later found favour with the Northern Soul crowd.

40. 24 SYCAMORE Wayne Fontana (1967)

The song was written by Les Reed and Mary Mason and had all the ingredients for becoming a hit, but failed to chart. The song was revived by Gene Pitney a few years later, and reached number 34 in 1973.

41. UNCHAIN MY HEART Ray Charles (1961)

Ray Charles learned to play the piano at the age of two, and between 1962 and 1963, he released three singles with 'Heart' in the title: 'Unchain My Heart', 'Your Cheating Heart' and 'Take These Chains From My Heart'

42. WALKING IN THE RAIN The Ronettes (1964)

The Ronettes only achieved one American top-20 hit – with the single 'Be My Baby'. This song also achieved a UK Top-30 hit – for The Walker Brothers' version (in 1967).

43. FUN FUN FUN The Beach Boys (1964)

'Fun Fun Fun' was the sixth American top-20 hit for the group – a batch of hits that included 'Surfin' U.S.A', which was the only one to have made the UK top 40.

44. BABY I NEED YOUR LOVING The Four Tops (1964)

This track was the first American chart entry for The Four Tops, who were originally named The Four Aims. Although 'Baby I Need Your Loving' failed to make it into the top 75, a Liverpudlian group, The Fourmost, successfully covered this song for the UK market.

45. THE LOOK OF LOVE Dusty Springfield (1967)

This was a top-40 hit in America. Although it wasn't issued in the UK as an A-side, the B-side, 'Give Me Time', became one of her lesser hits on this side of the Atlantic. It was featured in the 1967 spoof James Bond movie *Casino Royale*, starring Peter Sellers and David Niven.

46. YOU DIDN'T HAVE TO BE SO NICE The Lovin' Spoonful (1965)

This was the group's second single and the follow-up to 'Do You Believe In Magic' – both of which were American top-10 hits, but neither of which did any real business in the UK.

The Lovin' Spoonful, an American folk-rock band, had to wait until 'Daydream' and 'Summer in the City' before they could crack the UK top 10

47. PEOPLE GET READY **The Impressions (1965)**

This was also the title track to The Impressions' 1965 album and probably their best-known song, despite not being a UK hit. It was also the first time that Curtis Mayfield played lead guitar in the instrumental break on an Impressions' record.

48. DAWN (GO AWAY) **The Four Seasons (1964)**

The record stuck at number three in America for three weeks, being held off by 'I Want To Hold Your Hand' and 'She Loves You' by The Beatles. 'Dawn' was first offered to Atlantic Records, who turned it down.

49. THE RAIN, THE PARK AND OTHER THINGS **The Cowsills (1967)**

The Cowsills were an all-family group consisting of five brothers, a sister and mother, and were the inspiration behind The Partridge Family. Because the title of the song doesn't appear in the lyric, it was often referred to as 'The Flower Girl'.

50. THE MAN WHO SHOT LIBERTY VALANCE **Gene Pitney (1962)**

Written by Burt Bacharach and Hal David, the song was written for, but never featured in, *The Man Who Shot Liberty Valance*, the movie starring James Stewart. This was because director John Ford hated the song and refused to use it.

51. ANY DAY NOW **Chuck Jackson (1962)**

Another song written by Burt Bacharach and Bob Hilliard, this became Chuck Jackson's biggest American hit and was often sub-titled 'My Wild Beautiful Bird'.

52. CAROLINE **The Fortunes (1964)**

'Caroline' probably failed to become a hit as it was endorsed by pirate music station Radio Caroline and therefore all other broadcasters refused to play it.

53. MR PITIFUL **Otis Redding (1965)**

Written by Otis and Steve Cropper and recorded in the Stax studios in December 1964, the inspiration for the song came about after a local DJ referred to Otis as Mr Pitiful because of the sadness in his voice when singing ballads.

54. HEATWAVE Martha & The Vandellas (1963)

Their first track to make it into the top 20, this was Martha & The Vandellas' breakthrough single in the US. Martha Reeves, one of 11 children, was born in Eufaula, Alabama, on July 18, 1941. She moved with her parents, Ruby and Elijah, to Detroit, Michigan, before her first birthday. Reeves spent most of her childhood singing and working in her grandfather's church.

She attended Russell Elementary on Detroit's eastside and was taught vocals by Emily Wagstaff. Northeastern High School was where she studied voice under the direction of Abraham Silver, who also coached Florence Ballard and Mary Wilson of the Supremes and Bobby Rogers of The Miracles.

55. WINDY The Association (1967)

Surprisingly, 'Windy' – along with 'Cherish' and 'Never My Love' – failed to chart in the UK; but in 1968 The Association made it into the UK top 40 with the less likely theme song to the movie *Time For Living*.

56. A LITTLE BIT OF SOAP The Exciters (1966)

This is a cover of the original 1961 recording by American doo-wop group The Jarmels. The Exciters recorded the original version of 'Tell

Folk-rockers The Association, who specialised in what some termed 'sunshine pop', had US hits with 'Along Come Mary' and an American number one with 'Cherish'

Him,' a UK hit for Billie Davis. 'A Little Bit Of Soap' was successfully revived in the UK in 1978 by Showaddywaddy.

57. BACKFIELD IN MOTION Mel & Tim (1969)
A big turntable and club hit for cousins Mel Hardin and Tim McPherson who reached number 10 in America with this single.

58. BY THE TIME I GET TO PHOENIX Glen Campbell (1967)
Surprisingly, 'By The Time I Get To Phoenix' – one of Glen Campbell's most memorable songs – never actually made it into the UK charts.

59. FOR WHAT IT'S WORTH Buffalo Springfield (1967)
The song, sub-titled 'What's That Sound', became the first American hit for the group whose line-up included Stephen Stills (who wrote the song), Neil Young and Richie Furay.

60. I STARTED A JOKE The Bee Gees (1968)
The song, written by Barry, Robin and Maurice Gibb, comes from The Bee Gees 1968 album *Idea* and was released as a single in America where it reached number six. In the UK a cover version by Heath Hampstead was issued by the group's label at the time, Polydor, but despite substantial airplay, still failed to chart.

DANCE CRAZES

During the early Sixties, we were introduced to a new dance craze almost every month. Some lasted the course but most were just a passing fad. Here is a selection of some of them.

1. BABY DO THE PHILLY DOG **The Olympics (1966)**

By the time The Olympics had released this single, they had already worked their way through a number of dance fads in song that included 'The Mashed Potato', The Hully Gully', 'The Shimmy' and 'The Stomp'. 'The Philly Dog' was the last record by the group to make the American Hot 100. In case you feel like shaking your funky stuff, the basis for the dance is: With feet slightly apart, crouch down with arms bent and fists clenched. Move body and arms backwards and forwards with the beat. Jerk clenched fists over shoulders alternately, similar to the Hitch Hike movement, and jump to the left or right.

2. CINNAMON CINDER (IT'S A VERY NICE DANCE) **The Pastel Six (1962)** *UK No 25*

American record promotions man, the late Russ Regan (who later signed Elton John, Barry White and Neil Diamond in America), was approached by his DJ friend Bob Eubanks to write a song named after his popular nightclub in the hope of recording it with the club's resident band, The Pastel Six. Regan came up with the song 'Cinnamon Cinder' and a dance to go with it. The band recorded it in a small studio behind a record shop named Wenzels in Downey, a suburb of Los Angeles. The record began to sell in LA, which attracted airplay in other parts of the country. It eventually made the top 30, but after this one hit, little more was heard of The Pastel Six.

3. THE BOOMERANG **Don Covay (1965)**

This short-lived dance – the Boomerang – was very simple to perform. You just threw one arm to the side in the way you might throw a boomerang (and we all know how to do that, of course) and you then bend down as though you were picking it up – before throwing it again. You then tossed your head from side to side and up and down, as if looking for your boomerang. Finally, you put both arms up in the air as though you were about to catch it on its return. Actually, perhaps it wasn't so simple after all, on reflection...

Don Covay, the man who immortalized the 'Boomerang' dance craze in song

4. THE JERK **The Larks (1964)** *US No 7*

The group comprised three former members of Don Julian & The Meadowlarks, a Los Angeles close harmony group formed in the Fifties. As The Larks, they took 'The Jerk' into the American top 10 at the height of Beatlemania. Julian wrote the song after visiting his sister's house where the family were doing their own dance to Martha & The Vandellas' 'Dancing In The Street'. He asked them the name of the dance, to which they replied, 'The Jerk'. The dance is similar to The Monkey but with your hands and arms moving as if you're conducting a band, crossing your wrists in front of your chest and then sweeping out in time with your body.

5. THE DUCK **Jackie Lee (1965)** *US No 14*

Jackie Lee's real name was Earl Lee Nelson. He first enjoyed success in America in 1957 as the lead vocalist with The Hollywood Flames, who scored a top-20 hit with 'Buzz, Buzz, Buzz'. In 1959 he left the group and became one half of the duo Bob and Earl, scoring an international hit with 'The Harlem Shuffle'. In 1965 he signed to the new Mirwood label and introduced the nation to 'The Duck', produced by Fred Smith, who had also been responsible for 'The Harlem Shuffle'. So, for a few instructions... Stand straight with your feet shoulder-width apart, making sure you're at least two feet away from the person next to you, in order to avoid hitting them. Hold your hands in front of your shoulders with elbows bent at the sides and palms facing outwards. Bend your hands with your fingers straight and your thumbs below the rest of your fingers so your hands look like duck beaks. Bring your fingers and thumbs together four times. Now you're doing 'The Duck'.

6. DOIN' THE CONTINENTAL WALK Danny & The Juniors (1962)

The song was written by Danny & The Juniors' group members Dave White and Johnny Madara who were responsible for the group's biggest hit, 'At The Hop'. By the time this record was released, Dave and Johnny were also busy writing and producing for other acts. In The Continental Walk, dancers face a wall then move backwards, then forward, then to the right and then to the left. They jump forward and backward and click their heels. They do some quick tap steps and then turn to the left to face a different wall and continue.

Ever danced the Duck? No? Perhaps you should check out the musical works of Jackie Lee then

7. HITCH HIKE (Pt 1) **Russell Byrd (1962)**

Russell Byrd was the co-writer of such songs as 'Twist And Shout' and 'Hang On Sloopy'. He is best remembered as Bert Berns but over the years used a number of pseudonyms including Burt Russell and Russell Byrd, although his real name was Bertrand Russell Bernstein. On this 1962 release, he invites us to 'Hitch Hike' and all you have to do is stand in the upright position with feet apart, doing 'The Frug' movement; then 'hitch-hike' with your left thumb on the counts 1,2,3 to your right side. Clap on the fourth beat on the right side of your body; then 'hitch-hike' with the left thumb on the count 1,2,3, back to the left side. Or, to put it more plainly: With feet firmly placed, bend knees slightly and shake your hips. Place your hands at your sides and fist them, leaving thumb open and pointing up. Move arms up and down alternately, jerking your fist over your shoulder. Then, occasionally, jerk both fists together over one shoulder and jump to either side.

8. LOCOMOTION WITH ME **The Tornados (1963)**

The Locomotion became a popular but simple dance craze. It was a case of: slide, touch, slide, touch, slide, touch, slide, touch. Lock steps for eight beats. Walk forward with a kick; walk back with a stomp. Hop forward, hop back, hop forward, hop back, hop forward, hop back with a one-quarter right turn. Then begin again. 'The Locomotion' by Little Eva is the version you're probably familiar with. This one by the Tornados appeared on the B-side of their hit single 'Globetrotter'.

9. IT'S MADISON TIME
Alan Freeman and The Talmy Stone Band (1963)

'It's Madison Time', an American top-40 hit for The Ray Bryant Combo, was covered in the UK by The Talmy Stone Band, who decided, as in the American version, to include a voice giving vague instructions as to how to perform the dance. DJ Alan Freeman was chosen as being the ideal 'voice' for the dance instructions. Unfortunately, the record became one of the worst-selling singles in the history of the Decca record company. Just in case you want to try to dance to the record, the movements consist of a basic step and a series of figures. Each figure occupies a fixed number of beats, but they are all different. Don't expect the figures to start on the first beat of a bar or at the beginning of a phrase as they go all across the music.

The man who probably did more twisting than any other singer in the Sixties: Chubby Checker. He also liked a bit of Limbo, just for a bit of variety...

10. POPEYE (THE HITCHIKER) **Chubby Checker (1962)** *US No 10*

Chubby Checker introduced us to many new crazes during the era, not least, 'The Twist'. He has often claimed to have personally changed the way we dance to the beat of music. The simple dance is based on the 'hitch-hiker's gesture': waving the stuck-out right thumb three times to the right over the shoulder, clap hands; three times left thumb to the left over the shoulder, clap hands. All this is accompanied by shimmy body ripples.

11. LIMBO ROCK **Chubby Checker (1962)** *US No 2/UK No 32*

The Limbo originated in Trinidad, with the dancers competing by leaning backwards to dance under a horizontal pole without touching it. Should they touch it, or even worse knock it over, that person is out. After the attempt of each dancer, the pole is gradually lowered until only one person remains.

12. OH! MOM (TEACH ME HOW TO DO THE UNCLE WILLIE)
The Daylighters (1964)

The Uncle Willie was a dance born out of Chicago and swept across the Windy City in late 1963. This record by The Daylighters, who were also known as Delighters, became the most popular record promoting the dance. The group was started by school student Tony Gideon in the mid-Fifties and they cut tracks for a variety of different labels. It was in 1963 they went into the studio to record this ode to the dance craze that involved the shuffle of your feet heel-to-toe and side-to-side – that was 'Doing The Uncle Willie'. The song was covered in the UK by both Zoot Money's Big Roll Band and Brian Poole & The Tremeloes.

13. THE 81 Candy & The Kisses (1964)

The Cameo Parkway label unashamedly exploited many of the Sixties dance fads, such as The Limbo, The Twist and The Mashed Potato, with its roster of artists including Chubby Checker, Dee Dee Sharp and The Orlons. One of the late signings to the label were Candy & The Kisses who were originally known as The Symphonettes. Producer Jerry Ross renamed them for the release of 'The 81', a song he wrote with Kenny Gamble after they'd visited a dance club and saw the crowd engaged in a new dance to Martha & The Vandellas' record 'In My Lonely Room'. The less than comfortable movements involved the shaking of the head and arms, and walking in a sort of hop followed by high kicks, and then a complete turn of the body.

14. LET'S STOMP Bobby Comstock (1963)

'The Stomp' was one of the most simple of dances from the Sixties and could be learned in minutes. It was popular in Australian surf clubs, with teenagers pounding the floor with enthusiasm to the beat of records such as this Bobby Comstock release. The track came about after Comstock met up with songwriting team and producers Jerry Goldstein and Richie Gottehrer. At the end of a recording session with singer Freddy Cannon, they sneaked in Bobby's recording of 'Let's Stomp'. Cannon was so impressed with the record, he persuaded his label, Swan, to release it.

15. (DOING THE) HULLY GULLY Jet Harris & Tony Meehan (1963)

Co-written by Tony Meehan, this was the B-side to their top-three hit, 'Scarlett O' Hara'. The moves form a sort of unstructured line dance consisting of a series of steps that are called out by the master of ceremonies. Although each step is simple and relatively easy to follow,

The dapper Bobby Freeman managed to score a top-five hit in 1964 by casting his mind back to the days of swimming lessons

the challenge was always to keep up with the speed at which they had to be executed.

16. C'MON AND SWIM Bobby Freeman (1964)

Bobby Freeman, often cited as the first rock star to come out of San Francisco, formed a group named The Romancers at the age of 14, and then went on to assemble R&B band The Vocaleers. He will probably be best remembered for writing and recording the original 1958 version of 'Do You Wanna Dance' – which later became a major UK hit for Cliff Richard and The Shadows. For several years, he achieved a number of lesser hits in America. Then, after local DJ Tom Donahue signed him to his own Autumn label, he achieved this top-five hit in 1964, with a dance based on strokes used in swimming.

17. OLIVER TWIST MEETS THE DUKE OF OIL
Rod McKuen (1962)

This 1962 novelty recording by future celebrated poet, composer, performer and Jacques Brel-collaborator Rod McKuen, is one of the most truly obscure tracks in this book. During the height of 'The Twist' dance craze, McKuen recorded 'Oliver Twist Meets The Duke Of Oil'. Not surprisingly, it attracted very little attention at the time – but today is of high-interest value for its oddity alone.

18. I'VE BEEN TWISTIN' Jerry Lee Lewis (1962)

When 'the Twist' became all the rage in the early Sixties, many artists jumped on the bandwagon to record a song with that theme, not least of all Jerry Lee Lewis. By 1962, when this record was released, Jerry was struggling to maintain the chart status he had gained in the late Fifties. Taking Junior Parker's 1953 Sun Records' classic, 'Feelin' Good', Lewis adapted it to become this fine rocker, 'I've Been Twistin'' but, judging from its failure to enter the Top 100, one can only assume Jerry Lee and the Twist no longer appealed to the zeitgeist at that particular time.

19. THE PUSH AND KICK Mark Valentino (1962)

This dance was almost identical to 'The Twist' and was recorded in 1962 by Mark Valentino, a protégée of talent manager Bob Marcucci. It was Marcucci who introduced the good-looking teenager to producer Frank Slay at Swan Records in New York. 'The Push And Kick' climbed to number 27 in America towards the end of 1962, a hot period for new dance crazes in the world of popular music.

20. THE ROACH (DANCE)
Gene Wendell with The Sweethearts (1961)

This less than successful dance came out of Chicago and had a limited appeal to their black community. 'The Roach' was more of a 'stomp', mimicking the crushing of an insect followed by a backward flip of the foot, as in an attempt to dislodge the creature from the bottom of the shoe. This 1961 recording by Gene Wendell with The Sweethearts was co-written and produced by 22-year-old Steve Venet, younger brother of the late Nik Venet, the man who famously signed The Beach Boys to the Capitol label in 1962. Carolyn Willis, who sang on the record, went on to work with Phil Spector as a member of Bob B Soxx and The Blue Jeans.

KEEP IT IN THE FAMILY

This section takes a look at some of the successful acts that have brothers or sisters in their original line-up.

1. KEEP ON RUNNING The Spencer Davis Group (1965) *UK No 1*

The Spencer Davis Group's lead singer was Steve Winwood; his brother Muff played bass. After several minor hits they finally broke through into the top 40 with a song that had been written by one of Chris Blackwell's reggae acts, Jackie Edwards. He had written and performed it himself with a ska beat but the Spencer Davis Group turned it into a pounding rocker and it became the first new number one of 1966.

2. FLOWERS ON THE WALL The Statler Brothers (1965)
US No 4/UK No 38

Written by founder member, Lew DeWitt, The Statler Brothers were travelling at the time of release of this single with The Johnny Cash Show and it wasn't until they were reading through a music magazine and saw the American charts that they realised they had a hit on their hands. The group from Staunton, Virginia, were originally named The Four Stars before changing to The Kingsmen. However, in 1963 with the success of the song 'Louie Louie' by another group with the same name, they became The Statler Brothers – even though only two of them were brothers and neither were named Statler!

3. THE RAIN, THE PARK AND OTHER THINGS
The Cowsills (1967) *US No 2*

The group hailed from America's Newport, Rhode Island, and consisted of brothers Bill, Bob, Paul, Barry and John Cowsill with their younger sister, Susan. Their mother, Barbara, who died in 1985 aged 56, was also an original member. The family group were the inspiration behind The Partridge Family: they based their music on The Cowsills.

4. SUNNY AFTERNOON The Kinks (1966) *US No 14/UK No 1*

The Kinks were formed by brothers Ray and Dave Davies in 1963 and, as with all The Kinks hits, 'Sunny Afternoon' was written by Ray. It later appeared on their fourth studio album, *Face To Face*. The song was a change in musical direction for the band, a pattern they would follow for future releases. Recorded in very few takes during an early morning studio session, it had been written by Davies during a period when he was at home in his sick bed. 'Sunny Afternoon' is also the title of the successful West End musical based around the life story of the group.

5. SURFIN' U.S.A **The Beach Boys (1963)** *US No 3/UK No 34*

The title track to the second Beach Boys album was originally credited to Brian Wilson as composer. It was in fact a note-for-note copy of Chuck Berry's 'Sweet Little Sixteen'. A lawsuit prevailed and Berry was granted royalties on the record and a composer credit on future pressings. But the problems didn't end there as it later emerged that the lyrics to 'Surfin' U.S.A' appeared to have been inspired by a 1959 hit by Bobby Rydell, 'Kissin' Time', which mentions a number of American cities and also borrows a lot of its melody from 'Sweet Little Sixteen'. Great songs, all of them. Well, at least it kept the lawyers busy.

6. REMEMBER (WALKING IN THE SAND)
The Shangri-Las (1964) *US No 5/UK No 14*

The debut hit, both in the UK and America, for the girl group formed in Queens, New York, consisting of two sets of sisters: lead singer Mary and sister, Betty Weiss and twins Mary Ann and Marge Ganser (who died in 1971 and 1996 respectively). The group had already recorded as The Bon Bons before being placed under the direction of writer and producer, George 'Shadow' Morton, in 1963 when they were signed to Jerry Leiber and Mike Stoller's Red Bird label where they achieved International success with this single.

The Everly Brothers: 'Cathy's Clown' was one of the biggest of many huge hits for the boys, selling over eight million copies

7. CATHY'S CLOWN
The Everly Brothers (1960)
US No 1/UK No 1

In the first week of May, 1960, The Everly Brothers' own composition and first UK single release for the Warner Brothers label under its own logo, took over the number-one position in the UK. It remained there for seven weeks and also spent five weeks at the top in America when it became the first single to simultaneously make number one on both sides of the Atlantic. It sold in excess of eight million copies.

8. MASSACHUSETTS **The Bee Gees (1967)** *US No 11/UK No 1*

And so to one of the most successful bands of brothers: Barry, Robin and Maurice Gibb. Or, to us, The Bee Gees. This 1967 number one was written by all three members of the group, with its full original title being partly in brackets: '(The Lights Went Out In) Massachusetts'. It was a response to Scott McKenzie's number-one hit, 'San Francisco (Be Sure To Wear Some Flowers In Your Hair)' telling how the lights were all going out because all the hippies were heading for San Francisco.

9. AIN'T NOTHIN' BUT A HOUSEPARTY
The Showstoppers (1968) *UK No 11*

This was the first single to be released on the independent Beacon label. The Showstoppers hailed from Philadelphia, Pennsylvania, and were two sets of brothers: Earl and Timmy Smith and Laddie and Alec Burke. The record was re-issued in the UK in 1971 when it managed to make a chart position of number 33.

10. SUBSTITUTE **The Who (1966)** *UK No 5*

Reaction Records was founded in 1966 by manager and music executive Robert Stigwood and although the label only ever released three albums, one EP and eighteen singles, its short two-year existence included two of the most popular British bands of the Sixties: Cream and The Who. The label's first release was a record by The Who with the catalogue number of 591 001: their number-five hit, 'Substitute', which was primarily inspired by the 1965 soul single 'The Tracks of My Tears' by Smokey Robinson and the Miracles.

Pete Townshend became obsessed, particularly, with the line, 'Although she may be cute/She's just a substitute'. This had then led Townshend to celebrate the word with a song all its own. For the American single, released in April 1966, the line in the chorus 'I look all white but my dad was black' was amended to 'I try walking forward but my feet walk back'. The complete second verse and chorus were also erased from the US release, reducing the track's length to two minutes and 59 seconds. Robert Stigwood went on to form RSO Records in the Seventies and Eighties and as with Reaction was distributed through Polydor.

11. POPSICLES AND ICICLES The Murmaids (1963)

The Murmaids were sisters Carol and Terri Fischer and Sally Gordon. Their hit record, written by David Gates and produced by Kim Fowley, was remarkable in the fact that each time it was re-pressed in the US,

it contained a different B-side, a totalling four in all. None of their follow-up releases, on the wonderfully named Chattahoochee records, made any impact and after various contractual hassles they were dropped from the label. The trio resurfaced briefly during the flower-power era with a cover of Traffic's 'Paper Sun'.

12. BAD MOON RISING Creedence Clearwater Revival (1969)
US No 2/UK No 1

The Song was written by John Fogerty after he was inspired by a movie called *The Devil And Daniel Webster*, in which a hurricane wipes out most of a town. It was the first single to be taken from the album *Green River* and released several weeks ahead of the LP. 'Bad Moon Rising' was the second UK top-10 hit for Creedence Clearwater Revival, on which John sang lead vocals and his brother Tom is featured on rhythm guitar.

13. MY GOOD FRIEND The Paris Sisters (1966)

The Paris Sisters are probably best remembered for their 1961 recording of the Phil Spector-produced, 'I Love How You Love Me'. But the Paris Sisters' talents spread much further than that one hit. Real sisters, Albeth, Priscilla and Sherrell Paris were a talented singing and dancing ensemble who embarked on relentless amounts of stage performances through the entire Sixties and recorded for at least eight different labels during their career. This 1966 release on Reprise, produced by Jack Nitzsche (best-known for his work with the Rolling Stones and for composing soundtracks for movies such as *One Flew Over the Cuckoo's Nest*) was written by Priscilla and called 'My Good Friend'.

14. ISLAND OF DREAMS The Springfields (1962) *UK No 5*
The trio were formed in 1960 when Dusty Springfield left The Lana Sisters to join her brother Tom and Tim Field, who had been singing together as The Kensington Squares, to form The Springfields. They were signed to Philips in 1961, releasing their first single, 'Dear John' and then two which became chart hits, 'Break Away' and 'Bambino'. They eventually hit the big time with their top-five hit, 'Island Of Dreams', after which Field was replaced by Mike Hurst.

15. MICHAEL AND THE SLIPPER TREE The Equals (1969)
UK No 24
The third top-40 hit by the group, all written by lead vocalist Eddy Grant and on this occasion, with a little help from another founder member of The Equals, Derv Gordon, who joined the group with his twin brother, Lincoln. Not long after the release of this single, it was reported in September 1969 that all five members of the group had been injured in Germany, when their car ran off a motorway in a gale. Although a few more hits followed, more bad luck dogged Grant and, following a collapsed lung and heart infection that put him out of action at the beginning of 1971, Grant went home to Guyana before pursuing a solo career.

16. I'LL BE THERE Gerry & The Pacemakers (1965) *UK No 15*
Gerry Marsden formed The Pacemakers in 1959 with his brother Freddie, Les Chadwick and Arthur McMahon, who was later replaced by Les Maguire. Between 1963 and 1965 they achieved nine top-40 hits, three of which topped the charts. 'I'll Be There', written by Bobby Darin, became their seventh and final single to make the UK top 20 although The Pacemakers continued to tour both with and without Gerry.

17. CHAPEL OF LOVE
The Dixie Cups (1964)
US No 1/UK No 22

This three-girl group from New Orleans was originally known as Little Miss & The Muffets and they were discovered at a local talent contest by singer Joe Jones, who arranged for them to travel to New York. The line-up consisted of sisters Barbara Annn and Rosa Lee Hawkins plus their New Orleans-born cousin Joan Marie Johnson.

In 1964, they began to rehearse a song that had already been doing the rounds called 'Chapel

The Dixie Cups were the girl group who finally made a hit out of the previously unmanageable song 'Chapel of Love'

Of Love'. Two versions had already been attempted but left unissued by both The Crystals and The Ronettes because their producer, Phil Spector, wasn't convinced the song had hit potential. The Muffets renamed themselves The Dixie Cups, and were signed to Jerry Leiber and Mike Stoller's new Red Bird label. Soon after, their version of the song was released giving them a million seller, a US number one and a huge international hit.

18. SHAKE A TAIL FEATHER James & Bobby Purify (1967) *US No 25*

This single features the original James and Bobby Purify – two cousins named James Purify and Robert Dickey – who got together in 1965 and scored three consecutive American top-40 hits with 'I'm Your Puppet' in 1966 then 'Wish You Didn't Have To Go' and 'Shake A Tail Feather' the following year. Robert Dickey retired in 1971 and was replaced by Ben Moore.

The Honeycombs

19. THAT'S THE WAY **The Honeycombs (1965)** *UK No 12*

After scoring a number-one hit in 1964 with 'Have I The Right', The Honeycombs had to wait just over a year before they made the top 20 for the second and final time with 'That's The Way'. The group were formed in 1963, calling themselves The Sheratons and were spotted by songwriters Ken Howard and Alan Blaikley. They introduced them to Joe Meek who in turn produced their records. The uniqueness of the group was partly down to their female drummer Honey Lantree. The reason they are in this section of the book is that the rhythm guitarist was her brother, John.

20. BABY I LOVE YOU **The Ronettes (1964)** *US No 24/UK No 11*

Sisters Veronica and Estelle Bennett, with their cousin Nedra Tally Rose, formed The Darling Sisters in 1958, having sung professionally together since being in high school. In 1961 they changed their name to The Ronettes. Problems arose over the recording of their 1964 hit, 'Baby I Love You', as the girls were scheduled to tour on 'Dick Clark's Caravan Of Stars' across America. Lead singer Ronnie remained in California to record her vocals whilst the other two girls, Estelle and Nedra, went on the tour with Ronnie's cousin, Elaine. With two Ronettes unavailable for recording, Darlene Love and Cher were used on the backing vocals.

They sold a million

With so many records released, the chances of selling over a million copies have always been highly unlikely but this chapter looks at a mere 40 that achieved that status. Of course there are many others dotted about this book.

1. SUNSHINE SUPERMAN **Donovan (1966)** *US No 1/UK No 3*

Featuring Jimmy Page on guitar, this was Donovan's only American number one. He was one of the few British artists of the Sixties to have appeared on television before making his first record, achieving national recognition through TV's *Ready, Steady Go.* 'Sunshine Superman' was recorded with the American market in mind, and sold over 800,000 copies in its first six weeks of release, hitting a million sales soon afterwards. His album of the same name had advance orders of over a quarter of a million and soon after its release, passed the half-million mark. Not bad for a young hippy that many had previously dismissed as merely a Bob Dylan wannabe.

2. I SAY A LITTLE PRAYER **Aretha Franklin (1968)**
US No 10/UK No 4

This would have probably have been an American number one if it hadn't been for the fact that in its wisdom, Aretha's record label had decided to release the song as a double A-side with 'The House That Jack Built', thus splitting both the airplay and the sales.

3. SUNDAY WILL NEVER BE THE SAME
Spanky & Our Gang (1967) *US No 9*

Written by Terry Cashman and Gene Pistilli, the song had already been offered to The Left Banke and The Mamas and The Papas, who both turned it down before Spanky and Our Gang were presented it by their record producer, Jerry Ross. Lead singer Spanky McFarlane had previously been known in some American folk circles – in particular in Chicago, as a member of The New Wine Singers. In early 1966 she left the group and moved to Florida. One night a hurricane hit Miami in the area where she was living, in a one-room converted chicken coop. Two young men, Nigel Pickering and Oz Bach took shelter in Spanky's quarters and while they waited for the storm to subside, passed away the time singing together. And so the idea for Spanky & Our Gang was born.

4. SEE YOU IN SEPTEMBER **The Happenings (1966)** *US No 3*

The debut American hit for the group that was originally named The Four Graduates. They hailed from Paterson, New Jersey and, from 1964, they spent three years planning and practicing for their breakthrough hit. Trailing from one record company to another, they finally hooked up with the successful group The Tokens, who supervised their initial recording sessions that included 'See You In September', a song written in 1959 by Sid Wayne and Sherman Edwards, and originally recorded by The Tempos. The Happenings version initially started to sell, via airplay on radio stations in Boston, Massachusetts and quickly spreading across the whole of the US.

5. DUKE OF EARL **Gene Chandler (1962)** *US No 1*

The song was inspired by Earl Edwards, the founder member of the group The Dukays, with whom Gene was also singing. He was offered a recording contract with Vee Jay records and was allowed to release solo singles, provided he changed his name from Eugene Dixon. So he renamed himself after his favourite film star, Jeff Chandler: Gene Chandler was born. 'Duke Of Earl' was originally rejected as a single in favour of a track called 'Nite Owl'. Calvin Carter, a top man at Vee Jay was determined to have 'Duke Of Earl' released as a single and finally got his own way, resulting in the first million-seller for the label.

6. ODE TO BILLIE JOE **Bobbie Gentry (1967)** *US No 1/UK No 13*

She was born Roberta Lee Streeter in Mississippi and in 1958, at the age of fourteen, she saw the movie *Ruby Gentry* starring Jennifer Jones and decided to change her surname. By 1966 she was appearing with her own singing and dance troop in Las Vegas, for whom she wrote all the material. She then played some of her songs to publisher, Larry Shayne, who introduced her to Capitol records.

She recorded 'Ode To Billy Joe' on 10 July 1967, with the basic session lasting less than an hour and strings being added later. With the song running for over seven minutes, the record company made an edit and stuck it on the B-side of her single, 'Mississippi Delta'.

Aretha Franklin's record company decided to split the sublime 'I Say a Little Prayer' with 'The House that Jack Built'

However, DJs across America discovered the song and started playing it; six weeks later it topped the American Hot 100.

7. SHERRY The Four Seasons (1962)
US No 1/UK No 8

This was The Four Seasons' first hit in both the UK and America, where it topped the charts for five weeks. Many believed the group were an overnight success but in truth, lead singer, Frankie Valli had been working for ten

Bobby Gentry: her biggest hit and best-known song, 'Ode to Billy Joe', was actually a B-side

years before the success of 'Sherry'. Their first single as The Four Seasons was called 'Bermuda'; it failed to chart and they changed labels from Gone to Vee Jay where their fortunes turned. Writer Bob Gaudio was messing around on a piano at the end of a recording session and came up with the melody in fifteen minutes. Adding a few words to help him remember the song, he left the studio humming it. He then played it to the group with his made-up words that they decided to keep.

8. SAVE THE LAST DANCE FOR ME The Drifters (1960)
US No 1/UK No 2

This became the second million-seller for the group, following in the footsteps of their 1959 success, 'There Goes My Baby'. This song was written by Doc Pomus and Mort Shuman and soon after its release, The Drifters' lead singer, Ben E King, decided to leave the group in favour of a solo career. There was some speculation that Phil Spector helped out on the recording of the track as he was an apprentice to The Drifters' producers, Jerry Leiber and Mike Stoller, at the time and the production does have a certain Spector feel. But the truth may never be known.

9. CLOUD NINE The Temptations (1968)

This single was released at the beginning of November in the US but held back until 1969 in the UK. In the first month of its release, it sold over 800,000 copies, passing the million sales mark by the time it saw its British release. Written by Barrett Strong and Norman Whitfield, it had been interpreted in two different way: either with dealing with drug addiction; or imagining a dream world without discrimination. The listener was left to make up their own mind. The Temptations received a Grammy for the disc, winning the category for 'Best Rhythm and Blues Performance by a Duo or a Group'.

10. I'M LEAVING IT UP TO YOU Dale & Grace (1963)US No 1

Dale & Grace were Dale Houston and Grace Broussard, from Louisiana. 'I'm Leaving It Up to You' was a cover of a song originally written and recorded by Don Harris and Dewey Terry in 1957 as Don and Dewey. Dale & Grace had sung separately in local bars and clubs for years before teaming up, after meeting one day at a recording studio. Dale had tried recording the song as a soloist but couldn't make it sound right and suggested they tried it as a duet, resulting in a multi-million selling single.

11. THE TEARS OF A CLOWN
Smokey Robinson & The Miracles (1967) *US No 1/UK No 1*

The song was written by Stevie Wonder and Henry Cosby but, when they finished the song, they weren't happy with the lyrics, so they asked Smokey Robinson to come up with something better. Hearing the fairground noises that they had already added to their demo made Smokey think of Pagliacci the clown – and so he based his lyrics on the theme of a clown. At the time he was looking for a couple of songs to complete his 1967 album *Make It Happen* with The Miracles and decided to include the song as an album track.

Three years later, the British Motown office were looking for a follow up single to echo the success of 'The Tracks Of My Tears', but none of Smokey's more recent material seemed suitable. They were then delighted to stumble across another song mentioning tears – 'The Tears of a Clown' – and decided to release it as the follow-up. To everyone's surprise, it went to number one, inspiring the American office to follow suit, where the record also topped the charts.

12. JUST LOVING YOU **Anita Harris** (1967) *UK No 6*

Anita Madeleine Harris was born in the small village of Midsomer Norton in Somerset and at the age of eight took up ice skating. The manager of the ice rink was so impressed with her, that just before her sixteenth birthday, he offered her a professional job in Naples, followed by a stint in Las Vegas. On her return, she sang with The Cliff Adams Singers on the TV series *Song Parade*, before going solo in 1961, working in TV, radio, stage and cabaret.

Anita Harris, Somerset's million-selling singing ice-skater

She represented the UK in several European song contests in Montreux, Knokke-Le-Zoute and San Remo. She recorded for several labels including Parlophone, Pye and Vocalion before signing with CBS in 1967 and releasing 'Just Loving You', which remained on the charts for over six months selling more that 600,000 copies in Britain, topping the charts in South Africa to notch-up sales in excess of 200,000. Once sales from the rest of the world came in, it took the total to over a million.

13. YOU'VE LOST THAT LOVIN' FEELIN' **The Righteous Brothers** (1965) *US No 1/UK No 1*

The first single to sell in excess of eight million copies. The Righteous Brothers were two friends from Orange County in Southern California, Bobby Hatfield and Bill Medley and were given their collective name by a group of black marines who saw them perform in Santa Ana. Phil Spector approached songwriters Barry Mann and Cynthia Weil to come up with a song for the boys and, inspired by The Four Tops hit, 'Baby I Need Your Loving', delivered 'You've Lost That Lovin' Feelin''. This was not intended to be the title or the lyrics of the song but just dummy words to demonstrate the tune. Spector refused to allow them to change it, knowing when he was onto a good thing.

14. RAIN AND TEARS Aphrodite's Child (1968) *UK No 30*

The melody was based on a seventeenth-century classical piece, 'Canon In D', written by German organist and composer, Johann Pachelbel of Nurenberg. Greece-based band Aphrodite's Child were finding it difficult to achieve any real success in their homeland so decided to up sticks and head off for England. Being held up by a transport strike in Paris proved to be a lucky break. They happened by chance to meet up with a top French producer who worked for Philips who heard them play and signed them to the label. They recorded 'Rain And Tears' in English, which became an immediate hit in France, reaching number one, where it remained for fourteen weeks. The success spread right across Europe giving Demis Roussos and his group their only million-selling single.

15. HELLO I LOVE YOU The Doors (1968) US No 1/UK No 15

This was the second of three million-selling singles for The Doors, the first being 'Light My Fire' and finally, 'Touch Me'. 'Hello I Love You' came about when the group were trying to write songs for their third album, *Waiting For The Sun*. They started thumbing through poems written by Jim Morrison and came across 'Hello I Love You', which he had written one afternoon when he had watched a thin young girl walking across the beach. Morrison once said that he'd actually written a melody first but couldn't remember it.

16. JOHNNY ANGEL Shelley Fabares (1962) *US No 1*

She was born Michele Ann Marie Fabares in Santa Monica, California. Starting out as a dancer, she got a lucky break in 1953 when she was invited to appear on Frank Sinatra's TV show, but her big moment came when she was cast in the role of teenage daughter Mary Stone in the long running American TV series *The Donna Reed Show*. This led to a recording contract that in turn produced her debut single and an American number-one hit that went on to sell over a million copies.

17. HER ROYAL MAJESTY James Darren (1962)
US No 6/UK No 36

When Darren first heard the song 'Goodbye Cruel World', he didn't want to record it, thinking it was a stupid song. But finally his record label producer, Stu Phillips persuaded him that it sounded like a hit; it ended up selling close to two million copies. But Darren then complained that all he was ever asked to record after that were songs in a similar vain. Such was the case with the follow-up, the Goffin and King song, 'Her Royal Majesty'. Despite all his complaints, the record gave him another huge hit but perhaps that was the point where a change of style might have been the right decision, as he never managed to record anything as successful again.

18. I REMEMBER YOU Frank Ifield (1962)

Frank was born in Coventry but moved to Australia as a child. He returned to England in 1959 in an attempt to crack the British charts. He achieved a minor hit in 1960 with 'Lucky Devil' but further success eluded him until 1962, when record producer Norrie Paramor decided to give him one final shot – a song that was first heard in the 1942 movie *The Fleet Is In*. Frank decided to add some yodelling to his interpretation, which made the record stand out and gave him his first major hit.

19. THE LAST WALTZ Engelbert Humperdinck (1967)

This became Engelbert's second number one. Up until then, he'd been having hits with covers of older songs. This time he looked to the songwriting talents of Les Reed and Barry Mason, who came up with what would become the standard final song at every dance in every disco and church hall up and down the country.

20. GREEN, GREEN GRASS OF HOME Tom Jones (1966)

Songwriter Claude Putman was inspired to write this song after seeing the movie *The Asphalt Jungle*, which told the story of a convicted criminal waiting for his death sentence to be carried out. The original American version was by Porter Wagoner but Tom Jones decided to cover it after hearing another version by Jerry Lee Lewis. This gave him the 1966 Christmas number one, and probably only because The Beatles had decided not to make a play for it that year.

21. WE CAN WORK IT OUT/DAY TRIPPER The Beatles (1967)

This was the first of four singles by The Beatles to be officially released as a double A-side, giving them their ninth consecutive UK number one and the 1965 Christmas chart-topper. Both songs were recorded at the

The Seekers

time they were working on the *Rubber Soul* album, and no one could make up their mind as to which was the stronger song.

22. THE CARNIVAL IS OVER The Seekers (1965)

Tom Springfield wrote the song after a trip to Brazil, where he witnessed the Carnival in Rio. The tune is based on a Russian folk song that became popular in Russia in the early 1890s. This became The Seekers' best-selling single in the UK, selling almost 1.5 million copies and it has become an Australian tradition for the song to be sung at the close of major sporting events. Unfortunately, The Seekers were unable to do so at the end of the closing ceremony for the 2000 Sydney Olympic Games, as Judith Durham had broken her hip and was not able to appear.

23. TEARS Ken Dodd (1965)

This became the biggest-selling single in the UK in 1965. The song was written by Billy Uhr and Frank Capano in the Thirties; it gave Ken Dodd his most successful record of his career. It sold over a million copies and spent a total of 24 weeks on the chart, five of which were at number one.

24. WHITE ROOM Cream (1969) *US No 6/UK No 28*

It's quite amazing to think that Cream only existed for a little over two years, from mid 1966 to late 1968, but during that time they were amongst the leading pioneers of the evolving British rock scene. 'White Room' became the group's second American top-10 hit and was written by Jack Bruce who sings lead vocals and poet, Pete Brown. It wasn't released as a single until after the group had broken up, but ending up selling over a million copies worldwide.

25. WORDS **The Bee Gees (1968)** *US No 15/UK No 8*

The song first appeared in a movie called *The Mini Mob*, where it was sung by Georgie Fame who also had a starring role alongside Madeline Smith. The very limited distribution of the film and the pre-emptive release of the Bee Gees version eclipsed the Georgie Fame recording. It was the first Bee Gees single to feature Barry as the only Gibb brother to be singing.

26. WICHITA LINEMAN **Glen Campbell (1969)** *US No 3/UK No 7*

His first British hit and his first single to break through into the American top 10. Written by Jim Webb who had the idea for the song when driving home along the Kansas to Oklahoma border road and spotted a man up a pole fixing a telephone line. When Webb played Glen his demo of the song, he had accompanied himself on his Hammond organ, as a simple expedient. When it came to recording the fully-fledged arrangement of the song in the studio, Glen kept on feeling there was something missing. Until, that is, he remembered Webb's Hammond organ and added it to the backing track.

27. (YOU'RE MY) SOUL AND INSPIRATION
The Righteous Brothers (1966) *US No 1/UK No 15*

Although sounding remarkably like a Phil Spector production, this song was in fact the work of lead singer Bill Medley, who had clearly learned a thing or two from Mr S. It became the duo's biggest hit not to have been produced by Spector, both in the UK and in America. The record became The Righteous Brothers' second American number one and was written by Barry Mann and Cynthia Weil, who had also been responsible for their chart topping, 'You've Lost That Lovin' Feelin''.

28. THE CLAPPING SONG **Shirley Ellis (1965)** *US No 8/UK No 6*

This became Shirley's one and only UK hit and her third and final American top-10 success; it sometimes goes under the title 'Clap Pat Clap Slap'. The lyrics were adapted by Lincoln Chase, Shirley's then husband, from the Thirties song, 'Little Rubber Dolly' recorded by The Light Crust Doughboys. 'The Clapping Song' was successfully revived in 1982 by The Belle Stars, whose version reached number 11.

29. ANYONE WHO HAD A HEART **Cilla Black (1964)** *UK No 1*

Written by Burt Bacharach and Hal David, this was Cilla's cover of Dionne Warwick's American number-eight hit, which had originally been played to producer George Martin, with the suggestion that it would be a strong song for Shirley Bassey. However, George had other ideas and decided to record it with Cilla Black – resulting in a number-one hit that ended up being the best-selling female chart hit of the Sixties. Actress Sheridan Smith revived the song in the 2014 TV drama, *Cilla* and, due to popular demand, it was made available as a download, entering the UK top 40 a few days later.

30. PUPPY LOVE **Paul Anka (1960)** *US No 2/UK No 33*

A number-one hit in 1972 for Donny Osmond, the song was first recorded by its composer, Paul Anka, twelve years earlier. The song was dedicated to the actress and singer Annette Funicello, who he was dating whilst travelling on a package tour. But the affair was kept secret to avoid press coverage. After the tour, Annette recorded an entire album of Anka songs but didn't include 'Puppy Love'. Shortly after which, she married his manager.

31. BIG BAD JOHN **Jimmy Dean (1961)** *US No 1/UK No 2*

Jimmy Dean remained at the top of the American charts for no less than five weeks. Dean, by way of a joke, wrote the song about one of his friends, John Mentoe, an actor who was six feet, five inches tall. Pianist, Floyd Cramer was hired to take part in the recording but it was decided that a piano part didn't fit so he wound up hitting a chunk of metal with a hammer instead, a suggestion made by Dean.

32. YESTERDAY MAN **Chris Andrews (1965)** *UK No 3*

The man who wrote hits for Adam Faith and Sandie Shaw became a big star in his own right in Germany and over the years he's had a very successful career as a songwriter, singer and record producer. In 1965, he went into the studio to record his first single as an artist, resulting in 'Yesterday Man' becoming a multi-million seller around the world.

33. CONGRATULATIONS **Cliff Richard (1968)** *UK No 1*

It was on 6 April, 1968 that Cliff sang 'Congratulations' for the Eurovision Song Contest, held at the Royal Albert Hall in London. This

Bill Martin and Phil Coulter song was originally written by Coulter as 'I Think I Love You'. But Coulter was unhappy with the lyrics so he teamed up once again with Martin; they had written the previous year's winner, 'Puppet On A String', together for Sandie Shaw. 'Congratulations' was placed second in the voting, losing out to the Spanish entry, 'La La La' performed by female singer, Massiel. 1968 was the first year that the contest was transmitted in colour.

34. JE T'AIME...MOI NON PLUS
Jane Birkin and Serge Gainsbourg (1969)

Jane and Serge were two of the most famous stars in France, both on record and on the big screen, having met during the rehearsals for the movie *Slogan*. They became good friends. Serge wrote 'Je T'Aime' for Brigitte Bardot who, after recording it, decided it was too erotic and refused to allow its release; Serge suggested that Jane as a suitable replacement. The record, although performed in French, proved to be the most controversial release of the decade and was banned by almost every radio station in the world. After being released in the UK on the Fontana label, halfway through its ascent up the charts, Fontana ditched it, due to the thousands of complaints received by Fontana from the public; it was handed over to the independent record label Major Minor. The song's worldwide sales exceeded two million copies.

35. SNOOPY Vs THE RED BARON The Royal Guardsmen (1967)
US No 2/UK No 8

Written by Phil Gernhard and Dick Holler, the song was inspired by the comic strip *Peanuts* by Charles M. Schulz and the record was issued about a year after a story had been published featuring Snoopy fighting the Red Baron. Schulz and his publishers sued the band and won their case for using the name Snoopy without gaining permission – during which time they'd recorded an alternative version called 'Squeaky Vs The Black Knight', with a handful of copies finding their way into stores in Canada. But after agreeing that all publishing royalties would go to the owners of the brand, they were allowed to write and record further songs about 'Snoopy'.

36. OH PRETTY WOMAN Roy Orbison (1964) *US No 1/UK No 1*

Written by Orbison and Bill Dees, the song was recorded in Nashville Tennessee and gave Roy his third UK number one. Total sales of the record exceeded seven million and in 1999 the song was honoured with a 'Grammy Hall Of Fame' award; it is a regular in lists of the '500 Greatest Songs Of All Time'. The story goes that Roy Orbison was working with his songwriting partner at his house one day when his wife, Claudette interrupted and asked for some money to go shopping. Dees responded by saying 'A pretty woman don't need no money, honey'. Roy then started singing, 'Pretty woman walking down the street', and by the time she had returned from the store, they'd completed the song.

37. RHYTHM OF THE RAIN The Cascades (1963)
US No 3/UK No 5

This song was written by The Cascades' lead singer, John Gummoe, over quite a long period of time, beginning when he was serving in US Navy. The group came together in San Diego, California in 1958 as The Coastliners and each member of the group played an instrument as well as being able to harmonise. Signed to the American Valient label in 1962 formed by songwriter Barry DeVorzon, he insisted they changed their name and settled on The Cascades after a washing-up liquid. 'Rhythm Of The Rain' became their second single and was recorded at the famous Goldstar Studios in New York. The rainfall sound effect at the beginning of the record later inspired Phil Spector to use a similar gimmick on 'Walking In The Rain' by The Ronettes.

38. YEH YEH Georgie Fame & The Blue Flames (1964)
US No 21/UK No 1

Georgie Fame, whose real name is Clive Powell, was spotted by composer, Lionel Bart who heard him play in Islington, and introduced him to agent Larry Parnes. Powell changed his name to Georgie Fame at Parnes' insistence and was employed as a pianist in a group to accompany visiting American stars. One night, one of the stars failed to turn up and Fame was given a solo spot, shortly before the group were renamed The Blue Flames and began working exclusively with Billy Fury. After Fury decided to drop them, they earned a residency at London's Flamingo club whose owner, Rick Gunnell, became their manager and secured them a recording contract with EMI's Columbia label. Their first single, 'Do The Dog' was followed by a cover of Lee Dorsey's 'Do-Re-Mi'. Neither were hits, nor was their third release, 'Bend A Little'. But then came their version of the Jon Hendrix song, 'Yeh Yeh'. They had hit paydirt.

Georgie Fame made the leap from backing musician to million-seller with 'Yeh Yeh'

39. FRIDAY ON MY MIND **The Easybeats (1966)** *US No 16/UK No 6*
Formed in Australia in 1965, the band relocated to London the following year to record for United Artists. Their first release, 'Come And See Her', went virtually unnoticed. The follow- up, 'Friday On My Mind', written by group members George Young and Harry Vanda, was an immediate worldwide smash. In 2001, it was voted 'Best Australian Song' of all time by the Australasian Performing Rights Association.

40. SUNNY **Bobby Hebb (1966)** *US No 2/UK No 12*
In 1955, a soul group named The Marigolds achieved a top-20 American R&B hit with a song called 'Rollin' Stone'. The group's founder member, Hal Hebb, died eight years later after a mugging and in 1966, his brother Bobby wrote a song about his murder. That song was 'Sunny' reaching number two in the US. It was first recorded in 1965 for the Asian market by Meiki Hirohoto before jazz vibraphone player Dave Pike cut an instrumental version for Atlantic. In 1966, Bobby Hebb recorded the song himself, as an afterthought when he found he had a few remaining minutes of studio time at one of his recording sessions.